WHY ME?
An Autobiography by William Gargan

WHY ME? AN AUTOBIOGRAPHY BY WILLIAM GARGAN

DOUBLEDAY & COMPANY, INC., GARDEN CITY, NEW YORK, 1969

Library of Congress Catalog Card Number 68–10310
Copyright © 1969 by William Gargan and Arnold Hano
All Rights Reserved
Printed in the United States of America
First Edition

Suggestions for Dedication Page by My Son Leslie:

To Mary for far more than words can say.

To Mary who wouldn't take no for an answer.

For Mary—who else could have put up with me for forty years.

To Mary who gave me my second voice.

For Mary who put the right words in my mouth.

Dear Leslie: I like them all,
so friends take your pick.
Love, Dad

ACKNOWLEDGMENTS

When I finished writing this story of my life, I appreciated fully, perhaps for the first time, how many people have contributed to the making of that life. Mom and Dad, my brothers and relatives, friends, associates in the entertainment world, colleagues in the war against cancer (especially Lane Adams, Richard Mc-Grail, and Charles Taylor, my Crusade booking agent; these are the gentlemen who run the vast American Cancer society; also the late Robert J. Culton of the California Division; special thanks to Steve Barric, my paisano, who causes me no end of delightful trouble, and, of course, Mrs. Thomas Ray), the wonderful people I have met in every part of the globe—all of them are part of this story and, without them, it could not have been written. I thank them all. Some of them are mentioned by name in the pages of this book. Space would not permit me to include all those I wanted to include but I want them all to know how grateful I am to them for all they have meant to me over the years and, in particular, during my time of trial and sorrow. I would like particularly to acknowledge my indebtedness to Arnold Hano for his invaluable assistance in the writing of this book. Also, I would acknowledge the help so freely and so generously given me by my son, Leslie, during the time this book was being written. On another page, I have dedicated this book to my wife, Mary, and, of course, it never would have been written without her patience, understanding, and love.

CONTENTS

ILLUSTRATIONS

(*Following Page 120*)

1. My mother.
2. My brother Ed.
3. My mother, my brother Edward, and I.
4. Mom and Pop at Riis Park.
5. Mom and Pop, and my mother's sister, Agnes Wilson.
6. Mom and Pop, my Aunt Bina, and my Aunt Grace.
7. Three generations of Gargans.
8. Mother, my younger son Leslie, and I.
9. Barrie and Leslie.
10. My dear friend Leslie Howard with my son Leslie.
11. My wife, Mary, and Mother in Hollywood in 1932.
12. Mary and I in the living room of Gertrude Astor's house, which we had rented.
13. A picture of Russell Markert's Markettes, with Mary the third girl from the left.
14. Mary on her Pinto pony, Scotch.
15. Mary and I whoop it up at a Racquet Club party.
16. My two boys, Leslie and Barrie, in the uniform of St. John's Military Academy.
17. Bing Crosby and I on a fishing trip.
18. A photograph taken during my early years in Hollywood.
19. A scene from *Miss Annie Rooney* with Shirley Temple and Guy Kibbee.
20. A shot from *Four Frightened People* with Claudette Colbert, Herbert Marshall, Mary Boland and myself.

*Unless otherwise indicated all photos
are from the author's personal
collection.*

1

"You've Got Cancer of the Larynx"

While I was out playing golf one spring day in 1960, slicing not every drive, but every other, my wife Mary received a call from a friend of ours, Randolph Hale. Randy, who owns theaters on the West Coast and is a stage producer, was putting together a production of Gore Vidal's political comedy, *The Best Man*. He wanted me in it.

"Tell me," he'd said to Mary, "would Bill agree to have his hair dyed white?"

"Why not?" Mary said. "He's dyed it red all these years."

I was less willing. Randy Hale, who is also a Bohemian Club buddy of mine, wanted me to play the ex-President. You probably know the play. A couple of politicians fight over their party's presidential nomination on the eve of a national convention. One is a lofty erudite guy, with a nervous breakdown in his background, about to be exploited by the other fellow, who is a street-fighter type. Naturally the street fighter has an even more unsavory past, but the lofty erudite politician, supposedly modeled after Adlai Stevenson, is reluctant to make capital of it. The ex-President, who can throw lots of weight around, ends up washing his hands of both of them. That's the play. I should mention that the ex-President is dying of cancer. Yes, it's a comedy. Lots of laughs.

I had lunch with Randy at the Brown Derby. I told him I didn't want to do it.

"I can't picture myself a President of the United States, much less an ex-President."

"Lee Tracy did the role in New York," Randy said.

"I know. I can picture Tracy in the role. He looks like Harry Truman. I don't. It's not my style."

"It's the fattest part in the play."

I knew all this. I also knew I could use the $1000 a week (who couldn't?), though I was far from broke. But I'd more or less retired from active acting. I'd been acting professionally since 1925, when I was nineteen years old. Now, in 1960, I was fifty-four, soon to be fifty-five, and the notion of rehearsing every day, long hours a day, for a stage play, and then taking it out of town, up and down the Coast, and on to Chicago, as Randy Hale planned, sounded like more work than I felt like tackling. An occasional guest shot on television, that was different. That was easy, and remunerative. I kept busy enough, without breaking my back. We lived in a seventeen-room house in Beverly Hills that once was Jean Harlow's, and we'd just bought a second house in Bermuda Dunes, near Palm Springs, and I'd sent my two sons through college. The residual checks from *The Return of Martin Kane*, a television series I'd made on film in London a few years earlier, kept limping in. So did small-ish checks from investments in stocks and oil wells. Mary and I lived if not exactly high on the hog, a good ways up from the hoof. I belonged to a couple of stiff-priced golf clubs, and we ate well. We'd spent too many years—Mary and I— taking care of our nickels between my acting jobs, most of them in the days before the big salaries. For a spell I'd been a bootlegger, with Dave Chasen, because a man has to survive. When I wasn't selling hooch to a customer in the Algonquin Hotel in Manhattan, I was taking the subway down to a little church in Flatbush, to lay a Novena at the feet of St. Therese, begging for work. So now, thirty years later, Mary and I reveled in our good luck. We spent money at about the same rate as I made it. If I had a philosophy of life, in 1960, it was to search out the next laugh, either to find fun or give it. We were a couple of pleasure seekers. Seek and ye shall find. We sought. We found.

"Who do you have playing the two politicians?" I asked Randy.

"Gene Raymond and Leon Ames," Randy said.

I reached out my hand. "Why didn't you say so? Call me Mr. President."

Gene Raymond is an old, very close friend. I knew him when his name was Raymond Guion—very French—and the two of us appeared in *The War Song*, with George Jessel, so long ago I wouldn't want to jeopardize Jessel's latest romance. Gene and I had roomed together at Mrs. Quirk's famous boardinghouse in Chicago during the road show of *The War Song*. John Barrymore was at Mrs. Quirk's boardinghouse then, so you can see it wasn't exactly a meeting place of the WCTU, or the Girl Scouts. Or even the Boy Scouts.

And Leon Ames had been a close friend ever since I'd hit Hollywood back in 1932. Playing with Gene and Leon would be homecoming week.

We began rehearsing the first week of July in a little theater on La Cienega Boulevard, Los Angeles' well known restaurant and art gallery row. There is a sign in the theater men's room, "Do not flush the toilet while the play is on." The men's room wall is flush (if you will pardon the pun) with the stage, and you hear the toilet onstage and all over the house. The acoustics of the theater are great, especially if you like to hear toilets flush.

I was glad the acoustics were good. I'd had a siege of laryngitis a few weeks before, and I'd just got my voice back. I took it easy the first rehearsals. I also wanted to save my voice for the upcoming weekend, marking the annual summer encampment of the Bohemian Club. The Bohemian Club is a very special social group with a clubhouse at Post and Taylor Streets in San Francisco where you meet old friends and make new ones. The Club has a gorgeous sprawling grove of land among the redwoods of northern California, along the Russian River, and the Bohemians gather there every summer to let the world go to pot. The world also manages to go to pot when the Club's back in civilization, so we really weren't chancing much.

I'd told Randy Hale I would make the Grove, and as a fellow Bohemian he understood. He'd even written it into the contract. But he was mildly concerned. We'd be opening in less than a month, in Santa Barbara, and then we'd come down to Los Angeles for five weeks, if all went well, at the Huntington Hartford Theatre, and after that, up to San Francisco, and then to Chicago.

"You'll miss important rehearsal time," he said.

"Don't worry," I said. "I'm a quick study."

I went up to the Grove on Friday, relaxed for three glorious days and even appeared in one of our stage spectaculars—held in an open air amphitheater—the annual Hi Jinks show, which signals the end of each encampment. When I got back to Los Angeles and the little theater on La Cienega, I was refreshed and raring to go, except my throat was starting to hurt again.

The play was shaping up, my part was the meatiest, if not the longest, with a great tear-jerking second-act curtain, and ticket sales for the Huntington Hartford run looked healthy. Theater in Los Angeles is not quite like theater on or off Broadway. It is not quite like theater any place for that matter. You could open the world premiere of *My Fair Lady* in Hollywood, and after a good three weeks, you've had it. Yet something called *The Drunkard* can run for twenty-five years.

I'd been seeing my doctor, who had told me to quit talking for a week or two, which was impossible, so I whispered my way through rehearsals and took aspirin and gargled. I also was smoking two and a half packs of cigarettes a day, as I'd done most of my life, and peculiarly, the smoking seemed to soothe my throat. Perhaps the tobacco nicotinized what was starting to grow in my throat, unknown to me, shooting out its cells like a multiplication table gone crazy. I don't want you to think it was much pain or much hoarseness or anything much different from any laryngitis attack. I could handle it, and I knew when the curtain went up, I'd be bellowing in my usual style. I'd never had the pear-shaped tones of a Barrymore or an Olivier.

My tones were more like pineapples. But I could hit that second balcony, with plenty to spare.

To be closer to the theater, Mary and I had rented a small place on North Rossmore Street, between Beverly and Third, in the Mauretania Apartments, owned by Jack and Flo Haley. We had a distinguished neighbor upstairs. The 1960 Democratic convention began its raucous caucus in Los Angeles early in July, and Senator John F. Kennedy, with his aide David Powers, had made the Mauretania Apartments his special hideaway. Kennedy also had a security man, plus a couple of television sets and a clutch of telephones, so he could keep close track of the usual shenanigans of a nominating convention.

I'd seen Kennedy come into the apartment building one day.

"Hi, Senator," I said.

"Hello, Jack," he said.

"I'm not Jack Haley. I'm Bill Gargan."

We chatted briefly and I wished him luck. I'd run into him in the building elevator, and we got to leaving notes for each other. I'd tack a note near his floor button, "Is it true that if elected you'll have the Pope sanction meat on Friday?" And he'd answer back, "Yes, and tell the kids I'm all for a four-day school week."

On the afternoon of the balloting, Wednesday, July 13, after the papers and television people had ferreted out the hideaway of the past few days, Dave Powers said to me, "The senator wants to get the hell out and have a swim."

Kennedy's parents, Rose and Joe Kennedy, had rented Marion Davies' Beverly Hills villa, and I guess the vision of that swimming pool, plus a chance to see his folks, was pretty enticing. The problem was pulling out of the Mauretania Apartments unseen, and not leading a merry chase of newsmen all the way to Beverly Hills.

So I said to Powers, "I'll show you how to get him out of here." My television days as *Martin Kane, Private Eye*, plus my real-life months as a private detective back in Brooklyn, when I was tracking down ruthless credit welshers and daring deadbeats across the wastes of Canarsie, sprang to the rescue. Besides, as a Brooklyn boy, I knew all about fire escapes.

I took Powers around to the back where there was a wooden fence. We looked over the fence. On the other side was a driveway. The getaway route.

"Leave your car here," I told Powers. "Bring the senator down the fire escape."

He did.

But Kennedy couldn't scale the fence. His back bothered him. So we threw an old mattress over the fence, and he crawled up and over, with each of us giving him a boost.

Then he looked back from the other side, and he said ruefully, "I used to be very athletic, you know."

He and Dave got into the car and whizzed out to Beverly Hills, and the senator had his swim and a meal with his folks and his cousin, Anne Gargan, who—with that name—must be a distant cousin of mine. The meal, I understand, was Irish stew.

He came back the same way, at eight o'clock that evening, but, so Dave says, he managed to scale the fence himself this time. I think his pride had been hurt, or else he'd been buoyed by the dip and probably by the realization he was going to make it big.

That night Mary and I watched the balloting on our television screen, Mary in an old bathrobe, her hair in curlers, and me nursing a scotch. Came a light tap on the door, and when I opened it, the senator strode in.

"Do you mind, Bill, if I watch with you? Both our sets blew out upstairs."

Mary dashed for the bathroom, and set a world's record for female change. She came out, her hair all fixed, looking like a doll, in four minutes flat.

So we all watched together, Dave Powers by the phone, the security man at the door, and the senator nibbling his nails, or running his hands through his hair, truly nervous as he said, "I lost one there. Picked up half a vote there."

People will tell you that the Kennedys all knew the convention was a walkaway, no sweat, just a formality. If that's so, then John F. Kennedy was one of the greatest actors I ever saw. He was nervous as a cat.

When it became apparent Kennedy would go over the top on the first ballot, Dave said, "We'd better get over to the Sports Arena, Senator." They stood, and Mary said, "Congratulations, Mr. President," which may have been the first time anybody had said that to him. He bent over and kissed Mary, and as they went out, I grabbed Dave Powers and asked, "Who's it going to be for Vice-President?"

"He'd like Symington," Dave said, "but he's stuck with Johnson."

We opened *The Best Man* in Santa Barbara in early August, played a Friday through Sunday weekend, came down to Los Angeles for a few days of rest and then went into the Huntington Hartford. Our reviews were great, with Phil Scheuer in the Los Angeles *Times* particularly flattering to me—"Gargan was the head-and-shoulders standout as the ailing ex Chief"—and Abe Lastfogel, president of the William Morris Agency, gave me a ring and said he was trying to line up a television series for me, and we'd have to get together.

"Fine," I said, or maybe I whispered. My throat was raspy again, and very dry. It hurt when I swallowed, and I always wanted to expectorate, though there did not seem to be an inordinate amount of mucus. Nor was I coughing very much. For want of another word—and you know the word—I had a sore throat. It didn't matter much in the play, because this was an old man I was playing, dying of cancer, and if I sounded a little hoarse, so much the better illusion. Only I wasn't acting out the hoarseness. Still, it would subside at times, ease up, and I'd be my old bellowing self. My doctor, Harold Barnard, whom we called Barney, and who treated Wendell Willkie for his hoarse throat during the 1940 campaign, kept checking me out, giving me the usual treatments, and I felt fine otherwise. I kept right on smoking, and the smoking kept right on mesmerizing the pain, like a good narcotic should. The weeks at the Huntington Hartford flew by. I was delighted with the show and the response.

Abe Lastfogel and his people were scurrying all over town, dragging producers and network VIPs to the theater, to watch me.

We flew up to San Francisco in September, and opened at the old Alcazar Theatre, on O'Farrell, behind the Curran and Geary Theatres. *The Best Man* would be the last production at the Alcazar before they converted it to a Handlery Motel. We were determined to give the place a splendid wake. Opening night at the Alcazar was Bohemian Club night; hundreds of Bohemian friends of mine and their wives filled the theater.

Twice during the run at the Alcazar, something odd happened. I told you I had a great second-act curtain speech. The ex-President is sick and getting sicker, weaker, but in the tumult of convention activity, nobody notices, so it comes as a shock when I say to a girl, "I want you to pick up that phone and ask for Dr. Latham. Tell him to come quick and bring a stretcher because I can't move. I'm afraid the old man is just about dead."

Then the curtain falls, and after a moment of shock, audiences usually burst into applause. It's an easy line to win applause with. But twice at the Alcazar, something extra entered my voice, infiltrated the part. I said my lines, a little throaty, a little weak, yet strong enough to hit the balcony, and the curtain came down slowly, and you could have heard a pin drop. I waited for the burst of applause—why not? I'm a ham—but it didn't come. The quiet deepened, until now you could have heard less than a pin drop out there, you could have heard a heart beat in the balcony. Finally there came a sound like a giant sigh, and then they stirred and went out for the intermission breath of air or an orange drink. It happened once in a matinee, once in an evening performance, and each time I would get a call the next day, and somebody would say, "I thought you had actually died. I was relieved to see you take your curtain call."

Business was so brisk at San Francisco that Randy Hale canceled our date in Chicago and decided to stay on a couple of extra weeks, figuring he'd book a new house later. But on the last night of the extended run at the Alcazar, Hale told us he still hadn't located a Chicago theater, and we'd have to break up and get back together when he did find a house. Maybe two weeks.

I drove back to Beverly Hills with Gene Raymond, and when I got home I told Mary my throat hurt. She set up another date for me to see my doctor. Dr. Barnard shared an office with a heart specialist and very close friend of mine, Dr. Louis Martin. Dr. Martin had been my internist and Mary's for years. Now they both had me say, "Ahh."

"I'm concerned about your throat," Barney said. "I'd like you to see a laryngologist, Dr. Alden Miller. He's on North Vermont, opposite the Hollywood Presbyterian Hospital." They made an appointment while I was there.

Frankly I had become concerned myself. Perhaps I had polyps that would have to be scraped out.

Dr. Alden Miller turned out to be a steely eyed, no-nonsense man in his young forties. But a great, great doctor. He checked me into the hospital one evening, and then the next morning I swallowed a semi-knockout pill, to permit the doctor to slip a pipe down my gullet, equipped with a flashlight, a mirror, and half a hardware store.

He saw, I learned later, a mass of gray matter growing irregularly under the epiglottis, that piece of cartilage at the back of the throat, guarding the trachea, or windpipe.

He scraped away a piece of the gray tissue below the epiglottis for a biopsy, but, of course, he knew. Normal cells grow normally, in God's universe of order, neat and round and pure. This growth was wild, unruly, and though he had not yet slipped the tissue beneath his microscope's eye, he knew, or at least surely sensed, that these cells would not be neat and round and pure. Plus the color of the tissue. Tattletale gray.

Before he'd had the biopsy report, he called Mary.

"I'm terribly sorry," he said, "but it looks like a malignancy. Don't tell your husband until we know for sure."

This was a Tuesday.

I went home, and on Friday the doctor called, and asked

Mary and me to come down. Which means, unknown to me, Mary had carried this terrible weight on her mind for several days.

By now I was a little suspicious that it was more than polyps, though I honestly still had not permitted "cancer" to intrude. You fight off the thought of cancer, you, me, hundreds of thousands of people. You put off the thought. You cancel doctors' appointments, you refuse to have that X-ray taken, or the biopsy, or the Pap smear, because you don't want to know. This—more than anything else—is cancer's greatest ally. This refusal to face facts, this idiotic notion that cancer is something special that is best treated by ignoring it. They say a little learning is a dangerous thing. A lot of ignorance can be fatal.

We were ushered in, and Dr. Miller looked me squarely in the eye.

"You've got cancer of the larynx," he said.

Just like that. Talk about a straight line. This one jolted me right down to my socks.

I felt weak. My head swam with unseen terrors. Strangely, it all felt unreal. Dream sequence stuff.

"What's the procedure?" I asked. I didn't know that I had clutched Mary's hand until I felt her flesh quiver beneath my nails.

"We operate, you live," Dr. Miller said. "We don't operate, you die."

Thank God for frankness. A man has to stop hiding, stop shielding himself from truth. He shocked me out of shock.

"No other alternative?" I asked. I felt there wasn't, but a man tries.

He shrugged. "We could try cobalt, but it doesn't look hopeful. The position of the growth is such I don't think we can get to it."

"If you operate, what are the odds?"

His face brightened. "Better than even. There are some 20,000 laryngectomees in the country today"—that was the first time I realized there was a noun for what I was to become—"who lead relatively normal lives without their larynx. In most cases, the cancer does not recur. If it doesn't recur in five years, consider yourself cured."

"Will I speak?"

"Not the way you speak now. If you work hard, you'll learn to speak another way."

"But the operation means the end of my career?"

"Yes."

Stupid question. When man is born, is it written somewhere he must be an actor, and nothing but? Or a plumber? Or a policeman? My acting career would end. Was that all I could do? But I didn't think those thoughts then. Not until much later would I ever dare consider doing anything else. I was an actor. An actor without a voice was an actor without a profession, a baseball pitcher without arms, a night watchman without eyes, a ballet dancer pirouetting on one wooden leg. So Dr. Miller was wrong— Don't operate and die. Do operate and die. For acting, to me, was living, was life itself.

He had shocked me, but he had not cured me.

"I want to consult another man," I said.

"Good," Miller said. "I want you to."

He sent me to another man. He looked at my throat, he studied the biopsy report, and he said, "I concur fully and exactly with Dr. Miller's findings."

I went to another man. He also concurred.

Three or four days had gone by.

I knew my options were running out, like sand between the fingers, like water cupped in the hand, like life passing by. Dr. Miller called. "I'm getting worried about the delay. We don't want the cancer to metastasize." Metastasize means spread. Cancer cells sometimes lie quiet, in place, having eaten all they can until they are gorged, like swollen, sleepy beasts. But they usually wake up, hungry again, and they raven away, spreading here, then there, until you might as well forget it. Throw away the key; it's too late.

I went to Good Samaritan Hospital and talked to a radiologist. "How about cobalt?" I asked. "What chance do I have?"

"I couldn't guarantee a thing," he said. "It's in a tough spot.

It's below the epiglottis. We'd wreck everything just getting to it."

I'd run my options and nobody had picked them up. It was up to me.

Mary and I had our consultation, in the little coffee shop of the Hotel Tevis, in downtown Los Angeles. By now I had begun to get the full meaning. I told you I was a quick study. (That's supposed to be a joke, which was about the calibre of my humor those days.)

"Whatever you decide," Mary said, "is fine with me. It's your decision."

I called Dr. Miller.

"Let's cut," I said.

We made another date, to see Miller. While Mary and I waited, a little man came out of Dr. Miller's office. He had a brown bib over his throat. Miller followed the man into the anteroom and introduced him to me.

"I want you to meet this gentleman," Miller said. "Five months ago he had the same sort of operation you're going to have. He's just now beginning to talk. I want you to see that you'll be able to talk."

The man beamed. Then he began to talk. He'd been a tractor driver. At least, that is what I thought he said. What I really heard was a thick guttural incomprehensible goulash of breathy, raspy croaking sounds. Occasionally I'd pick out a word.

It was another shock. We had talked of an operation, and by this time I had resigned myself to it. But until that moment I had never heard a laryngectomee speak. Oh, boy, I thought, that's me, five months from now, five years from now.

It made me angry. I felt cheated, somehow. My voice was going to be reduced to—to that? To those sounds? That gibberish? I was sore, sore at Miller, sore at this poor unfortunate man, sore at the world, sore, very very sore, at myself.

"When can we operate?" I asked.

"In a week," Miller said. "Or ten days. You'll need time to put your affairs in order, your papers—"

"Doctor," I said, "I need twenty-four hours to put my life

in order. If you can't set it up in twenty-four hours, I'll go down the street and find a man who can."

And I walked out, Mary hurrying to catch up.

I am not sure I knew then, or I know now, why I was so angry. But I am glad I was. I think it was a healthy sign. I wanted to plunge in and fight this thing, I wanted to tear it out with my bare hands, if I could, and next best, with a surgeon's knife. And I had been challenged. I wasn't going to sound like that little tractor driver.

He'd got my Irish up, and speaking of getting my Irish up, Mary tugged at my arm outside the office, and pointed to an American flag hanging out of a doorway where people lined up on the sidewalk.

"Honey," she said, "we haven't voted."

So in the middle of it all, we steered our way to our precinct, and cast our votes for John F. Kennedy. And stayed up all night, rooting him in.

2

Pretty Flowers

At home—on 512 North Palm Drive, where we'd lived for over twenty years—I began to make those phone calls that put into movement the necessary acts a man must commit when his life and his career are at stake, and he still has time, energy, and mind to tackle them. The transfer of insurance policies, trust funds, bank accounts, property deeds—the sheets of paper that determine a man's wealth and the security of his family, his loved ones. Plus other more difficult calls, and a handful of letters.

I phoned my business manager, Noel Singer, one of God's great men, and broke the news. Noel had handled my accounts, my papers, for years. And still does. Mary and I had told no one. Not a single soul. Now we had to.

Singer began to arrange to transfer ownership from my name to Mary's and to my sons'. He would have the house we lived in refinanced, so we could have ready cash. At the same time he would put it on the market. We wouldn't be able to afford it. No profession, no money. As simple as that. In order to have some money, now, he would liquidate what assets I had, turn them into cash, so Mary would have something just in case I wasn't one of those who were operated on and lived.

I finished with Noel, and I called my closest friends. Walter Bunker, Dennis Day, Red Knorp, Pat O'Brien, Leon Janney,

Gene Raymond, fellow Bohemians, fellow golf-club members. I asked Wally Bunker, my Bohemian tentmate, to sell my Bel-Air Club membership. He did, for $3000.

Mary called the boys, Barrie, the older, in New York; Leslie, in San Diego. Barrie, then, was with Kenyon & Eckhardt, the advertising agency, and they'd just sent him out to the Coast on business, when he surprised me one day by dropping in at the Alcazar and catching *The Best Man*. Now he was stuck to his desk. But he promised to keep in touch; he did. He called every day. Leslie had just taken an assignment with a travel agency in San Diego, to write travel brochures.

"I'll keep you informed," Mary said.

"No you won't," Leslie said. "I'll come home." He quit his job, and he came home.

Some of the phone calls returned. Sally Kendall, sister-in-law of Walter Bunker, phoned me.

"Bill," she said, "I just got a dog, a perfectly marvelous miniature French poodle. He's yours when you get out of the hospital."

Which is how I got Patrick, a bristling, yapping, chocolate-colored bundle of Gallic joy, and as big as an eclair. Gallic? With that name Patrick he is more Gael than Gaul, and the love of my life. What a gift! And what a gift is friendship. Bless these people.

On Wednesday, November 9, Mary and I had cocktails and supper with Eddie and Frances Bernard, old and dear friends. Nobody talked cancer. We laughed, instead, and then Mary and I drove to the Los Angeles Eye and Ear Hospital, checking in shortly before 10 P.M.

When we entered the hospital, my heart sank. It looked like a dump. A very small private hospital, very unostentatious, a bit gray, dreary. Mary sat with me in my tiny room, and we talked. Idle talk, mainly. I don't remember too much of what we talked, far beyond the end of visiting hours. What does a man talk about at a time like that? It remains a blur, tinged with love and regret, like faded violets. I do know we talked more of the distant past than of the present. I asked Mary, "How come we got married?" and she said, "Because you were convinced two could live as cheap as one."

I shook my head, this time in mock regret. "If I'd known then, what I know now."

Once we laughed. Mary recalled the time I'd taken my folks to a theater in Brooklyn, to see Mary dance on stage. She got a job with *George White's Scandals*, just a slip of a girl sixteen years old, with a tiny lithe figure that set my heart pounding then and doesn't do my cool a bit of good today.

I was proud of Mary. She was my only real girl, the only woman I've been truly close to all my adult life. I took my folks to see her dance, a broad grin across my face, my dad on one side of me, and Mom on the other, and Mary came kicking across the stage, and I belted Dad in the ribs and squeezed Mom's arm, and said, "How about her? Isn't she something?" And then her shoulder strap broke.

What was worse, she didn't know it, she was so involved in putting on a show for us. She gave us a show all right. Her left breast began to peep out from under. You could hear the stage manager, in the wings, whispering hoarsely, "Put it in, Mary, put it *in*," but she thought he'd said, "Put it *on*," and she twisted and twirled and really turned it on. I tried to sink six feet and 200 pounds of Bill Gargan beneath the floor of the theater orchestra. The curtain crashed down early—thank God— but the night was a shambles.

So we laughed, and then the nurse poked her head in and said, "I'm afraid I've been too lenient." It was nearly midnight, and tomorrow was going to be a big day, and an early one.

I said, "You're a saint, darling. I love you." We kissed and she was gone, and those were the last words I ever spoke to Mary Elizabeth Gargan in what people call my "normal" voice.

Alone now, and not yet affected by the sleeping pill the nurse had given me, I had time for a few thoughts of my own. I had learned in the preceding hours that I was unafraid of death. That sounds like bragging, but it isn't. Smugness does not become the human animal, and I'd been smug enough when I had boasted earlier how I'd speak better than that little tractor

driver whose voice lacked any of the human warmth and reso-
nance we tend to associate with speech. Smug, proud, superior,
and a little bit whistling in the graveyard. But now I had relaxed,
and I found myself yielding to the moments ahead, unafraid.
It's not unusual. I have since met hundreds—thousands—of
cancer victims, and I find they also manage to sustain themselves,
most of them, in the dark moments before their operation, and
again, immediately after. Which is not to say that gloom, bitterness, waves of self-pity do not set in. They crash their way in,
and sit like vultures. But that is usually later, when you have
faced the news of your cancer, and then the operation, and then
the immediate convalescence, and you think (smugly, again)—
My, that wasn't so bad. Then, without warning, black bile crawls
up the throat, invades the heart. That's not quite true. There
is some warning. You have occasional fleeting bleak moments
when you turn your face toward the hospital wall, or you lie
alone on a pillow gone rigid in the hours before dawn, and you
cry a little, silently.

But most people have the strength and the courage, if that
is what it is, to face the music. They also have friends, wives,
husbands, lovers, children, parents. And they have God.

I have a little prayer I speak each morning, and by now—
Mary gone, the room dark and lonely—it was already morning,
though black as a grave. I wasn't sure what the true morning
would bring. I suspected it would bring what hospital mornings
are famous for bringing, people scurrying in and out of your
room, nurses, doctors, interns, ward boys, in that cross-traffic of
purposeful activity that cheerily announces that this place isn't
really for sick people, but for busy people. Get busy. And I
further suspected it would all be foreign to me. I hadn't been
really sick a day in my adult life. I wasn't too sure I'd be
operating too rationally, with a sleeping pill under my belt, and
anesthesia waiting for me upstairs. I just might not get that prayer
in tomorrow morning.

Besides, what's wrong with one extra prayer? I got out of bed,
and on my knees, I murmured:

"Look down upon me, good and gentle Jesus, whilst before

Thy face I humbly kneel, and with burning soul, pray and beseech Thee to fix deep in my heart, live sentiments of faith, hope, and charity." I tossed in a quick prayer for the sweet repose of my parents, dead nearly a quarter of a century, God love them, and I got back into bed, laughing quietly over that broken shoulder strap. I chuckled my way toward sleep, and just before I fell off, I hastily threw another prayer on God's lap. "Don't let that guy be a butterfingers."

A laryngectomy—the removal of a man's larynx, either partially or totally—is long and difficult. Mine was a total. Bear with these brief details; they will very likely disgust you; they would have disgusted me. But try to see beyond the blood and mucus to the marvelous invention and ingenuity of man. Forty years ago, when a surgeon told his patient what Dr. Miller had told me—cancer of the larynx—your chances of survival were extremely slim. Today, 90 percent of all laryngectomies, performed early enough, are successful. Victims who would have died, forty years ago, live on to old age. More, the quality of their lives has improved, because speech techniques have radically improved, and will continue to improve. Someday a surgeon will cut out a diseased voice box and slip in another larynx, made of lightweight metal alloys and plastic, or some new miracle fabric. Engineers shape new organs every day, and surgeons replace old diseased ones. Look what they're doing with heart transplants these days. So too with larynxes, someday, and perhaps someday soon. But even without a plastic voice box inserted in your throat, surgeons have figured ways to replace man's old speech with new.

The human body itself is responsible for much of the success of laryngectomies. The coils of the vocal cords are gone? Let's find something to replace them with. What's nearby? The top of the esophagus. Look at it. Where it joins the throat, you get a coiled mass of throat muscle. What would happen if air is made to pulsate as it passes these narrow throat muscles, shaped so much like vocal cords? Sound. That's what happens. Sound comes up on the wings of the passage of pulsing air.

So perhaps, when it gets down to it, we can lay the credit

where it ought to lie. With the Creator, who made man's body so that when a piece of his brain is destroyed, another piece is urged to do double duty, its old function and a new one as well. The working is intricate beyond the most facile engineer or surgeon. God has worked well, and the human body remains his greatest triumph. This is what God hath truly wrought. Not a telephone or a radio or a plastic organ. Man, and the web of blood, nerves, muscles, and bone, the mysterious interlocking of mind and fibre and soul.

Do not see only the mess of blood and mucus, though they are present in the operation and its aftermath. I breathe through a hole in my throat, today. A hole in the throat may sound like a disgusting thing to breathe out of, but the beauty of it is that I breathe. You blow your nose; I clear my stoma. I function. My body, God's body, functions.

They wheeled me upstairs at 8 A.M. and Dr. Miller went in with his knife, and totally removed my larynx, at the uppermost part of the trachea, or windpipe. With it went the cancer, for it had not metastasized. With the larynx gone, the connection from my mouth and nose to my lungs had been broken. A new connection must be made.

A hole is cut into my throat, about at the level of the Adam's apple (now removed). The trachea—that top part of the windpipe, precious avenue to the lungs—now is joined to the hole in my throat. Presto! I have an opening—like a nostril or a mouth, but called a stoma—that leads to the lungs. I can breathe.

The rest of the operation—six hours in all—is patchwork; delicate, exasperating, tricky, but patchwork. I made it more exasperating, because I turned out to be quite a bleeder. Every time Dr. Miller touched me, I spouted blood, which he then had to staunch. The usual laryngectomy takes three or four hours; I bled my way to six. But the extra hours still were patchwork. The major parts of the operation are removing the larynx, creating a new avenue from the stoma to the lungs, and closing off the old passageway from the mouth and nostrils to the lungs. Now when I take air into my mouth or nose, it leads only to my stomach. You know what happens when you swallow air into your stomach. You belch. So, I belch—thank God! That is how I speak.

And when I take food or drink into my mouth, it goes straight to the stomach, no longer able to wedge even the tiniest drop into my windpipe. You can choke over your food or your drink, inhaling a drop into your lungs. I can't. Chalk one up for me. Chalk up another one. You can drop a plastic bag over my head and keep it there for a week, and I'll still be around. Chalk up a third. You often breathe through your mouth. The mouth is the greatest repository of germs in the human body. The stoma is far more sterile. My breath, then, is purer than yours.

No, it is not fun. It is, frankly, a mess. It was a mess. All the while I was being worked over, Mary and Leslie stood outside in the corridor. The walls are thin. They could hear Dr. Miller asking to have the light moved or to pass him this or that instrument. And they saw me wheeled out, the afternoon of Thursday, November 10. My eyes were open; they don't give you a total anesthesia, because if they do, you may choke during the operation. Not that I felt anything.

Mary and Leslie also saw Dr. Miller, when he came out, his coat spotted with my blood. He held a towel, folded neatly. "In here," he said to Mary and Leslie Gargan, "is Mr. Gargan's larynx." He began to unfold the towel. Leslie (so I have been told) tightened a grip on his mother's elbow. In the towel, lying like a tiny chain, like a string of pearls, was the supporting structure of the larynx, tiny linked bloodless sections of cartilage. In the center of the necklace lay the larynx, the voice box itself, and shaped like a small box. Dr. Miller touched a long narrow very sharp instrument to a small wormlike bit of tissue. "This is the true vocal cord." He touched another worm. "And this is the false." He turned over the necklace. On the back of the boxlike larynx lay a lump, the size of a small walnut, gray-green, the color of a shrimp you buy at the butcher's before you clean and de-vein it. He poked at the walnut with his instrument. It would not budge. It lay embedded, as if in concrete, in the larynx. "And that is the cancer."

Mary and Leslie nodded.

"We will send all this to the lab, of course," Dr. Miller said. "But I wanted you to see what we took out. Do you have any questions?"

They shook their heads. But they knew, for sure, why the larynx had been removed.

Later that afternoon, I came to in my room, and saw figures hovering like ghosts, Dr. Miller, Mary, Leslie, a nurse. The room seemed strange, shimmering with colors, a psychedelic vision.

Dr. Miller's face loomed over mine. "So many flowers have arrived," he said, "we've had to move you to a bigger room."

I guess I nodded. Flowers. I couldn't have cared less. The feeling, again, was of stupor, the results of anesthesia, and the shock of all the tearing away at nerves and blood vessels. I floated off into another sleep.

When I came to again, I saw the flowers. I opened my mouth. I moved my lips, but nothing came out.

A nurse indicated a pad at my side, one of those magic slates of wax paper children write on and then lift up to get rid of the words and clean up the slate for another message.

I wrote on the pad, "*Pretty flowers*," and then I tried again, opening my mouth, because I was thirsty and I wanted a drink of water.

Now it registered.

No sound came out. Not because a tube stuck out of my nose and another lay in my throat. I couldn't speak because my voice box was gone. All the words of the past weeks about the operation and the loss of my speech had not really meant anything. I understood them, but I did not dig them, if you dig the difference. Now I dug.

I had lost the power of speech, that marvelous gift that separates men from animals. Gone. Totally gone. A man with a bellowing powerful voice one day and a mute the next. I felt my head start to turn, toward the wall. It was a feeling I would experience off and on for days, and then later, for weeks, months. Turn to the wall, away from life, toward blankness, death. The void of the wall, its blank face, expressionless, empty, like an idiot's mind, a blind man's sockets, held comfort. Hiya Wall, meet Mute.

But the nurse bent swiftly and she whispered, "Careful. The tubes."

So I didn't fully turn to meet Wall, my friend of nighttime hours and daytime bile, where I could whisper to myself (soundlessly, of course), "Why me?" and the wall stared back its idiot's vacuous grin.

I dozed off again, came to, and dozed off, and then it was night, my first night alone with my own black void, but a merciful injection slipped gently into my arm rode me blankly through to my first new morning.

Mornings are better. No doubt about it. They were pretty flowers. Mary was pretty Mary. Dr. Miller was the same no-nonsense man. I began to take stock, where I was, what was happening to me. I began to be interested.

Besides the tube sticking out of my throat, I felt a lump. To make my case slightly more exasperating, I am allergic to adhesive. Today if you slap a piece of sticky adhesive to my finger, the skin immediately puffs up. Usually the tube in a laryngectomee's throat is kept in place with adhesive. With me, it had to be held gently in place by rolls of gauze. The result was I couldn't move as much as most post-laryngectomy patients.

The tubes are like crutches. You breathe through the stoma, the hole in your throat just above the breastbone, slightly larger than a half-inch across, reasonably round, like the blowhole of a dolphin or a whale. But in the process of creating this new airway, the surgeon must adhere mucus membrane of the windpipe to the skin of the neck, and Nature resents the joining. Each tends to want to have nothing to do with the other, at least for a spell, until they become compatible. The stoma usually tries to shrink away. So a tube of silver alloy is inserted, to keep the stoma wide open.

The tube becomes encrusted with mucus and blood. The blood follows all the necessary destruction that the throat and windpipe undergo before the construction can begin. Surgery victims bleed;

it is the name of the game. I bled. The tube would fill with blood and mucus. If you leave such a clogged tube in a man's throat, through which he breathes, he won't. Breathe.

Every so often—several times a day in the beginning, and less often as the days went by and the healing quickened—Dr. Miller would remove the tube from my throat to clean it out. Later, nurses would remove it. Still later (and we are talking about the span of just a few days), I would remove it. The patient's care of himself is part of healthy convalescence. You get involved in yourself and in your recovery. A clean tube, a clean airway, is recovery.

But when the tube is first taken out, you panic.

I knew what Dr. Miller was going to do—he had told me but it didn't matter. I stiffened, and grabbed the sides of the bed.

"Relax," he said softly, as he slipped the tube gently from my throat. "I'll have it back in a jiffy."

He did.

But in that jiffy, I felt I would strangle. Breath came fitfully, in thin threads, to my lungs, and then too quickly expired back out. I would try to grab a huge lungful of air through my stoma, and instead I got a tiny gaspful.

Worse, the stoma begins to close. My stoma began to close.

Most stomas do that. Stoma skin resents mucus-membrane windpipe, and it begins to shut itself down. So the airway becomes smaller, and in the mind of a laryngectomee, you think it is no bigger than the eye of a needle through which you are drawing a slim thread of oxygen, about to snap.

Actually, the stoma becomes smaller, but it isn't as drastic as all that. It never closes all the way, and Dr. Miller cleans tubes in a jiffy, and the tube is back in before too many of those thready breaths have been inhaled.

Nor do all stomas react that way. In some people, the compatibility of mucus membrane and skin is achieved almost immediately, and the stoma hole remains wide and steady when the tube is out. In a few others, the incompatibility of the silver

alloy to the throat is greater than the other incompatibility, so
when the tube is removed, the stoma blessedly enlarges, thankful
at being free of contact with the silver tube.

But I would wager in all cases, in the beginning, a laryngectomee panics when the tube is first removed, no matter how
wide the stoma gapes, and breathing is reduced psychologically
to that faint thread.

Miller would take out the tube, clean it, examine and measure
the stoma, and replace the tube. But the tube, as I said, is a
crutch, and it would soon have to go. So the few-second interval
is gradually to a few minutes.

I remember on the second or third day, Dr. Miller said, "Now
we'll leave it out for ten minutes."

"*Ten minutes?*" I wrote frantically on my magic slate.

"Ten minutes," he said firmly.

"*You can't—*" I started to write, but he could and did. And
I could and did. Not well, Full of panic, sure the stoma would
close finally and surely, and I would strangle. I felt the stoma
closing, the skin contracting until the lips on each side were
now—I was sure—nearly touching.

Then the ten minutes ended, the tube slipped smoothly in,
and Dr. Miller said, "Fine. The stoma didn't change size at all
that time."

And the nurses! No matter how skilled a surgeon's hands,
they cannot match the cool feathery touch of a woman's fingers.
When Dr. Miller told me not to worry about the formation of
blood, that it was a normal thing, I believed him, and still
turned stiff as a board. When one of those exquisite things, those
angels in white (and the most exquisite, angelic was a plumply
pregnant matronly woman) said the same words, I believed
them, and though I won't say I remained loose as a goose, I
didn't turn to stone.

But whether you believe the doctor or the nurses, and turn
rigid or remain relaxed, the blood and mucus have to be cleared.
It is terribly uncomfortable, magnified in the patient's mind,
but still present, a lump that has to be removed for clear breath-

ing. Now enters the suction machine, a new tube, attached to a suction device, and leading to a glass jar.

At first the nurses operated it for me, clearing away mucus and other matter. Mainly, mucus, Nature's lubricant of the throat and gullet, but with less to do now that the passageway to the stomach has been separated from the passage to the lungs. So unused mucus accumulates, and the sunction machine must pump it out and deposit it, pinkly tinted, in a glass jar. I got to use it myself, within a few days, and in the perverse way of patients who want to get well, I enjoyed filling that glass jar. It is an accomplishment.

All this, I repeat, is a messy business, but especially so in the beginning. Tension seems to induce a greater mucus discharge. But it slowly stops being messy, and eventually it is as messy as a sneeze or a sedate blowing of the nose.

Eventually. Meanwhile I continued to feel I couldn't truly clear my throat of the blood I sensed forming there, and of the wad of mucus which I magnified in my mind to the size of a golf ball.

Yet beyond these feelings, one simple fact emerges, and grows stronger each day.

You're alive.

Every hour I felt better. I was and am blessed with a strong constitution, and I convalesced well. I would often ask that barren frustrating question, "Why me, God? Why, God, *me?*" I sometimes felt overwhelmed by bitterness, by discouragement, by the melodramatic notion that the curtain had fallen for the last time. Then panic and revulsion for myself would set in. The question, "Why me, God?" is common to cancer victims, and I am a common cancer victim. But I sensed that in the question lay the trap of self-pity. I fell into the trap many times, but I somehow knew enough to climb back out. Another question—common also to laryngectomees—would spring up in place of that whine of self-pity. I would say to myself (that's another joke; I couldn't say any other way), "All right, Gargan, you're here. What are you going to do about it?"

And I answered, "Nothing."
So I began to get well.

Everybody helped. I insisted on keeping the door open, and
my bed propped up. A lowered bed is too much like a casket.
And a closed door shuts out the life outside your room. So
visitors began to pour through that open door. My son, Leslie.
Gene Raymond. Wally Ford. Pat O'Brien. Eddie and Frances
Bernard. Dennis Day. George Murphy, who was later to become
United States Senator George Murphy, and who had had a
throat operation some fifteen years before, for the removal of
polyps, and later would have another, for the partial removal
of his cancerous vocal cords. Neil Reagan, advertising agency
executive and the brother of Ronald Reagan. Neil also has had
half his vocal cords removed. Today it is quite a sight to hear
the three of us together, me hoarse and croaky, and them
hoarse and high-pitched. I can outshout the two of them.
    And, of course, Mary. She kept busy in the room. The flowers
continued to pour in, like to an Irish wake, and she kept trying
to find space for them. They were awfully pretty flowers, but
along about the third day, I realized a new fact of life.
    I couldn't smell them.
    I couldn't smell anything.
    A laryngectomee loses his sense of taste and smell right away.
Taste nearly always comes back (mine has come back and is
stronger and more sensitive today than it ever was), and with
some laryngectomees, the sense of smell returns. But not mine.
If I take a rose or a heavily perfumed handkerchief and press
it to my nostrils, I get a faint far-away whiff. Otherwise, I can't
smell. It has its compensations. I can't smell garbage or smog
or body odor or bad breath or the smell of California's hills
when the weeds are cut down and begin to rot, or the smell of
oil wells that clog Southern California nostrils. I need not tell
you it poses problems. I have nearly burned down the kitchen a
half dozen times, because I couldn't smell something overcooking
ten feet away.

And I can't smell flowers, even a hospital room piled thick and high with them.

The door opened one day, and Mary helped a nurse in with three or four more pots. "Look, Bill," Mary said, a bright smile pasted to her teeth. "More flowers." Then her shoulders slumped. "More blasted flowers."

I reached for the bedside pad, and wrote, "*Thank them very much, but tell them I can't smell. Anything else would be acceptable.*"

"Like what?" she said. "Rubber plants?"

I shook my head and lifted up the sheet of the magic slate and wrote again. "*Tell them—'Can't smell. Send scotch.'*"

Mary grinned and showed it to the nurse.

The nurse was dubious. "I don't think Dr. Miller wants you to drink."

Now, there was a crisis. I wrote, "*Send in Dr. Miller.*"

But she couldn't, because he was not available. The next day when Miller made his visit I wrote, "*Doc, can I have a drink?*"

"I don't know, Mr. Gargan," he said. "Let me look at your record." He went out and came back a few minutes later. "You're coming along fine. Certainly you can have a drink. From what you've told me I know you have a tolerance for liquor."

And I'd say that was the understatement of the century.

I wrote on my slate, to the nurse, after Miller had left, "*Call Mary. Tell her to bring a bottle of scotch.*"

So the nurse called—a few minutes after six in the morning— and nearly gave Mary a heart attack.

Mary had a friend of ours, Mary Morrow, staying over, to help with the house, the shopping, and other necessities of daily living, while Mary spent most of her time at the hospital. When the phone rang, at 6:05, both girls leaped out of bed.

I heard the nurse say, "Mrs. Gargan, how soon can you get over here?"

And Mary said (she told me later), "Right away. Is he—?"

"Bring a bottle of scotch when you come."

So Mary and Mary Morrow threw on their bathrobes, and

marched right past the bar, where bottles of scotch stood in neat platoons, and they charged into Mary's car and drove to an all-night drugstore. Mary was near tears. Dr. Miller, she knew, was death on cigarettes and liquor.

Still, Mary was Mary. Here she was, in a drugstore at dawn, wearing a bathrobe, and asking for a bottle of scotch. She had to be, in the clerk's mind, an alcoholic who'd run out of the stuff. But then she said, "And gift wrap it, please." Not an alcoholic. Just a nut.

She and Mary Morrow rushed to the hospital, parked in the visitors' lot, and ran to my room.

"What's—wrong?" she asked the nurse.

"Wrong?" the nurse grinned. "Dr. Miller says your husband can have a drink, and he's not waiting on ceremony."

Mary mixed a milk punch, an ounce or so of scotch and a couple of ounces of milk, and a nurse poured it down the tube in my nose, and I want you to know that that milk punch was one of the best drinks in my life.

That night I got a new nurse, an absolute raving beauty, and after I'd finished enjoying just the look of her, I got down to more basic pleasures. I asked her, on my magic slate, where my nightly drink was.

"I don't know what you mean," she said haughtily.

"*Check my record*," I wrote.

She did, and came back with the bottle. Maybe she was sore at me (all I'd done was *looked*), or else she knew nothing about drinking, because she didn't mix the milk and scotch. I was busy watching a television show, and she threw the booze in, straight. A piece of flame hit my stomach and I hit the ceiling. If I could have screamed, I would have shattered every glass window in the hospital. Fortunately she knew enough to toss in the milk right after it.

The scotch punch was not my only sustenance. I was fed intravenously for a few days—more tubes—and then I began to take soft foods, like an infant. I wasn't hungry, and I'm not a big pablum man, so I didn't put my soul into my fare. The result was I kept grandpawing my food, dribbling like a baby or a toothless old man. Actually, it was strange. My throat was still sore, from the operation, and the structure of my throat and esophagus had been drastically changed. I was eating with a new instrument, and I had not mastered it. So I dribbled my soft cereal and my soft-cooked egg, my farina floating in cream and butter like blobs of fat, and today when I hear patients tell me they didn't like their hospital steak because it wasn't rare enough or their *coq au vin* lacked garlic, I think of those days I sucked baby food past my battered throat. I feel no sympathy.

Mary did more than put an end to the run on the florist shops and provide drink and company and love. One day I had another visitor, a woman who wore a flat gold necklace at her throat and who carried a handful of pamphlets.

Her name, she said, was Teckla Tibbs, and she said it in a voice deep and vibrant, very husky, with that mechanical quality all laryngectomees have. Let's face it, it is not human speech as you and I know it—but hers was very clear, very understandable.

She wore that piece of flat jewelry at her throat to conceal her stoma.

She had a real estate business in Los Angeles, but she was not here to sell me a new house or buy my old one. She was a volunteer worker for the American Cancer Society, and California's delegate to the board of directors of the International Laryngectomee Association. Dr. Miller had mentioned her to Mary, and Mary had asked her to come to see me. Mary sensed it could not all be well. She was right. She always is. I was getting better every day, but part of it was like a blind man who has learned to walk with a cane, and now runs (blindly) very fast, straight at a stone wall. Drinking wasn't talking. Whenever Dr. Miller mentioned esophageal speech (even if I could have talked, I couldn't have pronounced it), I seemed to stiffen. Mary notices everything. One of my senses had been ripped away; hers—all of them—had correspondingly increased. She knew I was resisting the notion of speaking. Mary had found Teckla Tibbs, without telling me, and now I lay in bed, a captive audience, listening with growing amazement.

No, it wasn't a human voice. It was mechanical. But I understood every word. She seemed to take a breath, though with little effort, and then the words rolled out, and then another breath, and four or five more words, and oh, so clear.

I hurriedly scrawled, *"Will I ever talk like that?"*

She smiled. She actually laughed, except that a laryngectomee can't make a laughing sound. To balance things, in God's way, he can't make a crying sound, either.

"Well," she said, "you'll talk, but not like me. Yours will be deeper, like a man's speech."

And I laughed, for the first time, a silent laugh. Her voice was deep as a well.

But she had given me the notion that I really had a chance to speak clearly enough that I could communicate. Man has that precious miracle of speech, that separates him from the beasts, and I wasn't going to have to join the beasts after all. Speech. Human speech. Real magic, not a so-called magic slate, a pad for mumblers and mutes. Speech, spoken words. I could— perhaps, cross my fingers, pray to God, trust to Him, and to luck—I could, someday, maybe, phone my sons, order a drink at a bar, tell a joke, and say, again, to Mary, "I love you."

"You can learn to speak, like me," she said. "You swallow air and then you expel it"—expel came out exbel; laryngectomees can't say the letter "p"—"to make sound with the pharynx, the muscles in your throat. The blue pamphlet"—bamphlet—"shows you how."

She talked some more, and I sat there fascinated. She gave me the feeling I had a chance to speak, and speak fairly well. By God, I thought, I'll make it. Before that, I had heard Dr. Miller, but I did not believe him. Oh, I'll talk, and better than that tractor driver, but how much better? Miller told me about speech school, and I felt, All right, I'll go, I'll talk, I'll mumble. So what? I still wouldn't be the William Gargan of the past. The tool of my trade was gone.

Teckla Tibbs, at the bidding of my wife, had given me a lift.

When she left, Mary came back in. She bent over and reached for my pillow, to straighten it.

I shook my head. I would straighten it myself. I grabbed the pillow. I was not an invalid.

Mary stepped back and grinned her love right into me.

I was getting better. Or so I thought. But you think you've covered all exits when along comes a setback from an angle you've never noticed. You couldn't have noticed.

A few days before I checked in to the hospital for my operation, Clark Gable had suffered a heart attack and was taken to Hollywood Presbyterian Hospital. I kept check of Clark's progress, in the papers and over the radio, and after a few days it seemed he had it licked. Meanwhile, he must have heard about my operation. We knew each other quite well. I'd beaten Clark out of a job back on Broadway thirty years earlier, and we'd kept in touch ever since. We had something in common. We both had a mad passion for Carole Lombard, which was not strange; so did every man who ever met Carole. Mine, of course, was confined to working with Carole. Clark—no fool, he—married the girl.

On the morning of November 17—my seventh day—I walked out to the nurses' station, to flirt with the nurses, especially the plump pregnant one, Mary Brosnan, and to pick up my mail. My own Mary had picked it up every other morning, but I was getting pretty itchy by this time. I do not much enjoy sitting around doing nothing; I wanted to go home. Dr. Miller had said at least two weeks, and probably three, but I could not see how I could last that long, on my back. So I collected my mail, took a little walk, and went back to my room.

In the mail was a golf book, with an inscription, "*Hang on fast. Love, Clark.*" Well, I thought, that's nice. I got into bed and began to turn the pages. At the same time, I'd turned on the television set, and with a remote control unit, I picked up the early news.

And the first thing I heard, and saw, was the news of Clark Gable's death. Some time before midnight, he'd been reading a magazine, turning the pages, and in between one page and the next, he'd died. Like that.

I froze. Terror struck an icicle into my heart.

Clark. Me. Hospital. Death. Magazine. Book. Death. Hospital bed. Instant death.

I am ashamed to say, I went crazy. I clawed my way out of bed; I tore my tubes out of throat and nose. I scrabbled for my clothes. A nurse looked in and screamed. She rushed for the phone. She tried to get Dr. Miller. Miller was in surgery. She called Mary. "Mrs. Gargan? Can you came down right away? Mr. Gargan is tearing the place apart." I reached for a pad. With trembling hand, I scrawled, *"I'm going home. Get clothes."*

The nurse stared at the pad. "He says he wants to leave. No, I can't give him a shot. There are no orders for a shot."

I'd have liked to have seen her try. I'd have ripped her arm off. That's how crazy I was. Where in hell were my pants?

I sat on the edge of my bed, panting. Mary showed up, within minutes, it seemed.

"You look like a chipmunk," she said. I still was bandaged, with just my cheeks, eyes, nose, and mouth showing. I had a touch of edema, so my face was swollen. Chipmunk was probably accurate. "What are you acting like one for?"

I shoved the book at her. She saw the inscription, and briefly closed her eyes.

"Clark's gone," she said. "There's nothing we can do. Get back in bed."

Dr. Miller also arrived. So did a young intern who calmly lifted me and laid me on my back, in bed.

Suffice to say, I cooled down. But the terror had not fully left. For the first time, I had truly connected my own sickness with death.

On the eighth day—the next day—I wrote on my pad, *"When can I go home?"*

On the tenth day, I went home, earlier than had been planned. I guess the hospital personnel were relieved. When I walked out of the hospital, I looked around. The place that had looked like a dump, gray and dreary, when I entered, now had another look. Unpretentious, business-like. Like Dr. Miller. No nonsense. It had a job to do. It had done it magnificently.

I went home, clutching my blue pamphlet, *Your New Voice*, put out by the American Cancer Society.

When Mary and I got home, a television repairman, Howard Singer, was in the house; Howard has kept our sets in working order for years. Leslie had let him in, and as I clumped up the stairs, he was just finishing tuning the set in my bedroom.

"Look, Bill," he said, "it's fixed." The screen began to flicker; he tuned up the sound, and the first thing I heard was my voice, in an old movie.

Singer turned white. Frantically he twisted the dial.

I raised my hand and slammed it down on the set. I couldn't say what I wanted to say, but inside I was screaming, "Off. Off. Turn that damned thing off."

I sat on the bed, shaking, the terror once more at my heart. I looked down and there still clutched in my hand was the blue pamphlet, *Your New Voice*.

Self-pity flooded over me.

3

Sand in Our Sandwiches

. . . All my life, I wanted to sing. If they'd ever let me, of course, I would have emptied the theater.

Not that I haven't had my chance. In 1945, while making *The Bells of St. Mary's*, directed by that wonderful funny man, Leo McCarey, I'd stand around during a break on the set and admire Bing Crosby as he whipped up an impromptu quartet to harmonize. Once Bing couldn't find a fourth, so he asked me to step in and sing bass. Why not? We rolled right along until it came time for me to join in, and after a few seconds I noticed I was singing alone.

Crosby looked at me queerly. "Are you ill?" he asked.

That ended my semiprofessional singing career.

The odd thing, my only brother, Ed, had a marvelous voice, good enough to get him onto the stage in the spear-carrying chorus at the Metropolitan Opera, where the Met's general manager, Gatti-Casazza, wanted to pay his way over to Italy for voice lessons. But Ed wouldn't go. Singing was a lark, to Ed. He was the kind of guy who woke up laughing. That's how he sang. Laughing. He'd sing at a concert and he'd go along beautifully, his big voice swelling, and then for the hell of it, he'd let loose a blooper. He couldn't have cared less. Later, he became an actor, playing Irish cops in over a hundred films, doing them exceedingly well, but never giving the work much more than the time of day.

But he could sing. Right from the start. My father once took us out to Canarsie when I was a kid to hear Ed sing at a beer festival. This was before Ed developed his talent for hitting clinkers. When he finished people stood up and cheered, and other people banged their heavy beer steins against the wooden table. It was funny; Dad, Ed, and I all had identical speaking voices. People always confused us, on the phone, or between rooms, or whatever. But the similarity ended there. If I'd have sung at a beer festival, people would have banged their beer steins before I finished, to drown me out.

My father and mother had had seven children, but only Ed and I survived childbirth or early infancy. In fact, I was a twin. Perhaps this made me closer to Ed, though he was four years older. He traveled with an older crowd, played with other, older kids, and went to work while I was still in high school, pretending to study. All in all, we spent little time together, though we did share a bedroom wherever we lived in Brooklyn, taking turns to bank the coal at night and clean out the ashes the next morning. Sometimes we didn't take turns. There'd be a sign Mother would put up near the front door—FIX FURNACE!—and whichever of us got home first would head for the basement and go to work. But as often as not, the other would come down, too, and Ed and I would work down there, filling each other in on the day's doings, he maybe a runner on Wall Street, and me a slow walker to school. We had to squeeze in these meetings; there was so little time. He'd be up at the crack of dawn, to go to work, or take off for somewhere, and I'd go to school, or else I'd go to work. Still, we were close. When I was born—on July 17, 1905—an uncle on my father's side, Big Ed Gargan, felt my brother Ed's nose might be out of joint by my arrival. So Uncle Ed came to the house with a small puppy nestled in his coat pocket. He handed the puppy to my brother; Ed promptly named the pup Prince, and because Ed was that kind of guy, he more or less shunted the dog over to me. Prince and I grew up together. Big Ed Gargan, by the way, was called Big Ed because he stood some six feet three or four inches in his bare feet. Which is how he died. He stepped on a rusty nail, in his bare feet, developed blood poisoning, and died.

Maybe Ed and I were close for other reasons. We were a lone-wolf family. My father was a gambler, which did not sit well with his in-laws. It seems to bother other people as well. Whenever a press agent or a publicist at a movie studio would put together a biographical sheet on me, he'd insist on listing my father as a "building contractor and a member of the Secret Service."

He was a gambler. A bookmaker and a gambler. He knew Joe Adonis and Little Augie and even Al Capone. He made book in the copyroom of the New York *World*, and made book in Room 9 of City Hall. The house we lived in the first years of my life, at 427 Henry Street, the same street on which Winston Churchill's mother was born, was a big brownstone, four stories high on the edge of Brooklyn Heights. Dad had won it in a poker game. He also owned a piece of a burlesque theater, and several saloons. When I'd come home from grade school in the afternoon, nine or ten years old, I'd manage to go by way of his saloon on 49th Street and Third Avenue in Brooklyn, where my father would give me a small glass of port wine or two or three ounces of beer. That was the beginning of my drinking. I can't say it ever hurt me. Whether it ever helped me is another question.

So Dad was the black sheep of the family, and *he* couldn't have cared less. In fact, he gloried in it. Mother was more strait-laced, a bit of a prude on the surface, but in reality a vivacious quick-witted woman who ran with Dad all her life and his. When Mother died in 1937, the undertaker said to me, "We will proceed slowly from the church to Holy Cross Cemetery—" and I interrupted. "Mr. Dunnigan," I said, "begging your pardon, but let's have none of this eight-mile-an-hour stuff. Mother went fast all through life, and I'd appreciate it if she could go fast on this last trip." You never saw such a wild caravan. She would have clucked her disapproval and wrinkled her nose, but she would have loved every careening moment of it.

Dad was Bill Gargan, a rosy-cheeked man whose auburn hair turned pure white while I was still a kid. Mother was Irene

Gertrude Flynn before she married, with dancing blue eyes and light brown hair, and a pug nose that said she was Irish. Actually, they were lace-curtain Irish, born in this country. I've never had the feeling that Ireland was my home. This country is my home. Dad would take me to church on Sundays—he liked to try different churches, all over the city—and if the sermon was delivered in a thick brogue, Dad would whisper to me, "Greenhorn! To get that guy over here, they had to tie him down and put shoes on him." Then he'd defiantly slap a dime in the collection plate. He was a critic of style. When he liked a sermon, particularly one delivered in bombast with all the flourishes, he'd place bills on the plate. I've seen him leave two one-hundred dollar bills when he was particularly pleased. He never used the envelope that came with the plate. "What am I ashamed of?" he'd say. A dime or a hundred dollars, he did it in the open.

We knew we were Irish, of course. Mother would take Ed and me to Sea Gate, one of the bathing beaches near Coney Island. Each nationality had its own part of the beach. The Italians sat there, the Jewish families sat there, and the Protestants over there, and if you crossed the invisible line in the sand, a bunch of boys would rise up and the fight would be on.

Not that we spent much time on the sand. We all burned badly from the sun, so we'd crawl under the boardwalk in the shade and eat our sandwiches. Mother would save shoeboxes all year, and then on a Sunday outing pack them with sandwiches, and we'd eat them, washed down with a nickel cup of coffee and condensed milk, under the boardwalk. People would pass over our heads, and sand would sift through the cracks and into the sandwiches and coffee. I've never much liked sand since. Yes, I knew we were Irish. While Mother saved up shoeboxes, I saved up rocks, and on a given day, the Irish kids in Bay Ridge would do battle with the Italian kids, on a vacant lot. I have scars on my chin from those rock fights.

I was a rowdy kid and a big kid, though they called me Tiny Bill. Why not? Ed was bigger, like his namesake Big Ed, six-three at his full growth. Still, I was big enough, and far bigger than the average kid. I played catcher on our kid baseball team, with-

out a mask or shinguards, on a rock-hard diamond beneath Manhattan Bridge, and I played basketball on our school teams, at
St. Francis Xavier grade school, run by the Franciscan Brothers,
and St. James High, run by the Christian Brothers. I shot pool
and billiards at the St. Francis Lyceum, where I won a cue for
three-corner billiards, and I'd ditch school in the spring to scale
the fence at Bedford Avenue to sit in the bleachers at Ebbets
Field, rooting for Zack Wheat and my particular Dodger hero,
Ivan Olson. The cry those days was, "Hit it on the nose, Ivy!"

I never was much of a student, and I couldn't have cared less.
I horsed around in class and I took my licks from the Brothers.
Not all the Brothers. Brother Denis, my first year teacher at St.
James High, on Jay Street in downtown Brooklyn, seemed to like
me. We had a common interest. My father would get theater
tickets from the reporters either at the *World* or at City Hall,
and I would take Brother Denis to a Saturday matinee. I liked
the silent movies, too. Our local movie house was an old one-
story building, where you could pack a couple of hundred people,
mainly squealing kids, and for a nickel you'd see the show. On
Saturday I'd take 6¢, so I could buy a penny jawbreaker, and I'd
sit in deep bliss, watching *Stingaree*, a silent serial with a great
horseman, for three shows, or until the manager would come
down the aisle, growling, "Young Gargan, get out of here." My
mother had come for me.

I got my first job in a silent movie when I was a kid. Vita-
graph Studios, operating out of Flatbush, was shooting a film
with John Bunny and Lillian Walker. A friend of Ed's, a boy
named Paul Kelly, had a part. Paul went out and recruited Ed
and me to play tiny bits in the film. I had to put on a baseball
uniform and stand in the outfield, as though I were catching
flies. I was maybe six or seven years old. For the one day's work,
I got $3.85. Which made me rich, and the envy of my friends.
Paul Kelly, who was Ed's age, went on to become a fine actor,
but his violent temper threw a black shadow across his life. That,
plus drink. In the 1920s, he met the actress Dorothy MacKaye,
and fell in love. Unfortunately, she was married, to Ray Raymond,
a musical comedy star. Paul got drunk, and in his cups, en-

gaged in a bloody fist fight with Ray Raymond, over Dorothy. Raymond fell and hit his head against a radiator, and died. Paul went to jail on a manslaughter conviction, and was released in 1929, after two years. He and Dorothy MacKaye married in 1931, but a few years later, she was killed in a car crash. Paul pulled himself out of the abyss of these tragedies, and eventually went on to a distinguished career, starring finally on Broadway in *Command Decision*. I knew him when he was a friendly Brooklyn boy with a bright grin, but when he got sore and set his jaw, you had better watch out.

Despite this first movie "role," it was the stage that really attracted me. I remember seeing *Uncle Tom's Cabin* at the Grand Opera House, and I was hooked. I began to appear in school plays—I played Shylock in my first year in high school, and then Horatio in *Hamlet*, and Macbeth, and played somebody—not Romeo—in *Romeo and Juliet*. Naturally I appeared in the Christmas plays, but when it came to sing the carols, a Brother would walk down our row and he'd say, "Somebody is croaking," and pretty soon they found out who. I became a listener.

The theater got me in brief trouble. One day I said to Brother Denis, "Father, I have two tickets for next Saturday's matinee. Would you like to go?"

Whack! He hit me smack in the kisser.

"You'll stay in after school, Billy Gargan. Don't you know Wednesday is Ash Wednesday. You will write on the blackboard, 'I will not go to the theater during Lent,' a hundred times."

I wrote it and I didn't go.

But I liked Brother Denis. So did most people. Years later, when I appeared on the Maxwell House radio show with Frank Morgan, Frank and I sat on the edge of the stage signing autographs after the program. A youngster with a fresh Irish face came up and said, "You had Brother Denis, and so did I. He said if I ever saw you, I should say, 'Hello.'" The youngster was Dennis Day, and we have been close friends ever since.

But not every Brother was like Denis. In my second year at St. James, my teacher, Brother Anthony, took snuff, and I used to imitate him and break up the class. I was becoming quite a ham. Brother Anthony did not seem to mind, but another Brother—let's call him Michael—got wind of my behavior and he said to me one day in the corridor, "Wait till I get you in the third year, William Gargan."

That same year, with Brother Anthony, I entered the school elocution contest competing with third- and fourth-year boys. All those Saturday matinees came in handy. I won the contest. But my reputation was working against me. Nobody gave me the pocket watch I was supposed to get. Not in the second year. And not in the third year, either. In the third year, I was lucky. Brother Michael, waiting in the wings, was shifted to the fourth year, so I had Brother Anthony and his snuff for a second season. During the third year, my father would say, "Have they given you the watch yet?" and I'd say, "No." Dad began to growl about it. Then in the fourth year, I got Brother Michael, and he got me. He made life in school as miserable as he could. I'd turn in a paper, and if it was a good paper, which it usually wasn't, he'd still knock off ten points for "sloppy work," and I'd fail. He kept me in after class, gave me the tough chores, handed me extra assignments, and treated me like dirt.

I didn't make it easier for him. I'd snarl back at him, and then one day he belted me a couple of times, and I shouted, "You can go to hell!" and he chased me right out of the room and out of school. Officially, I was put on probation, but I never went back.

Which didn't stop my father. Perhaps because he was so close to the downtown political bosses, he knew you *could* fight City Hall. He kept growling, "Where's that watch? When are they going to give you the watch?" and after I was chased out of school, he marched off one day and came back and said, "You be outside the school tomorrow afternoon at three."

I was, and they slipped me the watch, on the street corner, like a guy buying black market goods or Parisian postcards.

Later, I had a small measure of revenge. I was in Boston, playing my first show, *Aloma of the South Seas*, at the Wilbur Theatre, and living in the Fenway Park section. One day, coming home from the theater on the street car, I saw Brother Michael across the aisle, in street clothes, a dame on his arm. I was shocked, furious. "You dirty hypocrite!" I said, "you dirty son of a—"

"Wait a minute," he said. He was terrified. He must have thought I was going to slug him. I was. "I left the Order. I never took my final vows."

I sat back, satisfied. I hadn't finished my school. He hadn't finished his. We were even.

So I really have no education, and, yes, I regret it, but it wasn't as important then as it is today. Today you need the knowledge, to survive. Then, you could get it on the street, in jobs. You could work, then, when you were a little kid. Today there are laws against child labor. I always had jobs. I worked for Ringling Brothers circus when I was eight or nine years old, carrying water and selling soda pop, just to get an extra ticket and maybe 50¢ a day. Later, when the circus moved to Bedford Avenue, Brooklyn, a friend and I opened a small wooden stand outside the tent, decked out with bunting, and we sold a mixture of lemon extract and orange extract, with ice and sugar, for 5¢ a cup. We mixed the drink in a garbage pail, and at the end of the day we threw what was left in the street. It was an outlaw operation—we were not part of the circus selling crew—so we didn't last long.

I delivered dry cleaning for a tailor on 7th Avenue and President Street, I swept out one of Dad's saloons, I worked for a florist as a delivery boy on a bike, all while I was in school. We were independent kids, Ed and I. My folks went up to Saratoga Springs every August, for the thirty-day racing season, and most years I would go with them. When we stayed home, they gave us $30 each, to last the month. We'd buy steak for three days, and then eat spaghetti the rest of the month. The result was, we both became good cooks. Today I do the cooking in our family, and though we don't have to, I still can make a mean bowl of pasta and stretch it out for twenty-seven days.

Mother was never much for cooking or keeping house. She liked to sally forth, and though she made it appear that Dad's drinking was more than enough for one family (it was!), years later I found out she could put down a stiff manhattan or three, when they were out.

Mother liked to do the proper things. She played the piano and often invited other musicians to our house, where she'd hold violin and piano concerts. One year we spent the summer in East Setauket, Long Island, and Mother would be the gracious hostess for a Sunday afternoon musicale. Meanwhile, I'd spend the day clam-digging.

Back in Brooklyn, Mother practiced the usual social amenities. We had a back parlor, for family gatherings, and a more exclusive front parlor, for wakes or wedding receptions. You had to marry or die to get in the front parlor. Mother kept it immaculate. Like other people living in the city, we had straw mats we'd throw on the stone stoops, to sit on in warm summer evenings. Window awnings had come along about the turn of the century; they quickly became status symbols. So Mother bought awnings, but she also had a sense of thrift that kept her levelheaded. She just bought awnings for the back windows; that's where the afternoon sun was.

We always had a boarder living with us, in a room on the top floor. One guy gave us trouble. He wouldn't pay his rent, and he refused to clean his room. Or even allow anyone else to clean it. Mother's sense of thrift and cleanliness both were shocked. She had the guy thrown out. The boarder I remember best was a skinny dark roustabout who worked down on the docks when he wasn't drinking or going to the movies. His name was Al, and in return for his board, he served as handyman, keeping the house clean, for which he also got 15¢ a day. He kept a bag of nickels in his room, and when he filled the bag, which took about six months, he'd go to the movies, fortified with a couple of bottles of booze. He liked to drink while watching the show. He loved the cops and robbers movies, but the fantasy got too much for him, and he'd start yelling and fighting in the audience. Then the real cops would take him to the precinct house and give us a call. "Come and get him," they'd say, and we'd come and get him.

He had a cough, and I used to hear him coughing quietly up

in his room at night; maybe he had tuberculosis. He lived with us for years, dying in 1930, of pneumonia.

Al wasn't the only one in our house we'd have to go out and get. Dad too had a drinking problem. He was a periodic drinker, not a steady one, but it was often enough, and when he'd go on a toot, he'd be gone sometimes ten days. Saloonkeepers would call us, and say, "He's down here," and when I got to be fourteen or fifteen, I'd be the one to go for him. I could handle him.

He'd drink either at one of his saloons, or at Sasso's, a hangout for Little Augie, the local counterpart of Capone, and where Capone himself drank when he came to Brooklyn. Or Dad would drink in Joe Adonis' saloon down the street. Once Dad got stewed at Sasso's, and I was summoned. I remember going through the swinging doors and seeing him leaning up against the bar, with money strewn all over the sawdust floor. As soon as I got there, several men—and mind you, they all were in the rackets, or nearly all—collected the money and gave it to me. They had waited for me to arrive, so I could see how basically honest they were, with their own kind. Dad was not a racketeer, but he gambled and he owned saloons and he made book, and he paid off his bets. He never welshed on a penny in his life. This was, I guess, part of the code. He became, in their eyes, a man to be trusted, one of their own.

Years later, this reputation came back to help me. I was playing in Chicago in a play called *Chicago*, with Francine Larrimore, at the Harris Theatre. As I walked out the stage door one day, a man stepped from the shadows and said quickly, "We're forming a protection association. It'll cost you $20 a week."

"I don't need any protection," I said, and I brushed right on by.

A week later, he was back, with the same request for protection money, and again I told him No. But this time I inquired of the cast. It turned out everybody was paying ten or twenty bucks a week to the guy.

I still wasn't going to kick in. Protection money was a big Chicago racket. Gangsters controlled a huge piece of Chicago business. They controlled the dry cleaners and dyers, the bakers, barbers, electrical workers, garage men, shoe menders, plumbers, garbage collectors, window cleaners, undertakers, milk salesmen. You name it; they had a piece of the action. You paid an extra 50¢ to have your pants pressed, because the tailor shop was paying protection money. The dry cleaners collected an extra 50¢ from the customer to cover what they paid to Capone or a rival gang. All in all, they say, protection cost Chicagoans over $130,000,000 a year in those days.

Now these hoods were moving in on the stage. Joe E. Lewis wouldn't pay one day, so they carved up his face and left him to die, except they didn't quite carve deep enough.

I didn't know any of this, then. All I knew was I didn't see the sense in paying some guy $20 for protection. I'd protected myself well enough for years.

One night I went to Colisimo's, at 22nd and Wabash, a hangout for gangsters, mainly, and I had a drink. The next thing I knew, I woke up on the table, my wallet gone, and with it, a couple of hundred dollars. I'd been slipped a Mickey.

The next week, the guy came by the theater again, after a Saturday matinee, and he grinned and said, "I told you you needed protection. Now, how about it?"

I realized he had arranged for the roll. "Let me think about it," I said, and he grinned his wicked grin and walked off.

I went back to my hotel and I called the only man I knew who might help. My father. I told him the story. He was silent for a half minute. Then he said, "Where are you staying?" I told him. "All right," he said, and he hung up.

A few days later, I got a phone call.

"Your name Gargan?"

"Yes."

"Your father phoned. Come up to the Lexington Hotel. Top floor."

I went.

I was ushered in to the top floor suite. A little guy sat behind a desk, dark hair, big round eyes, round face, ruby red lips, like a woman's, a scar on his cheek.

"You Gargan?"

I nodded.

"I'm Capone."

Al Capone was angry, he told me, at what had happened. "Some punk has his own racket," he said, "and I'll be blamed. I don't like it. I'll turn you over to one of my men."

I found my voice. "I'd just as soon you forgot all about it." What was I getting into? A couple of rival rackets, with me in the middle? I'd pay my $20.

He shook his head, his big round eyes sad as a hound dog's. "We have to teach these snotnose kids a lesson. Don't worry. We won't kill him." He laughed sadly.

So he introduced me to another man who told me what to do. When the protection man came around again, I was to take off my hat, to identify him. Meanwhile, the Capone henchman would be across the street, watching. That was all.

On Saturday, the protection guy stopped me again, at the stage door.

"Well?" he said. "How about it? You wise up any?"

"Nope," I said. I took my hat off. I wiped my brow. I wasn't faking the sweat. "You'll never get a nickel out of me. Get out of here."

He shook his head. "You'll be sorry." He walked away.

Four days later I got a call, to go up to the Lexington. Capone had a wallet on his desk. "Is this yours?"

"Yes," I said.

"This the money you had in it?" He shoved some bills across the desk.

"I guess so," I said. I began to stuff the money into the wallet.

"Count it," he said.

So I counted it, with shaking fingers, and I said it was exactly right—I had no idea—and he grunted, and I walked out, and that was the end of that. I never saw the protection guy again. I don't know what happened to him. I don't want to know.

So my father's connection had come in handy, in that one incident and I had seen one of the dark sides of his life.

Another dark side was his drinking problem. He'd take the pledge, but it didn't always stick. Sometimes it got so bad we'd lock him in his room, with bars on the window, but he always had a way to lick the system. He'd somehow phone a saloon, and a delivery boy would climb up to his window and slip the bottle between the bars, and he'd wink an eye and slip the boy a sawbuck.

But most of the time, he remained a light figure, not a dark one. He and Mother never had a fight, never a quarrel, in front of Ed and me. They managed to fill the house with love and warmth, and the house we lived in, whether we lived there for a few weeks or a few years, Dad was always itching to move, the house always was a home, and I remember my childhood with fondness. It was my home, and when people today ask whether I have ever been to Ireland, and I tell them "No," they are wasting their sympathy. I once tried to go to Ireland when I was in London, making a film, but the usual fog socked in, and we couldn't get out. Somehow it doesn't bother me. I never knew the Gargans or the Flynns of the old country. Perhaps if my folks had been born in Ireland, it might have been different. But they weren't. America was their native land. So too is it mine. I feel no other pull. My roots, as such, lie in Brooklyn, in the saloons and movie houses, in the brownstones won in card games, in the bittersweet memories of my father, drinking at Sasso's, or gloriously alive, striding off to church with me, where some new pastor would shake his fists and harangue in high fine style, and Dad would press a hundred-dollar bill into the plate. My memories and my roots are the top floor where Al, the boarder, coughed away his life, treasuring his bag of nickels that got him drunk at the movies, where fantasy transported him, sometimes too strenuously.

4

I Never Was a Big Ginger Ale Man

I cannot kiss my father off so lightly. I am my father's son. (And Ed was my mother's.) My mother was the solid member of the family, but Dad gave the family color and style. Not that Mother didn't have flair. She also could fight City Hall. She'd been a schoolteacher before she married, and in 1914, when I was nine, there was a teacher shortage, and she'd gone down and taken the exam to be a substitute teacher.

She got word she'd flunked the test.

Naturally we consoled her, pointing out it had been nearly twenty years since she taught, and people just get rusty.

"Nonsense," she said. She put on her hat, and she bustled into the Board of Education office and demanded to see her paper.

It was unheard of, they told her.

You're hearing it now, she told them.

They dug up her paper. She looked at it quickly, and then she snorted.

"You've added it up wrong," she said.

And they had. They'd made a ten-point mistake. Instead of failing by four points, she'd passed by six. She got a job, teaching the third and fourth grades, in a school on 13th Street and 4th Avenue, in Brooklyn. People tell me she was one of the best teachers in the school system. I believe it.

But though she was a good teacher, I received my arithmetic

lessons from my father. He would come home at night from his bookmaking and empty his pockets on the dining-room table. Ed and I would straighten the crumpled bills, and then we would sort them—tens in one pile, twenties in another, hundreds, even thousands. One night I saw my one and only $10,000 bill that way. Then we'd count the money.

Dad had a fantastic mind, a miracle mind. He could add three columns straight up. Even before he took all the bills from his pockets, plus the slips identifying the bettor and the bet, and we had sorted and counted them, he knew within a few dollars what kind of day it had been. A very good day, he might make $5000 or $10,000. A very bad day, he might lose that much. Or more.

The next day, he'd pay off at the track, standing at a little shed beneath the grandstand. My father was scrupulously honest, which helped when the bettors broke him, as they occasionally did. He had a credit rating of $100,000 at the track—he could bet or borrow up to $100,000, so he could recoup and pay off his debts. He seldom bet when he made book; he seldom bet when he had money. He'd bet when he had to, and then he bet with a cold shrewdness. He knew the jockeys, the grooms, the trainers, the owners; he knew what horse was ready and what horse wasn't, and why. But he usually reserved his betting for those moments he needed money to pay off his debts. Otherwise, he was a bookie.

I said he was scrupulously honest. Within the context of his trade, that is. Bookmaking was illegal off the track, and in some states, at the track as well. In New York, the law was fuzzy, and bookmakers accepted bets in a state of quasi-secrecy, on the grass in front of the grandstand. This was the Betting Ring. The police usually left the bookies alone. Some of the policemen were on the bookies' payroll.

Dad resented the semi-secrecy of his life, as though it were something sinful. He felt it wasn't, and one day in 1914, with the advice of lawyers, my father tested the law against gambling at the track. He openly accepted a bet at Yonkers, in full view of the track stewards and police. He was arrested, the case came up in court, and the law was upheld. He had tested the law—his sole purpose—and he had lost. He paid a small fine, and that was that. He kept right on accepting bets, but it again had to be done undercover.

Dad was an imposing figure, though he stood but five feet seven or eight inches. He walked very straight, and he dressed to the teeth. His friends called him "The Senator," and he looked like your stereotyped senator, preferably one from Virginia. He wore a wing collar and florid bow tie, and beneath his single-breasted suit was the inevitable vest. The vest was terribly important, with all those extra pockets, for crumpled wads of money and slips of paper. He had two rules: Never get on a sucker list, and Never carry a wallet. He scorned those people who donated money to churches and other charities, with their name attached. He deplored their attempts to get publicity for what should have been a charitable gesture, but more, he pitied them because now they would find themselves on the sucker list. We'd go to church, and there'd be names on the church board, announcing the contributors who'd helped make up a year's deficits. "Showoffs," he'd sneer. Which was another reason he never used the envelopes they passed around on Sundays with the collection plate. You would slip your donation into the envelope, and put your name on the front with a flourish. Look at me, it announced, I gave, I gave. Today I see he is right. A few people give money to charities just to get publicity out of the gift. Naturally they are using Uncle Sam's money, not their own, because they write it all off when income tax rolls around. Real charity, as I define it, begins when you run out of Uncle Sam's money and dig into your own pocket.

Dad's stricture against carrying a wallet came out of bitter experience. He was riding a trolley in Flatbush one day, hanging onto a strap, when he felt his back pocket brushed. By the time he turned around, the guy who'd ripped out the pocket and removed the wallet, with $6000 inside, was gone. Today, as a result, you couldn't give me a wallet.

Dad had been born with a physical deformity, which on another man might have changed his way of life. He had a shortened right hand, lacking one row of knuckles, so the hand was tiny. It would have looked grotesque on another man, except Dad could never have looked grotesque. Instead of catering to the dwarfed hand, he exercised it. For a spell, in his youth, he was a court stenographer, scribbling away at a fantastic speed with his tiny hand. Like all his other talents, he later put the shorthand to use. When the cops would periodically crack down on book-making, Dad would stroll along at the track behind two other bookmakers, John Walters and Tom Shaw. Bettors would come up to Walters or Shaw, and quietly ask, "What's the price on Number 7?"

Walters, or Shaw, would say out of the side of the mouth, "Four to one."

"I'll take $2000."

Quick nod of the head, and the two bookies kept walking, with Dad behind them.

His tiny right hand, buried in a pocket, had written down the bet.

Or he and I would go to church, and when Mass was over, he'd whip out a piece of paper, and read back from his shorthand notes the parts of the sermon that had impressed him.

He made me part of his life, taking me where he went, as though we were friends and not merely father and son. And we were friends. I remember once walking along Times Square with Dad and a distinguished gentleman, very lithe and trim, with a wonderful face and clear eyes and a spring to his walk. He dressed somewhat like Dad, except even more floridly. And with that wonderful fresh face and those clear eyes and light step, you might have thought he was a sissy.

A fire bell clanged behind us, and one of the fire department's salvage trucks came rolling along, in heavy traffic.

The salvage truck was supposed to get to fires ahead of the fire-fighting trucks ostensibly to protect the property, to pull it out of the way and keep an eye on it. Instead, they stole every-thing they laid their hands on.

So my father's friend cupped his hands and hooted, "There go the forty thieves!"

In the heavy traffic, the truck came to a stop, and a burly fireman got out.

"What'd you say?" he demanded.

The remark was repeated.

"Why, you—" and the burly fireman threw a punch.

Dad's friend stepped out of the way daintily, and the fireman tossed another haymaker, and again it was cleverly evaded, and finally after three or four more punches, the fireman stood still and puffed, "Quit moving, you dandy!" and the gentleman stood still until the fireman tossed another punch. Then he stepped aside, and with the back of his hand, flattened the fireman.

It was James J. Corbett, former heavyweight champion of the world.

There were other friends, less distinguished, yet more fascinating. Some of them remain brief blurs in my memory; they came and went. One year, instead of the family going down south, to the Miami tracks and then to Havana, we stayed up north, and Dad ran a book in a rented apartment in Buffalo. Don't ask me why. Perhaps there was pressure on at the Florida and Havana tracks. Or maybe Dad didn't have the cash for the trip to Florida for all of us, plus an expensive hotel or boardinghouse.

A man lived in the same Buffalo apartment house, and I'd see him on the front porch in the morning, sitting in a rocking chair, with a pair of dice in his hands, picking at them, loading them. Yes, he was a friend of my father's. The dark side. Later, we had the fellow over for dinner when we were back in Brooklyn, and after dinner, because something was wrong with his car, he'd gone to a garage on Troy Avenue, one of the tougher neighborhoods in Brooklyn. While the car was being repaired, he wandered over to a crap game in the garage, where one man was beating the chauffeurs and the workingmen out of their wages. Dad's friend could see the man was using loaded dice. It takes one to know one. So he asked to sit in on the game, and he gave the man a dose of his own medicine. When he'd cleaned out the game he gave the money back to the chauffeurs and workingmen, and he said, "This man has been using loaded dice," and he got up and started to walk off. The man shot him in the back, dead.

For a spell, a bookmaker named Bill Torpie moved in with us. His talent was "doping"—the track word for "figuring out," or "handicapping"—the international tracks. He knew who was running in London or Paris or even Brisbane, Australia, and who would win. But he had other talents as well. When they built old Belmont Park, in Long Island, Torpie thought the track looked a little strange. One deserted night he went out with a steel tape measure and he measured the track. It was 165 feet short of a mile. He figured the horses accordingly, knowing that the horse who might tie up in the last yards of a mile race would not lag at Belmont, and the horse who needed a long stretch to put away the sprinters had less stretch to do it in. He cleaned up. He had an odd betting method. He'd watch the horses for ten or fifteen days—just watching and handicapping—and then he'd walk into a betting ring, and he'd say, "Take your pick, 3-to-1." He'd give you any horse in the race, at 3-to-1 odds. Naturally bettors hastened to plunge on the favorites, for they'd get 3-to-1, instead of even money or perhaps 6-to-5. But Torpie had handicapped the race perfectly. He knew a 6-to-1 or 7-to-1 horse had to win it, and the horse did, and he'd cleaned up again. Had you bet the winner, of course, you'd only have received 3-to-1.

One year Torpie, my father, and a bookie named Charlie Secret—what a Damon Runyon name!—took the boat from Florida to Havana, to spend the season at John J. McGraw's track. McGraw, of course, also managed the New York Giants baseball team.

Torpie, Dad, and Charlie Secret went to Havana, to have a run at McGraw's horses. Secret also got into some dice games, which was his specialty. He was the only man I ever knew who could take a dice pot, scramble the dice, and announce the number he'd throw. My dad had quaint friends.

At Havana, Torpie—the international expert—kept watching the horses. "Don't bet today," he'd say.

One day, he said, "I think I've got it doped. Here are the six winners. But don't bet them. I'm not sure."

All six horses won.

Every day he'd go to the paddock area early, near the jockeys' rooms, and then he'd come back and say, "No bets today." One day, halfway through the meet, he nodded. "All right. Here are the winners. Bet 'em."

So they did.

It was a jockey frameup. Torpie had cracked the frame, and he knew every winner. But in the excitement of one race that day, Torpie yelled out, his horse miles ahead, "Don't win it so far, Eddie," or whatever the jockey's name was. "Make it look close." A track plainclothesman came over and tapped Torpie on the shoulder. "Buddy," he said, "be on the boat out tonight." So Charlie Secrel, Bill Torpie, and Dad came home that night. But richer.

Dad didn't spend all his days at the track. He had his saloons, with his brothers Charles and James, and for a spell he owned a burlesque theater in Philadelphia he'd also won a piece of in a card game. Mother made him get rid of that; it offended her.

One of the bars Dad owned in the years just prior to our involvement in the World War was near the Todd Shipyards, at the Brooklyn waterfront. Through his connections at City Hall, he learned one day that the government was going to declare all the saloons in the shipyard off limits.

So Dad hastily put his thriving waterfront tavern up for sale and got a good price from a man named Brown. Then the government shut down the bar, and Dad moved out of town for a few weeks.

All this seeps into a boy, and makes him the man he is to be. Prohibition threw its long shadow on our lives, and it was a distorted, distorting shadow. Carry Nation had earlier taken her ax to the saloon bottles and mirrors, the movement had picked up steam, and now people began to sing:

"O, it won't be long, is the burden of our song
  Till we get our wagon started on the way,
  And our friends who vote for gin will all scramble
    to jump in,
  When we get our big bandwagon, some sweet day."

But it wasn't so simple. You could declare a law against drink, but not one against thirst. So people drank, illegally from 1919 on, and some drank legally, because they were smart. With foresight when Prohibition was about to become law, some private clubs laid in enough bottles to last for years, which was legal. But saloons weren't. So the swinging doors were shut, and a different door went up, with a peephole. Saloons became speakeasies. It was an exercise in semantics. No, it wasn't simple. Al Capone, in booze all his life, legal and illegal, died of paresis—syphilis of the brain—as did Jimmy Walker, which may prove something. But the ladies of the WCTU who sang out for Prohibition, swigged down Lydia Pinkham's remedy for female ills, which happened to be 40 proof. Hitler was a teetotaler.

A man—or a boy—could drink, if he wanted to. I took to reading the papers to see who had died, and then I'd call up a few friends of mine, and we'd smuggle our way into the wake, where liquor flowed freely. Into my bones was being hammered a philosophy of life, epicurean, though I did not know it had a name, then. Go out and enjoy life. Search out the fun, the laughter. I was a big boy, with curly red hair and my folks' laughing blue eyes, and where the drinks were good and the cigars long and fine (or short and cheap), I'd be there. The body, at a wake, would be laid out in the parlor upstairs, and we'd pay our respects, and then we'd go downstairs where the party was raging. Off in the kitchen would be a ham and a turkey, and vats of poteen—Irish malt whiskey—plus soft drinks for the youngsters. Even when I was a youngster, I passed the soft drinks by. Let's face it, I never was a big ginger ale man.

I remember a wake for a fireman who had died. After paying my respects to the deceased, I went to the kitchen, where the turkey had been stripped to the bone, but a great ham lay pink and tender. My friends and I poured out drinks of whiskey and we laid the knife to that ham, the air so thick with cigar smoke you really could have laid the carving knife to it as well. It was a fine wake, a splendid wake, and the hours passed, and the ham slimmed down, until the fireman's brother burst into the kitchen, grabbed the ham from us, slammed it into the icebox, and said,

"For goodness sakes, boys, leave some for breakfast." Only he didn't say goodness!

No, we weren't chagrined. We roared with laughter and went out into the night, and if I could have sung, I would have sung. Life was delicious.

Yet God was laid into my bones, as well. I'd made my First Confession and received my First Communion when I was six, and I went every week and spoke my sins into the priest's ear and God's. I knew, early in life, that there are just two ways of life—the right way or the wrong way. There was no rationalizing, no middle ground, and I questioned none of it. Not until much later did I question any of it, and then only faintly, because the feeling becomes embedded deeply, and the questioning is mild, transient, fleeting. There is no in-between.

Which does not mean a man—a boy—does not err. He should not, but he does. I was no angel, as if that needed telling. When I snarled my disrespect at Brother Michael, I felt he deserved it, but I sensed I had done wrong, and I confessed my sin. I should have obeyed, done my studies, been a good student. But then I would have been a different person.

So like millions of other Catholic youngsters I went to confession, and it was as bad in my youth to say, "I swore five times, Father," as it would be today for a young man to say, "I slept with a woman."

Yes, I did swear five times, and I went to confession, and it was as bad as if I had stolen. I would leave confession properly humbled, chastised, and cleansed. I had talked with God. I began to believe that God could do anything. He has that power to forgive, and I had that power to petition.

Which is not to say I also believe God will make life easier, just like that, if He is asked. Too early in the game I learned this wasn't so. Life has its apparently meaningless moments, its unsought tragedies that strike savagely and, to us, senselessly.

I had an uncle, on my mother's side, named Tom Wilson. Together with a man named Jackman, he owned and operated a roller coaster in Coney Island, called Jackman's Thriller. It was a nickel ride. Because he was my Uncle Tom, I rode it free, and rode it and rode it.

He was a bachelor, and he would invite the whole family—on Mother's side—to his place every Christmas Eve. He always had a tremendous tree, and beneath it lay presents for the whole family. Our own family didn't go in for big Christmas trees and pretty presents but we were close to one another and had a great spirit of kinship. One year, 1919 or 1920, when I was fourteen or fifteen, we spent Christmas Eve at Uncle Tom's, and just as we came home there was a phone call from my mother's sister Agnes. Tom Wilson had opened a cellar door, to go down into the basement, and he'd fallen down the steps and hit his head against a waste pipe. He was dead. I'll never forget that Christmas.

Then there was Big Ed Gargan, whom you know about, stepping on a rusty nail. Big Ed used to work at one of Dad's saloons, and when a Swede sailor got a bit feisty or else passed out from drink, Big Ed would sling the sailor over his shoulder and take him outside until he quieted down or sobered up. Yet a rusty nail killed him.

Yes, I knew about the senseless tragedies of life. Maybe they helped me handle my own tragedy, later on, when I would momentarily yield to self-pity and wonder, "Why me, God? Why me?" Too often, there seems to be no answer. Or at least no answer for a long, long time.

5

Yellow Charleston, Shorty Hines, and Pinkerton Finks

Far and away the highlight of my youth were the summers at Saratoga Springs. For ten years, with rare exceptions, from 1911 to 1920, Dad would take us to Saratoga in August, for the racing meet. Yonkers would close on a Saturday, and Saratoga would begin on Monday, and we'd all rush on board the Cavanagh Special, named after John Cavanagh, the betting ring czar. If a gambler had a dispute with a bookie, he'd take his complaint to Cavanagh who would listen patiently. If Cavanagh believed the gambler, he'd say to the bookie, "Pay him." You were off the track if you didn't. Or if Cavanagh thought the story unlikely, he'd say to the gambler, "Sorry, I don't believe you," and that was that. The gambler was marked down as a liar and a bad bet; bookies scratched him. Cavanagh was one of the most powerful men in the betting world, and the train was well named.

The trip was a social event. They served cocktails before dinner, and wine with, but in between drinks and meals and chitchat, bookies busily handicapped the horses.

One year my brother Ed persuaded Dad to wait until Sunday and go up to Saratoga in Ed's new Hupmobile. Ed was great with cars. He enjoyed figuring out how things worked, and then keeping them working, or making them work better. In later years, he'd collect and rebuild antique clocks; he even took out a patent on a violin clock, called Fiddle Time. He was always a good photographer. In his last years he took up water colors and created some lovely canvases. He painted pastoral landscapes, but the Brooklyn boy in him won out; the finest water color he ever did, I think, was a rendition of the Brooklyn Bridge at night.

In his youth, cars were his specialty. He attended Commercial High, in Brooklyn, for two years, and later took a two-month course in a YMCA Airplane Mechanics' School, run by the Army. He held jobs in garages, as a mechanic and machine-tester.

Which was the only reason Dad allowed Ed to talk us into the Hupmobile, instead of the Cavanagh Special. Dad had one instruction for Ed. "Never lose sight of the railroad track. I want to bet tomorrow."

A fine new highway extended from Brooklyn to Kingston, and another good road from Kingston to Albany, and a not bad road from Albany to Saratoga Springs, but Ed couldn't lose sight of the rail tracks, so we lumped over rough fields and cowpaths and on an occasional frontage road chuckholed and narrow. Dad trusted the railway; he didn't trust the car. It took us eleven hours to go less than 200 miles. We never lost sight of the Delaware & Hudson tracks gleaming beside us, and Dad bet the next day, but it was the last time we took the Hup. Both Mother and Ed were crestfallen at this turn of events. Mother loved the car, or any car, and enjoyed getting all dressed up, with a feather duster and a big floppy sun hat. Ed missed tinkering with the car. He was a great mechanic. Later he worked for a dealer handling the Isotta-Francini. He'd tune up those foreign motors so fine the dealer would put a glass of water on the hood while the engine was purring, and the water lay still as a sheet of glass.

At Saratoga we'd either stay at Mrs. Moriarity's boarding-house, on Union Avenue, or in a furnished house on Lincoln, near the railroad siding where they let the horses off. It depended on how Father had done at Yonkers. If we had money, we stayed at Mrs. Moriarity's, a magnificent huge mansion, where you paid $35 a day, even if you were a baby, and you got all your meals, all your whiskey, and all your cigars (even if you were a baby). If Yonkers had licked Dad, we'd stay in the four-room furnished house, for $125 a month.

Dad always rented the furnished house in advance, just in case he went broke during the Saratoga season. That was how you knew the state of our finances. Were we at Moriarity's or at the furnished house? And did Mother have her diamond ring? The first thing that went, when things were tough, was Mother's three-carat (slightly flawed) ring. Another tipoff was Mother's hands, and not just the ring finger. If she was doing the cooking and the dishes, Dad was in trouble. (And so were we; cooking was not Mother's forte.) All the other rules applied as well. Dad would bet, if he was broke; he'd book if he had money.

It all added up to one of the more exciting afternoons of my life, in 1919, August 13, 1919, to be exact, and if you are a race-track buff, you know the date. Dad had been booking the first week of the meet, but in very bad luck, and we had moved into the Lincoln Avenue furnished house, the diamond ring was in hock, and Mother's knuckles were red. On Wednesday, August 13, Dad's luck began to turn. He bet and won the first race; he bet and won the second; he bet and won the third, and by now he was back on his feet, with a fat bankroll. So he shifted roles. Now he booked. The feature race that day was the Sanford Memorial, three-quarters of a mile for two-year-olds, and one of the two-year-olds was Man o' War.

Philadelphia Jack O'Brien, the legendary race-track gambler, was at the track, betting his usual ultra-conservative wager, picking favorites in the third hole—in the show position. Betting, in other words, for the favorite to finish third or better. For which he'd win nickels to every dollar he bet, but he'd win, and he bet big enough so that he'd win a lot of nickels. Three, four, five thousand dollars worth of nickels.

But on this Wednesday, Man o' War was odds-on to win, so if you bet a dollar in the first hole on Big Red (who happened to be a star-blazed chestnut, and not accurately red), you'd win peanuts. You couldn't bet the second hole or the third—place or show—because no bookie would accept a bet on Man o' War to finish worse than first. He never had—finished worse than first, that is.

So Philadelphia Jack O'Brien bet $19,000 on Man o' War to win, and he bet it with my father. If O'Brien won, he'd win a few thousand dollars. It looked like the surest few thousand dollars this side of the Mint. If Dad lost, he wouldn't be troubled seriously (it had been a *very* good day), but then O'Brien was not the only gambler at Saratoga betting on Man o' War with Dad.

There were seven horses in the race. The only other notable horse was Golden Broom, who spent most of his career chasing Man o' War. Golden Broom was equally weighted with Man o' War, at 130 pounds, which shows you how good he was. Golden Broom went off at 11-to-5 that afternoon. The next rated horse was Upset, with 115 pounds, and the bookies had him listed at 8-to-1. The rest of the field ranged from Donaconna at 30-to-1, to a couple of nags at 100-to-1. But to the crowd, the race would be between Man o' War and Golden Broom, if it was to be a race at all. Usually Man o' War, with his classically quick start, just ran off and hid from the others.

Johnny Loftus rode Man o' War this Wednesday afternoon, and there have been better rides. Though frankly it wasn't all Loftus' fault. The regular starter, Mars Cassidy, was ill that day, and one of the placing judges, C. H. Pettingill, took Cassidy's place. Pettingill butchered the start.

They didn't use starting gates in 1919. The starter laid out his horses with a piece of tape in front of him, and waited until they were all fairly straight before he dropped the tape and let them go.

Pettingill fidgeted so long with the tape, Golden Broom broke three times before the tape was officially dropped, and Upset tried to break a couple of more times. Meanwhile, the placid Man o' War got bored with the proceedings and finally started to turn away, until he was faced ninety degrees to the rest of the field. At which time Pettingill sent them off. The lightly regarded Upset, with Willie Knapp up, flew away from the pack, while Loftus wrestled Big Red back around and finally set off after the horses far ahead. You probably know the rest. Upset began to hang in the stretch, wobbly-legged and spent, and Man o' War ran an incredible race, coming from so far back it looked as though he'd started the next race, not this one, but he never closed the whole gap. A neck separated the two, and Dad had taken $19,000 from Philadelphia Jack O'Brien, and other thousands from other bettors, and he carried home $57,000 that night. The next day Mother had her diamond ring (with a little yellow flaw), and we all were encamped at Moriarity's, enjoying the food and whiskey and cigars, even the babies.

I worked at the track that year. Dad got me a job as a sheet writer on what they called the "Back Stretch." After all, I was fourteen, and a big kid.

The Back Stretch was off limits, a place where the guys who were barred from the track would congregate to bet. I wrote up the sheet, marking down the name of the bettor and his bet, for a bookie named Shorty Hines. I guess Shorty had welshed a couple of times in the past. Now he worked the Back Stretch, and with him were other bookies who had welshed, two-bit touts, pickpockets, and all sorts of low life, including Pinkerton finks. The place crawled with Pinkertons.

Mainly, Shorty Hines took bets from the stable boys—50¢ and $1 bets—and at the end of the day I'd get $10. When I got it. This is how it worked. We'd nail the prices of the first race to a tree, I'd mark down the bets, and Shorty would collect the money. Then when the race would start, we'd run into the infield and with binoculars watch the race. On the way back, we'd figure out how much Shorty had won or lost, and we'd plot the prices for the next race. I'd tack up the sheet and Shorty would collect the bets, and from the bets placed on the second race, he'd pay off the winners on the first.

One day plenty of guys won that first race, so Shorty had to scratch up extra money to cover his losses, and then we ran into the infield and watched the second race, which turned out to be worse. On the way back, Shorty said, "Post the prices on the third. I'll be right back." I began to post, and he took off, which didn't please the guys who had money coming to them from the second race. One man in particular didn't like it, and I couldn't blame him. His name was Yellow Charleston, a tall, lanky, very pale Negro, and he came up close to me and he said, "Where's Shorty?"

"He'll be back," I said, because I believed he would. I was big, but I was just fourteen, and I guess I still was naïve.

"Yeah?" Yellow Charleston said, and by now a crowd of bettors began to close in.

"Yes sir," I said, and then I said—so I wasn't that naïve—"There he is!" I pointed and yelled, and everybody turned. I ran like hell.

That was the end of my betting days on the Back Stretch, and my one and only connection with Yellow Charleston, who later was electrocuted for murder at Sing Sing.

It was not all gambling at Saratoga. This was the social season, and every night there'd be a concert, usually at the Grand Union Hotel, a very posh spot that could cost you $75 a day for a room, complete with a rope in case of fire. You threw the rope out the window and climbed down. Everything was simpler in the old days. John McCormack sang one year and immediately after him, Sophie Tucker came on, which is like pairing champagne and root beer. Chauncey Olcott, another great tenor, lived in Saratoga Springs all year, and he often gave concerts. Every Sunday in August he sang at 11 o'clock Mass, and you should have seen the mob of people throwing fifty and one-hundred dollar bills into the plate, as though money were going out of style. Olcott's "benefit" paid for all the coal the church used every winter. In 1917, Caruso made an appearance, and he sang "Over There," and I guess that was the greatest ovation I ever heard a man receive. My flesh crawled. Caruso had us over for supper one night in Saratoga, and he sang again, for his supper, I believe, judging by the way he put away the spaghetti. I never saw a man eat so much in my life.

On Sundays, we would gather at the Grand Union, the men in straw hats and white pants, and the women in their dusters, and while we waited for the horses and carriages to be assembled, the men would discuss the next day's races and the world situation, in that order. We'd ride to Halfway House, between the

Springs and Lake George, and eat chicken and biscuits, and at the next table would be Eva Tanguay and her daughter. I remember helping the daughter into her chair, because that was the polite thing to do.

Oh, it was a different world, a simple world, an innocent world, a lovely, lyric world, for all the welshing gamblers and all the men who went shuffling off to the electric chair at Sing Sing. I do not pretend people were any better. They just seemed to be.

In the world I would one day enter, the theater, you could see Ethel Barrymore on the stage one year, and Otis Skinner and Eddie Foy, and Elsie Janis and Billie Burke; the next year you could see Laurette Taylor in *Peg o' My Heart*, and Al Jolson and Jane Cowl and Grace George and Douglas Fairbanks. In 1914, some 176 plays were presented on Broadway. Today there are about forty. And Henry Ford and Thomas Alva Edison launched an odd crusade against smoking, "The Cigarette Must Co." But nobody listened, nobody cared. The world was lyric; it sang and it danced and it went gaily, giddily, gorgeously to hell. Caruso singing *Over There*, had sent goose bumps crawling over my skin, but not until later did anybody think of the World War for what it was—mile after mile of muddy holes where men were blown to bits.

We had our heroes and heroines, great men and villains, and the lines were clear. My father was a great man, in my eyes, a hero. I have surely exaggerated what he did and how he did it, but I have told it as I remember it. He never wore field glasses to the track; he could call a race with the naked eye. He knew all the silks, all the jockeys, and all the horses. I remember once seeing a horse Dad had bet on come in, first by two or three lengths, and I yelled, "We won, we won!" and he leaned over and very lightly slapped my face.

"We have not won," he said.

The jockey—he said—had crossed over at the eighth pole, and interfered, and sure enough, the inquiry flag went up, the names came down, and Dad's horse had been disqualified. He had a marvelous eye. The moral of that little slap was, "Don't count your winnings until they're hatched."

They all were great men, and some remain so today. Dad had a friend, Francis Dunne, who today is a dear, honored friend of mine, the steward representing the New York State Racing Commission, a charming man, a beautiful man. He'd been a young clerk when Dad was a bookmaker, and today he is one of the most knowing men in the racing world. I went up to Saratoga with him in 1949 or 1950, when I was vacationing from *Martin Kane, Private Eye,* and Francis would reminisce about the race-track world. He'd take off on the man who'd built Aqueduct Park, with the shortest turn of any track, a track that broke more horses' legs than any track in the world.

"A cruel track, a murderin' track," Francis Dunne would call it, and he'd call it to the face of the man who had built it. "You're a disgrace to the profession," he would say, and the man would remain silent. What could he say?

Dunne and I once theorized how a race track ought to be built, and our theorizing took us through years and years of planning on tablecloths in one nightspot after another. We decided to build our track on Welfare Island. Why not; you'd only improve the place. We'd level the island, build our track, the parking lots and restaurants, and then because of the weather in New York—rain and heat in summer, and snow and slush in winter—we decided to put a dome over it all. Other people got into the act; they would join the discussion, and they would say, back then, "You can't put a dome over a field."

"Why not?" we'd say.

"Because," they'd say, "it just isn't done."

Well, our track, drawn on a hundred tablecloths over the years, had a dome. It had everything. It had a hotel. It had gift shops, a mall, small parks. One day I said I liked it so much I might want to die there.

And Francis found an unused corner of the tablecloth and drew in a cemetery.

Eventually we took time off to figure what it would cost— $475,000,000.

"Let's do it," I said.

But we hadn't figured all the costs, because the track kept growing.

"How about a muddy track?" Francis asked. "What's a track without occasional mud?"

So we planned to truck in mud and build a separate inner course, and run two races a day in the mud.

I still think it's a good idea. But it's the dome that bothers me. Those doubters were right. I *know* you can't put a dome over an athletic field. If you could, some big-mouth Texan would have done so by now.

6

I Am Fired . . . Again

As I got older, and bigger—I was six feet tall when I was fifteen—the days of playing became fewer, and the days and nights of working became many. Which is not to say I didn't have my fun. Or that I didn't play while working.

I wangled a job brushing the ice at a skating rink in Prospect Park when I was thirteen, for a free ticket to the rink. One afternoon a lithe young thing went flashing by in a seal coat and bright red skirt, and I fell into a hole out of which I have still not climbed. Nor do I want to.

I took after this young thing in flashing seal and red skirt, showing a bit of round young calf, a tam o' shanter perky on her blond head, and in my elephantine way, I managed to brush her with my broom and knock her flat. On purpose, of course. Mary Elizabeth Kenny climbed right back up, her eyes spitting fire and her mouth not doing badly either, and I knew I was in love. Mary admits it was a big moment for her, too. "He knocked me on my fanny," she says, in her loving, elegant way, "and I'm still on it." Pure poetry!

I was a hulk of a kid, big and brawny, and Mary got to calling me Fatty Grogan. She knew my name, but that was who I was to her. When her phone rang, and it was her cousin Wally Summerville on the other end, trying to arrange a double date, she'd say, "Who with? Fatty Grogan?"

He'd admit it was with old Fatty, and she'd say, "No chance. Ring somebody else."

But Wally persisted, and she and I would go out, with Wally and his girl. I was fourteen, going on fifteen, when I began dating Mary. She was a year younger.

Mary lived in Manhattan, but she often spent weekends with the Summervilles, at 86th Street in Bay Ridge, which made us practically neighbors. We'd go to Coney Island, and spend my nickels at Feltman's—dimes, actually; Feltman's served the best hot dog I've ever had in my life. It had to be good. They charged a whole dime, while every other place sold franks for a nickel. Or we'd go to Lundy's, on Sheepshead Bay, and buy a sack of baby lobsters for a dollar, and broil them at home. Or as I got older I'd take her to the local vaudeville houses in the area, the Loew's Met or Keith's Prospect. A hot date was dinner at Key's Gardens, a Chinese restaurant on the corner of Flatbush and Fulton, where you could also dance. I was a lousy dancer, and she was a natural. But she'd get my courage up, and I'd stumble about the floor.

It almost didn't matter how graceful you were, what with the new dances we had. The two-step and waltz had come along at the turn of the century, but the time was out of joint, and so were a couple of hipbones, trying to waltz or two-step in hobbleskirts. Ragtime became the rage, and with it, skirts climbed, and gentility was for wallflowers. Irving Berlin wrote *Alexander's Ragtime Band*, and the new music was no longer restricted to honky-tonks down South. It spilled over onto Manhattan's Ritz-Carlton ballroom, and with it came a host of new dances anybody could dance if he enjoyed hugging women—the Grizzly Bear, the Bunny Hug, the Turkey Trot.

So I danced, and even if I didn't know the dance, I would have tried. It is like the very bad joke about the vaudevillian who walks into a greasy spoon and says, "Give me a piece of apple pie," and the counter girl says, "We're out of apple pie," and the vaudevillian says, "Fake it, sister, fake it."

If I didn't know the dance, I would fake it, because it meant holding Mary Elizabeth Kenny, and pretty soon, nothing else in the gay, giddy, gorgeous world mattered as much.

Prohibition came into our lives during our early courtship, and with it I began my drinking days in earnest, Mary right behind me.

A bunch of fellows would buy a quart of alcohol for a buck and a half from Rappaport's Drug Store on Bergen Street in Brooklyn, and we'd add a 15¢ tube of juniper juice and two quarts of water, and for $1.65 we had three quarts of gin. We'd take it with us, to the restaurant or the dance hall, and sneak it in under the girls' coats, and then Mary and I, and Wally and his girl, and whoever else was along, would drink the three quarts of gin. We had cast-iron stomachs. I don't recall ever getting plastered in those teenage days. When I felt a buzz, I was wise enough to stay away from home until the giddiness passed. My folks never knew I was drinking. Mother would have had my scalp. One drinking man was enough in our family.

Having a girl meant finding money of my own, and not just money from delivering dry cleaning all over Brooklyn for $1 a day after school, and $3 on Saturday, plus tips which in Brooklyn were never considerable. I had to find a job that would pay for those Chinese meals and my share of the gin and the midnight snack at a restaurant in Flatbush where we'd have round-bone ham and eggs sizzling in a platter, with a blob of potatoes, before going home.

I never minded work. Before I met Mary, I had worked at a Brooklyn department store, Abraham & Straus, wrapping packages during Easter week and Christmas. I even had a small romance in the delivery room. A very pretty older girl worked in the wrapping department, and I began taking her out for lunch and to the movies, until one day we met a friend of mine who happened to look like an ordinary thirteen-year-old. My girl got suspicious. "Just how old are you?" she asked me, and I told her, and she dropped me, horrified.

The experience—wrapping, that is—helped. Today I wrap all the packages at home. I suspect this is Mary's revenge for my ever having looked at another girl.

I squeezed a job as a Wall Street runner into my school schedule, which made it easier and easier to cut out of school more and more often, and made it easier still to stay out for good when Brother Michael chased me from the room one day.

I worked for a brokerage firm, Williams, Nicholas, and Moran, at 30 Broad Street, and they paid me $12 a week to deliver stock to customers and run messages from the floor of the exchange, or from the Curb, to brokers and clients. I gave Mother $3 of the $12, which was a great investment. When I needed it back, at the end of the week, she had it for me. Giving your mother part of your weekly wage is good therapy, even if you don't let her keep it.

While working on Wall Street, I got to eating lunch at the Exchange Buffet, a cafeteria that operated—and still operates—on the honor system. You'd go in and pick out what you wanted and when you were finished, you told the cashier on the way out what you'd eaten and she'd tell you the price, and you'd pay. Usually I'd just have a ten-cent plate of French fries and a cup of coffee, and that's what I'd claim, but I finally succumbed to the E-B's popular name—Eat it and Beat it. One day I stood before the cashier, and she smiled sweetly and said, "What have you had?" and I said, "The usual. French fries and coffee," and there was a tap on my shoulder, and a man stood there. "Just a minute, Buddy," he said. "Haven't you forgotten the hot roast beef sandwich, the peas and carrots, the green salad, and the apple pie with the slice of cheese on top?"

"No cheese on top," I said firmly, and I paid, and went back to being honorable again. The theory is conscience doth make cowards of us all, and we'll tell the truth. In practice, a sharp eye like that guy's made a coward of me.

I'd deliver stock up to two o'clock, and then with the closing delivery hour at 2:15 upon us, runners would get what was called the Pork Chop. If you could squeeze in another delivery —the Pork Chop—you got an extra dollar. You had to know the short cuts in Wall Street; I learned, and ran my legs off, and eventually I became head runner of the firm, earning a fat $15 a week, sending the other runners out.

The firm I worked for specialized in handling GM transactions, and when I became head runner and lost out on the fringe benefits of Pork Chop deliveries, the firm permitted me to buy five shares of GM stock at $13 a share, out of wages. I gave the five shares to Mother, and years later, after they'd split so often you could have built a pyramid with the shavings, she sold them for $1500.

For all the gambling fever of the Exchange, being a delivery boy was not quite what I had in mind as an ultimate profession. A private detective came closer, and Dad managed to get me an interview with the Burns agency, for a job as an investigator. The job fell through, but I did land a position as an investigator for a clothing store, the Mentor Clothing Company, at Fulton Street, near Loew's Met. I worked from 8 A.M. to 6 P.M. for five days, and then on Saturday I worked from 8 A.M. to 10 P.M. I was allowed a half-hour off for lunch, but because much of the work was on a commission basis, I seldom ate. It adds up to over sixty hours a week, for which they paid me $30. I had to check the credit of customers who wanted to buy a suit but couldn't or wouldn't pay all of it at once. Maybe they'd put $5 down on a $25 suit, flash a couple of references, and arrange to pay the rest in small installments. It was the beginning of installment buying, but without the sophistication of credit cards and the like.

So a man would buy a suit, and want to take it along with him, except the salesman always found something wrong with the cuffs or a shoulder that had to be lifted. Meanwhile I'd be on the phone or on the subway, tracking down an uncle or a boss or somebody who could vouch for the customer's credit. That was one part of the job. No job I ever got was one-sided. They also gave me a sheaf of deadhead slips—customers who had failed to meet the installments and had disappeared, with a Mentor suit. If I came across any of these deadbeats and managed to collect any part of the old debts, I kept 50 percent. Which was why I ate no lunch. I'd carry 75–100 slips, and those pre-processed court summonses you used to be able to use on old debt cases, and I'd go up and down brownstone steps, looking into vestibules at the names of the tenants upstairs. If I spotted a last name that was the same as one of my deadbeats, I passed myself off as an insurance claim adjustor with a settlement, and the faces would brighten and they'd say, "That's my nephew. He's living in Coney Island." And I'd be off to Coney Island, or Canarsie, or Bensonhurst, or up into Manhattan, the Bronx, or Staten Island, figuring how to make an ex-customer cough up what he owed, or a good part of it. The summons, of course, was just a threat. A man would rather pay than go to court.

It wasn't always the safest work. I spotted the name of a deadbeat one day in the Bushwick Park district. I walked to the top floor of a tenement house, and knocked. A man growled, "Who is it?" and I handed out my spiel about the World Indemnity Insurance, checking out a bequest, and from behind the door the man said, "Wait a minute. I'll get dressed." He opened the door a few minutes later, and I said, "I'm from Mentor Clothing. Here is a summons," and I slapped him with a summons. He let out a howl. "You dirty rat!" He ran inside the apartment, and I took off, because I had my suspicions. Out he came, bounding down after me, a gun in his hand. He let out a shot, and I broke Man o' War's record.

It worked the other way, too. I tracked down a woman who owed $30-35, and when she opened the door, I began saying, "I have a summons—" and she put her finger to her lips and said, "Please be quiet. Come in." She led me into the kitchen of a little railroad flat where a coal-burning stove was operating on a couple of clumps of coal. A baby lay in a crib, wrapped in what we used to call a pneumonia vest.

"I know I owe the money," the woman said, "and I intend to pay it back as soon as I can." But times had been hard. Her husband had left her. The baby had been sickly, and now he had pneumonia, and this was the crisis day. "I've been hoping and praying all day," she said, and I growled, "Listen. If you ever get the money, send it in, but don't worry about it. As far as I'm concerned, you're deceased." I wrote across the card, "Located and found deceased," which was what we were supposed to write, and I walked out, feeling pretty good because I hadn't dunned the woman out of her kid's medicine.

Some people I didn't mind dunning. Or at least seeing they paid. I had another sideline at Mentor. Occasionally some one would plunk down $10 on a suit, and in the day or two before he came back to pick it up, we'd checked him out as a total phony. So the boss and I worked up an act. The poor soul would walk in for his suit, and the salesman would have him wait in one of the dressing rooms while the salesman got the suit, and the boss would whisper, "Okay, Bill, go into the act."

As the world will tell you, I've always been a pretty loud fellow. I'd go to the back of the store, and I'd let out a bellow, "Where is he? Where is that lousy phony and thief, that two-timing deadbeat crook? Coming for his suit, is he? I've got the goods on him." I'd go stamping through the back of the store, heading for the dressing rooms, and he'd hear me and get into his old clothes and take off. Mentor would be $10 richer, of which, naturally, I got $5.

No matter how you sliced it, it was dreadful work, bullying people out of money, whether they deserved it or not, and pretty soon I quit. This time I landed a real private detective job, with an agency on Wall Street. The usual work was guarding payrolls or making deliveries of cash or other valuables, for $10 a day and expenses. My first assignment had me tailing a man who'd terminated his employment as a butler for a family in Port Washington, Long Island, at the same time the family jewels disappeared. The family didn't want the police involved, so we were hired. I had to tail the guy from his top-floor railroad flat at 101st Street and Park Avenue where he lived with his wife, and report back any unusual activity. He had a routine. He'd take the streetcar to 42nd Street and buy an out-of-town newspaper. I got close enough one day to see he was buying the Cleveland paper.

He was an impeccably dressed man, in his late fifties, the perfect proper butler. I finally was able to rent an apartment next door and with another detective and a stenographer, I'd listen at the wall of my apartment to what went on next door. Pretty soon we figured he was reading the personals, looking for the word to go to Cleveland with the jewels, where some fence, obviously, was ready to receive them. The thief was eventually picked up by another detective from the agency at the railroad station with the jewels in a suitcase, ready to board a train for Cleveland.

I worked eight months, and then I was assigned to protect a salesman carrying uncut half-carat and quarter-carat stones from 48th Street and Fifth Avenue to an office on Fulton Street where he showed the diamonds. I then would accompany him back to 48th Street and Fifth. No sweat. Except one day when I got to Fulton Street with the salesman and he went into the office, I realized I had to go to the john. Usually he would be in the office, concluding his business arrangements, for ten or fifteen minutes. I flew into the men's room and was back out, sitting on the stairs, as I always did, waiting, within two or three minutes. I waited a half hour, and then I knocked on the door of the office, and found he'd been gone nearly that whole half hour. When I sheepishly reported back to the agency, they said, "Take your pill out," which meant take your card out of the time clock, you were fired. I was fired.

Getting fired was my true trade. Next I got a job selling Wesson Oil to grocers in Brooklyn. I'd carry big cardboard placards for shop windows, and I'd take orders, and when I'd get rid of all the placards and file enough orders for the day, I'd catch the new show at Loew's Met or the Prospect. Vaudeville was now in my blood. The sight of men and women prancing onstage, with a little patter, a song or a dance or a bit of magic, turning the world brighter for the people in the broken leather seats made my heart beat faster. I was earning $35 or $40 a day in commissions, which was really big money, so I never felt I was skimping when I blew myself to the afternoon show. Still, the company expected me to work all day. When the lights went on one day at the Met and I looked around, there was my boss sitting right next to me. I said "Good show, wasn't it?" and I bowed to him and got up and left. I don't pretend it was a great line, but then I am not the greatest ad-libber in the world. I admire the quick inventive lines that some people seem to have lying on their tongue in abundance. I am reminded of one of the funnier ad-libs I know. It happened in the middle of another great disaster. Bing Crosby's house in Toluca Lake, California, burned down one night many years ago, and if you don't think that was a disaster, you should have seen Bing crawling around, looking for his golf shoes. He was in his bathrobe, all the Crosbys were in bathrobes, standing around, and the house an inferno. There was no danger to anyone's person, but the house was a total loss, and Bing had misplaced his golf shoes, which not only was going to keep him from the club the next day, but he also kept his handy cash in his shoes. The story has nothing to do with golf or cash, but with the fire. Dave Shelly, in business with Bing, wandered over to the fire when the word got out, and as Crosby stood there, open-mouthed, watching his beautiful home being engulfed in flames, the whole family silent and stunned, standing on the lawn in robes, Shelly tapped Bing on the shoulder and he said, "Hiya, Bing, what's new?"

To this day friends of Bing never say, "Hello." They say, "What's new?"

I said, "Good show, wasn't it?" which couldn't have been a very funny line, because my boss nodded and said, "You're fired."

Which is how I got into show business.

7

Mr. Bob. Heap Big Coconuts

In 1921, while I was endearing myself to Brother Michael at St. James High, my brother Ed saw an ad in the paper, announcing a tryout at the Met for roles in the chorus. He auditioned and when he let loose his rich baritone, they signed him for $1 a night. Ed was working regularly as a garageman in Brooklyn during the day, but he could use the extra money. He now had a girl, Catherine Conlan, a round, pretty thing whom everybody called Cooee, and whom Mary and I call Cuddles today. Her father had given her the Cooee name, because, he used to say, she cooed in her sleep when she was an infant. Ed met her after a church basketball game and dazzled her because he had a car. She must have dazzled him as well, because when Ed took her home that night, he asked, "May I kiss you goodnight?" which may not sound so daring today, but was pretty swift then. (And Cooee said, Yes.)

Ed stayed with the Met for two years, and then in 1924, he got a job in the Rudolf Friml operetta, *Rose Marie*, as Sergeant Malone. Show business appealed to Ed, which turned out to be a great break for me. I would drop over to the Imperial Theatre once in a while, and watch Ed rehearse for *Rose Marie*, he and Dennis King warming up their voices in the empty theater, and I'd get a bang out of Ed. Dennis King had a pleasant-enough tenor, but when Ed really got warm, he could have blasted King right off the stage. In its raw state, it was a magnificent voice.

One day he was going to the Lambs Club for lunch, with Arthur Deagan, whom Ed was understudying in *Rose Marie*, and Ed asked whether he could bring me along. I was between jobs, as they say, and bored, and when Deagan agreed, I was delighted. Not so much to be with Ed or Deagan or to eat at the Lambs, but to be doing something. I'd just been fired from the Wesson Oil job, and I badly wanted to be working again. I went to lunch with them, and I remember Ed pointing out the fine old actor George Nash, and nobody needed to point out John Barrymore, whom everybody called Jack. A man named Le Roy Clemens came over to our table; he knew Ed and Deagan, and I was introduced to him, and he said, "And I suppose you want to be an actor, too?"

"Yes, *sir*," I said, with a good show of enthusiasm, not because he'd said "actor," but because he'd really said "worker." Had he said, And I suppose you want to be a plumber, too? I'd have said, Yes, sir, just as fervently. He could have said baker, candlestick maker, tree surgeon, or shoe salesman. I wanted to be something; I wanted to be anything. I'd got out of school in 1922, and this was 1924, and I'd already been a delivery boy, a package wrapper, a skating rink cleaner-upper, a Wall Street runner, a private detective, a credit collection dunner, a shortening salesman, and probably four or five I've forgotten. I never was between jobs long. A day or two, or a week at the outside. But I wasn't making a profession out of any of them, and perhaps I was a shade more enthusiastic about "actor" than I might have been about tree surgeon. I'd surely chop down the wrong branch, if not the wrong tree.

Vaudeville had been in my blood for some time, and I always enjoyed a trip to the movie house to see the silents, and I loved getting tickets to stage plays from Dad. But I also loved going to ball games and dances; I loved eating in restaurants and drinking in speakeasies; I was thrilled by the sight of horses rushing down the stretch, especially when the horse I'd bet on was leading the way. Lots of things were in my blood. Life was in my blood.

So Le Roy Clemens smiled at my boyish enthusiasm, and read it all wrong, fortunately, and he said, "Why don't you go down to the Lyceum rehearsal hall? They're trying out for a play I've written." I said, "Yes, *sir*," and I got up and started out. "Wait a minute," he said dryly, "you can finish your lunch."

So I bolted my lunch, and I was at the rehearsal hall an hour later, and they told me to come back the next morning, for my tryout.

I returned the next morning, and I read a line, and somebody said, "That's fine. You're hired."

I would remember more about it, the thrill of getting my first acting job, if I thought in terms of acting as my own special and precious way of life. But I didn't think that way. It was the Wesson Oil company saying, "Fine. Grab those placards and hit the grocery stores on Willoughby Street tomorrow." Or Mentor saying, "Fine. Now take these deadhead sheafs and dun them until they bleed money."

A job. The play was *Aloma of the South Seas*, by Clemens and John B. Hymer. I had to say the line, "Mr. Bob. Heap big coconuts," my body smeared with thick brown goo, to make me look like an Islander, and for this I would get $30 a week.

I was fascinated. It was another world, and I liked it. I had my line to say, but there was much more to be absorbed, so I began to study what was going on. I watched the actors, the director, the stage manager, even the company manager. I didn't realize then I was a quick study, but I was. I soon knew every part, I knew all the stage directions, and I especially knew just when you were supposed to tell the backstage man to pour the rice on the sheets and shake the sheets to make a sound like a great driving rainstorm about which the play revolved.

So I quickly developed another sideline. I became the third assistant director, in charge of the storm scene. We opened in Baltimore in November of 1924, at the old Ford's Theatre, and on opening night, one of the Island girls came to my dressing room and said sweetly, "Would you help me with my make-up?" I was delighted. I had to smear her smooth back from a bucket of this brown goo, and she obliged by smearing my back with her tender little hand, and as we were smearing each other and giggling madly, the door opened, and the producer walked in. It turned out he had a special claim to the girl, and just before I went on stage that night, to say, "Mr. Bob. Heap big coconuts!" the stage manager came up to me and said, "Gargan, here's your notice. You'll do the Baltimore run, but that's all."

It was just like all my other jobs. Easy come, easy go. I don't remember that I was particularly crestfallen. Crestdroopy, maybe, but not fallen.

The Baltimore run lasted two weeks, for which I received my $30 a week, and I kept watching other people, to see what they were doing and how they did it. I didn't much worry about why they did it the way they did. I've usually left the "why" of acting to the Method boys. If I'm told to cross a room and open a window, I can get across the room without a session in psychoanalysis, thank you. If the playwright has written the play well, there's motivation for what's going on. Just do it. I especially watched Arthur Vinton, who played the lead, Red Molloy. Vinton was a great stock actor, which is not the same as saying he was a great actor. He could do any role of any play with scant notice, and he always did them with a great sense of authority. He had wonderful stage presence; he knew what he was doing. The reason he knew what he was doing was that he did every role exactly the same way. He'd bellow a line, take two steps, bellow a line, and take two more steps. He kept moving this way, and the part always had a liveliness, a sense of activity. It was *one*-two-three; *one*-two-three; *speak*-walk-walk; *speak*-walk-walk. I thought it was wonderful; I immediately absorbed Vinton's style, and pretty soon I was bellowing, "Mr. Bob," and I'd take two steps, and I'd bellow, "Heap big coconuts!" and I'd take two more steps. This is known as fattening your part. It is also known as hamming it up, and it makes other actors hate you, though I did not know it then.

So I kept busy, while working my first and last two weeks,

and then we closed in Baltimore and the troupe got ready to go to New York, to open at the Lyric Theatre, on West 42nd Street. I got ready to start looking for work, when A. H. Van Buren, director of *Aloma of the South Seas*, suddenly discovered nobody else knew the storm scene. It was a great scene, in the old noisy theatrical tradition, the kind of thing playwrights no longer write into plays, because the movies do it better, and theater audiences will not accept a handful of rice across a shaking sheet to depict the downfall of rain. But forty-plus years ago it was great stuff, and *Aloma* never would have made it without our typhoon. I was the typhoon man, knowing when to shake the sheet, spill the rice, bang the drum for thunder, and flash the lights for lightning.

Reluctantly, I was kept on. Perhaps the producer also found out nothing had transpired between his girl and me. Still, it was reluctantly. I remember one night A. H. Van Buren saying to a group of people, "And that fellow over there is Mr. Gargan. If we could do without him, we would." I started toward Van Buren, my fist crawling back, and an actor named Frank M. Thomas, who played Bob Holden ("Mr. Bob," to me), grabbed my arm and said, "Do you want to get out of this business?"

I did not. It was a job, and I'd been rehired, so to speak, and until they found a better reason for firing me, I'd stick around.

We lasted six months on Broadway, and frankly I never really knew what I was doing. I said my line, that kind of idiotic line that represents the happy savage talking to his superior, and the play whirled on, with me always swinging my arms backstage to get the storm stirred up something fierce. Meanwhile, I'd memorized every part, and pretty soon I was understudying every male part, and they made me assistant second director, still in charge of the storm, but with other directorial chores as well. More important, I replaced Arthur Vinton as Red Molloy three weeks after we opened at the Lyric.

After six months, two road companies were formed, the first to go to Chicago, and a second to Philadelphia. The better people made the trip to Chicago. Naturally I was with the Philadelphia group. I went up to the producer, and I said, "I can direct the Philadelphia company." For reasons that baffle me still, he said, "Good. You are the director." Yet it wasn't so baffling. Actors were versatile people, in those days. You learned the craft of the entire theater, not just the craft of acting. My brother Ed, in *Rose Marie*, was not only singing and acting the role of Sergeant Malone, but he filled in as assistant stage manager, buying all the props and costumes, and later as stage manager, running a company of eighty-five players.

So I became director of the Philadelphia company, for which they paid me a flat sum of $300 and raised my pay to $75 a week. (A. H. Van Buren, who directed in New York, had received $1000 a week, so you can see how they rated my worth.) I got the rehearsals started, and pretty soon I had everybody saying their lines and taking two steps, and we had a lively production. We opened at the Walnut Street Theatre and immediately had a raging hit on our hands, every performance sold out, with people standing in the back of the theater and behind the boxes. Meanwhile, in Chicago, the number one company laid an egg and folded after three weeks.

Eventually A. H. Van Buren hurried down to Philadelphia, and undid the more foolish bits of business I had instilled in our cast, and I returned to my part, "Mr. Bob. Heap big coconuts!" But I also became stage manager, and I played every other male part as well, at one time or another, Red Molloy, the second lead, the third lead, every part. When Jack Mooney, our manager, deserted the company because he loathed Philadelphia, I was taught to take over the box office. Mooney had a small gimmick going for him. He'd sell standing room at $1.65 a ticket, except there were no tickets. Mooney would turn in his statement every night, and the last line would read: "Sixteen standees @ $1.65," though anybody who could count knew there were closer to 116 standees. So I sold standing room at $1.65 a standee, and I pocketed my share, extra. Just as Vinton's acting style was the only acting I knew, Mooney's box-office style was the one I knew.

I was a hardshelled kid. I was nineteen years old, going on

twenty, and it was a job. No, I did not have stardust fever.
I had never looked at acting artistically, and except for rare
moments, I never would look at it artistically. Later on, I would
feel upset before a show, even vomit before a show. But in
1924 and 1925, on Broadway and on the road—Wilmington,
Boston, the eastern seaboard, and out into the near-Midwest—
it was a job, one-two-three, one-two-three. Selling Wesson Oil
was a job; even scaring the wits out of a poor deadbeat in a
dressing room at the Mentor Clothing store was a selling job.
Now I was a salesman, on stage and behind stage and in the
box-office, selling myself and my goods, my alleged wit, my
muscle, my quick memory, my love of life and of liveliness.
My life had taken on steam; it had begun to careen like a
wonderfully colored carousel of prancing horses; and I danced
to the tune of a childish calliope. The tune was mine, the
carousel mine, the life. Yes, it was a job, but it had its magic
dust. We spun dreams, and every so often I would remember
those Thursdays I had sat in the Loew's Met or the Prospect,
watching the new vaudeville show, marveling at the patter, the
dance, the song, the joke, the acrobatics, the juggling, the *magic*.
Now I was on the stage, and down below were the lonely
souls who needed to be dusted with my magic, who needed
to be swept into a dream world. No, it wasn't artistic, it
seldom would be, though later I would do more skillfully in
other plays and films what I did in *Aloma*. But it had that
magical quality to it, that dream-making quality. It wasn't artistic,
and later, after six months or so in the same part, it became
a crashing bore—acting did—but always, then and later and
now, it held out moments when you felt like a god, sprinkling
your bits of pleasure down on an audience unfolding to receive
you. "We are the music makers," Arthur O'Shaughnessy sang,
"and we are the makers of dreams . . . we are the movers and
shakers of the world forever, it seems."

8

Or, How to Handle a Lionel Barrymore

Aloma played forty weeks on the road, a not unusual feat for those days. Ed spent eighty weeks with *Rose Marie*. I can't say this was the heyday of the theater in terms of the quality of the written drama. Surely *Aloma* was not the greatest play since *Hamlet*. But it was a period when people flocked to the theater. And theater flocked to the people. Road companies crisscrossed the continent; stock companies filled every barn and meeting hall, and not just in the summer months. Man must be entertained. The movies had not yet fully caught on; it would take the dramatic changeover from silents to sound before a silver screen replaced the stage as America's mass medium of entertainment.

Naturally it was heady stuff to me, still not twenty-one years old when *Aloma* finally folded and I'd heaped my last big coconut. I'd seen a new piece of America, a less sophisticated piece, the wide-eyed people of the East and near-Midwest—Ohio, Indiana, Pennsylvania—who brought into the theater the smell of strong soap, an obsession to laugh at our labored jokes, and a simple susceptibility to our melodrama. These were hiss-the-villain audiences, cheer the good guy, and hurrah for the Red, White, and Blue.

Mainly, they wanted fun. The whole country wanted fun. The war had ended, and nobody in his right mind dreamed there'd be another. Normalcy was in full swing, and normalcy meant the Roaring Twenties, the Jazz Age, twenty-three-skidoo, and oh-you-kid.

I had money, and then I didn't have money. As soon as it came in, it went out. I spent it. Not all of it, but pretty close. Ed used to do me one better. He spent it all. I remember the night the four of us, Mom, Dad, Ed, and I, had dinner at Cavanagh's on 23rd Street, to celebrate Ed's return from the *Rose Marie* road company. Dad wanted to know how Ed managed to spend all his money, and Ed got pretty vague about it. Well, Dad said, just take last week's salary. How did Ed spend that?

Ed broke it down, or tried to. So much for laundry, so much for phone calls back to Cooee and to the folks, so much for meals, tips, shoeshines, newspapers, and so on. But when he'd finished, he still hadn't accounted for the last $22.

"What'd you spend the twenty-two dollars on?" Dad wanted to know.

Ed, nonplussed, thought and thought. Finally he had it, his face breaking into a huge grin. "I spent it on chewing gum!" he announced triumphantly.

"Twenty-two dollars' worth of chewing gum?" Dad shrieked. He picked up a handful of cherries softening in a bowl on the table, and he flung them in Ed's face.

Which only made Ed laugh harder. Life, to Ed, was a bowl of cherries.

I didn't spend my money on chewing gum. My special vice was slot machines. But what the heck—if I spent it today, there'd be a nice paycheck tomorrow. I needed tomorrow's paycheck, because I also spent money on long-distance calls to my girl, Mary, who'd started to make her way in show business. Yes, she was my girl, and I was her beau, except we had no formal understanding, and we were young healthy people. She had a stagedoor johnny in every city she danced her lovely legs off. I'd phone her from Pittsburgh or from Boston, and I'd hear her mother say, "It's your long-distance Romeo." When I'd see Mary, I'd tell her, "I'm going to marry you one of these days," and she'd shake her lovely head (which, incidentally, had violently changed from blonde to titian, right out of the dye bottle), and she'd say, "No, you're not." She kept it cool; she kept it from becoming overly serious when neither one was ready for marriage. Yet it was serious. Beneath my bantering threat to marry her was a deadly serious statement of fact. I intended to marry her. And beneath her, No, you're not, was the unspoken word, *yet.*

But it was far too soon. I came back to New York, *Aloma* behind me, and I looked for an agent. Agent was something else I had learned. An agent found work for you. *That's* magic. I went over to the Brown brothers office—Chamberlain and Lyman Brown, the most wanted agents in town. Particularly Chamberlain. They had a woman named O'Reilly; I never knew her first name; I doubt that she had one, a square-jawed major-domo who kept people out of the Browns' hair. I told her who I was and what I'd done, and that I'd like to be part of the Brown stable. She liked me well enough. But the Browns preferred wealthy kids from snooty families, not a Brooklyn boy with a Brooklyn accent, out of a bookmaker by way of a substitute grade-school teacher.

So I didn't sign with Chamberlain Brown. I wound up with Mike Connolly, of the Jenny Jacobs agency, and I was delighted. Mike said to me, "You want to go back to work right away?" and I said, "You bet," and he said, "There's an Earl Carroll show—*Laff That Off*—that's going on the road, and they're hiring. I think they'll like you."

I went down to read and they liked me. I played a fellow who's lost his girl, a part of 125 sides, which made it one of the very good parts of the play. A side, for the uninitiated, is a small sheet of paper, with your cue and lines on it. I met a lovely young girl, also in the show, a fluffy-haired grinning thing with a slightly odd voice, a cast to one eye, and a delightful sense of humor. She must have been a year or two younger than I, but she was already making it big. She had whatever it is you have to have—star quality, quicksilver, whatever you want to call it. She had it. But she was going to go with another road company, so Shirley Booth and I played together just three weeks before we split. Had I been there earlier, when the play began rehearsing for Broadway, I'd have met another young actor starting out, a laughing-eyed Irishman named Pat O'Brien. But Pat got fired before I came along. We made contact later.

Laff That Off, again, would never drive Bernard Shaw out of show business. It was farce, pure and simple-minded, and because it used just one set, it was an easy play to bundle up and take along with you. We played a week each in Philadelphia, Baltimore, and Boston, and then took off on a series of one-, two-, and three-night stands. Usually we lived in a big Pullman car, with a Baker heater the porter would keep lit, so we wouldn't freeze to death on the siding of some small town. I hit it off with Norval Keedwell, who starred in the play, and after the show he and I would search out the local speak. In Cumberland, Maryland, we didn't have to. Keedwell knew a colonel who lived in Cumberland, and the colonel invited the whole cast to his place, an absolute mansion, with colonial pillars, huge windows, and a handsome staircase of polished oak. He also served us pepper whiskey, which I found delicious. Just as we were ready to leave, Keedwell and I wandered into the kitchen, and there was a keg of the stuff, and an empty milk bottle. We put the two together, filling the milk bottle with pepper whiskey, and clumsily wrapping a piece of paper about the neck of the bottle. I stuffed it into my overcoat pocket. All went well until I got to the car. I bent to get in, and the whiskey sloshed out of the bottle and onto the ground, next to the colonel's immaculate boots. He stared at me gravely. "Why didn't you tell me, son?" he said. "I would have given it to you." I felt miserable, for a few minutes, and then I felt fine, and Keedwell and I laughed all the way home.

On the stage, I'd begun to have some feeling for what I was doing. I wasn't much of an actor, but I worked hard, and I picked up what lay around and discarded what didn't work. I also learned to defend myself. A girl named Miriam Sills joined the cast after we'd been on the road thirty weeks or so, and she and I had a scene together in which I sit in a chair next to her, and she consoles me for losing my girl. One night as I turned to her, I noticed she had moved back a bit. To see her and speak to her, I had to turn my body so I faced away from the audience. Naturally she was looking the audience right in the eye. I figured it was nothing, but the next night she'd moved farther back, and pretty soon in order to see her I had to turn my back on the audience.

After the curtain one night I said, "What's up, Miriam? I've got my back to the audience. Get back where you belong."

She smiled sweetly. "I feel more comfortable back there."

"Okay," I said. "You just stay there."

So the next night when I turned to talk to her, and found she had skedaddled halfway to the rear of the stage, I picked up my chair and strolled over and sat down again, next to her and a hair behind her. I smiled sweetly at her and picked up her hand and patted it, and she got the message. If she moved, I'd move. The next night she was right where she belonged.

You come across tricksters like that. It's part of the business. Some actors have to hog the scene. With the good ones, you don't mind too much. Years later I made a film for M-G-M, *Night Flight*, a featured play thrown into such company as Helen Hayes, Robert Montgomery, Spencer Tracy—a great trickster, by the way—Myrna Loy, and those two super scene stealers, Jack and Lionel Barrymore. Had they wanted, any of them could have eaten me up, green as grass to the ways of moviemaking. I played Myrna Loy's husband, which is pretty nice playing. My first day we had a scene in which I meet Jack Barrymore, with Lionel sitting at a desk between us. Clarence Brown was the director, and we began rolling. After a few lines, I noticed Jack Barrymore's face stiffen slightly, and then he blew his line. Brown yelled, "Cut!" and we took a brief break and Jack called me over. I'd met Jack at Mrs. Quirk's boardinghouse on the Chicago North Side, and later with Leslie Howard on a couple of social evenings, but this was the first time I'd worked with him.

"Have you noticed that sweet sonofabitching brother of mine?" he asked pleasantly.

"Not particularly. My scene is with you."

"The charming bastard is trying to steal it. He's moving and scratching and mugging all over the place. It's your scene. Don't let him do it."

"What should I do?"

"If you see him moving when I'm talking, you blow your line. If I see him move when you're talking, I'll blow. Okay?"

I shrugged. If Jack Barrymore said it was okay, it was okay with me.

So we started in again, and as Jack spoke, I could see Lionel squirming. I blew my next line. We tried it once more, and I guess Lionel scratched his nose, because Jack blew. Then he tugged an earlobe, and I blew. Then Jack. Then I. When we reached Take 55, and Lionel hadn't begun to run out of scratching room, Clarence Brown finally said, "All right. It's funny. We get the point. Now can we settle down and get a good take?" He looked at Lionel. "Get the scratching over with before we shoot, Lionel." Lionel grimaced and grunted. "Eh?" he growled, his wonderful seamed face twisting and changing shape, "Scratch?" he said, digging into an armpit. "I haven't moved."

So we shot Take 55, and it was perfect. I met Jack and Jack met me, and we started out of the room, and Lionel followed us, and just as he reached the doorway, he reached around, and he scratched his behind.

Brown broke up. "Print!" he said, and Lionel had stolen the scene anyway.

But you don't mind it in great company. Later I allowed myself to appear in another film with Lionel—an odd movie called *Sweepings*, with much of the action shot behind a department store, the street covered with rags and debris, from which the title came—and Lionel and I had to do our scene with a small trash truck between us. He pulled the Miriam Sills bit on me; as he'd talk he'd move back a few steps, and the big cameras mounted in great safelike boxes kept the focus

on him, which meant I was becoming a blur. The director was
John Cromwell, and when I saw he was letting Lionel have
his way, I began walking back with my lines, and pretty soon
the truck between us was out of focus. Cromwell finally had to
place a wire behind us to keep us from backing up, while
Lionel kept saying, "Eh? Move? I haven't moved an inch."

You protect yourself as well as you can. Sometimes you can't.
I once played in a cornball drama, *The Greatest Thing in the
World*, written by the wife of a wealthy Chicago gynecologist, a
woman with nothing better to do than finance her creative itch.
I was hired with two days' notice. *The Greatest Thing in the
World*, by the way, turned out to be Motherhood, which gives
you some idea of the calibre of the play. We lasted one performance, at the Triangle Theater in Greenwich Village, for
which I received a lordly $20. Years later I met the author
and her husband. They were good friends of Norval Keedwell,
my buddy of *Laff That Off*, who also appeared in *TGTITW*.
The gynecologist husband vaguely recalled me from the play.
"Goodness," he said, "that was a very expensive play." It turned
out the producer had received from the doctor and his wife—
who angeled the whole production—$150 for my services, of which
I got $20. That's a nice commission.

There is something childish about all this. It is as though
bright, naughty children wrote the rules. Acting is childish. Who
else prances in front of the public and says, "Look at me!
Ain't I a kick?" Children play make believe, for fun; we acted
it out, for money, which simply made us very bright children,
or lucky. And it made the producer of *The Greatest Thing in the
World* brighter or luckier, or some other word. We brought
dreams to life, which is what children do so well that they
wake up screaming at night, or they giggle in their sleep. It all
fitted in with the time—a childish, irresponsible period in America's life, and in the world's. Nor did we keep our playing confined
to the stage. Life was our playground. I mentioned that I finally
made contact with Pat O'Brien. He and Spencer Tracy and I
began to pal around quite a bit, and when Spence hit it big in

The Last Mile, as Killer Mears, he and Pat lived at the Lambs Club, and I'd meet them there and we'd start on the rounds of the actors' hangouts. We'd wind up at Helen Morgan's club, where she'd climb on the piano, and break your heart with a blues number. But one night we weren't in the mood for broken hearts, and Pat took it on himself to insult all the customers in the place, 90 percent of whom were gangsters. Finally the bouncer came over and asked Pat and Spence and me to leave. He didn't ask. He told.

So we weaved to our feet and stumbled through the door, in boozy hysterics, and Pat began to call for a cab. The night was young—dawn hadn't quite cracked—and this was New York, Broadway, a trio of actors all working, which was like defining heaven. A cab finally hove into view, and Pat asked the driver what had taken so long, hadn't he known that we three actors wanted a cab, and pretty soon Pat was taking off on the cabby, who began to dish it right back. Finally Pat called him an un-charming name, and the driver got out of the front seat and he said, "What did you call me, Buddy?"

Pat repeated it, and the cabby took out a tiny whistle, and he blew it once. If I knew where the guy got that whistle, I'd buy up the lot and, become a millionaire. Because instantly, out of nowhere, twenty-five cabs descended on us. You can't ever get a cab in New York; that's a cardinal rule. Here were twenty-five unasked-for cabs. Twenty-five cabbies got out and began throwing punches. They more or less surrounded Spence and began belaboring him, and I tried to run, like the wise coward I am, but they caught up and began to beat up on me, and finally the three of us regrouped again a dozen blocks away, and counted our wounds. Spence had busted his right arm. For three acts he'd have to carry Killer Mears' gun with that broken wing. I was bleeding from the neck. Between the two of us, we had two or three dozen bruises. O'Brien? Not a scratch. Ah, the luck of the Irish!

So we played at life, and if I'd been done out of the money I should have been paid for *The Greatest Thing in the World*,

I couldn't complain much. They were paying me for playing a game, acting, and we actors were what Alfred Hitchcock calls "the most grossly overpaid players in the world."

Except when we weren't paid at all. It happened.

9

Why Don't We Get Married?

I'd spent forty weeks of one-, two-, and three-night stands when *Laff That Off* finally closed, and I returned to New York. Perhaps it had come too easy. I had regular money and regular work and regular and even irregular laughs, and I'd become used to it. I was an actor. Not a plumber or a tree surgeon. An actor. I'd never spent so long on one job before. It spoiled me.

I landed back in New York in the spring of 1927, and I holed up in the apartment of Jim Carroll, brother of Earl Carroll of the *Vanities*.

Jim had an apartment in a four-story brownstone in what is today Rockefeller Center, and where the Center Theatre would stand. I would climb the four stories and come out on a little sun garden on the roof, where the *Vanities* girls used to sun themselves in their brief costumes. There are less pleasant ways to spend a summer. Meanwhile, the Jenny Jacobs agency was trying to find work for me; I figured each afternoon in the sun might be my last before going down to another rehearsal hall. I couldn't imagine that play producers were not actively competing for my services.

One actor who came up on the terrace was a peppy little bushy-haired fellow in horn-rim glasses fellow who'd just returned from a southern tour of the *Vanities* with Joe Cook. His name was Dave Chasen, and today Dave is a superb restaurateur in

Hollywood. He became and remains a close friend, and while he waited for Joe Cook to round up another *Vanities*, and I waited for Jenny Jacobs to call and say, "Kid, they want you for the lead in Bernard Shaw's latest comedy, for $1000 a week," we decided to fill the interim and our yawning pockets with money. We became bootleggers.

I'd made booze before, and would make it later. On occasion my folks made their own, or Dad's own. They'd pour a quart of sugar alcohol into a gallon jug, peel the skins of three oranges and three lemons and toss them in for twenty-four hours (or longer, if you really wanted it aged), and add three quarts of boiled water. You had a gallon of tiger's milk, slightly orange. Add ice and ginger ale, if you insisted, and drink.

Then there was Mary and her folks. The Kennys had moved to Eastchester, at the upper end of the Bronx, 225th Street and Gunhill Road. Mary's dad—Pop Kenny—was a bricklayer, when he wasn't a saloonkeep, and when he wasn't either, like at midnight or on weekends, he made his own whiskey. He and Mary's mother, whom we called Nana, made Irish poteen in a little copper still, and stored the whiskey in wooden half barrels. When Nana went in to make the stuff, right in the kitchen sink, she very daintily pulled down the kitchen shade. You knew when she was mixing, especially on an otherwise bright Saturday morning. Down would go the shade, and pretty soon they'd corked up another keg or two and stored it in a closet. Pop Kenny would give the keg a kick every so often, to age it. Pop also had to get rid of the mash. Usually he drove to an empty lot and dumped it in the middle of the night, but one evening, a bit polluted, he didn't quite reach the lot. He emptied it in the backyard of a neighbor who kept a flock of ducks, and the ducks gobbled down the mash. The next day the neighbor stormed up to Pop's door and knocked it in and dragged Pop and Nana to see the damage they had wrought. The ducks were either staggering around woozily or else spread out in stuporish sleep. Drunken ducks. I bet they would have tasted delicious. The sauce was already in.

When I was broke, I would tastefully "borrow" a pint of

Kenny poteen. I eventually paid for those pints. Nana Kenny died in 1942, and Pop Kenny came out to Beverly Hills to live with Mary and me. He helped out at home, doing odd jobs and keeping busy, which was more therapy than work. He also took to cleaning up after a party, straightening out the bar. He was a great cleaner-upper of bars. Not only did he finish what was in the glasses, he didn't like to see any left in the bottles. He was a neat old man, and a grand guy.

So Dave Chasen and I rented an apartment, for $100 a month, at 10 East 50th Street, opposite the side door to St. Patrick's Cathedral, and where a Saks Fifth Avenue shop now stands. Mary would come over, with her wealth of experience, and help us make the gin. Because we made it in quantity, we used the bathtub, just like in the pulp stories. We bought most of our labels from a dealer on 40th Street and Ninth Avenue. The label determined the price. You bought an Ambassador scotch label, and you naturally charged more than you did for any ordinary scotch, though the stuff inside was exactly the same.

We had one good customer, over at the Algonquin Hotel, who took six bottles of our gin every night, labeled Booth's High and Dry. He paid our rent. Gin, of course, was the basic alcohol, plus juniper and glycerine. Scotch was the alcohol, plus creosote, caramel, and prune juice. Gin was the big demand, because it was cheapest. Sometimes you got a fussy drinker who had a more esoteric notion of what he wanted. One guy asked for a bottle of Irish whiskey, which is a swell drink, but I had no idea how to make it. By this time I'd met another fellow who's been a friend ever since, Irving Pinsky. When Mary and I were finally married, and dead broke, Irving came over one day with an armload of paper bags, each one emitting a more piercing odor. Out tumbled exotic spicy items, such as pastrami, lox, knishes, bagels, and six or seven other foods totally foreign to me and Mary, then.

"What's this?" I asked Irving.

"Jewish food," he said. "Eat. Look how you look."

So we ate, like we'd never eaten before. Irving hooked us.

We also met Irving's mother, and she taught us a thing or two about food. Mama Pinsky was a connoisseur of schmaltz herring, in the barrel. You know those big barrels, filled with brine, dotted with peppercorns, bay leaves, cloves of garlic, in which a couple of dozen schmaltz herrings float about blissfully. Mama Pinsky would slip her arm into the barrel up to the elbow, and pull up a herring. She'd toss it back with a sniff. Too fat, she'd mutter. She'd fish up another. Toss it back. Too thin. This one had too much tail and that one too big scales. This one's eyes were too wide and that one's too close-set. "Ah," she'd finally say, pulling up a winner. "Look." So I looked, and pretty soon I learned to distinguish a great vintage schmaltz herring from just a pretty good one. (There are no bad schmaltz herrings.) Now when I go into a delicatessen, I pick my own. I am an expert, thanks to Mama Pinsky.

But it was as a bootlegger I really knew Irving, those days. I called and told him I had this nut who wanted Irish whiskey.

"Come on down," he said.

So I went over to Kings Highway, in Brooklyn, where he had a still.

He poured a fifth of scotch into a barrel and emptied in a pint of bourbon.

"Presto!" he said.

Irish whiskey.

Plus, of course, the clincher. He slapped on a Jamison label.

Why did we do it?

I like to think it was a means of survival, and it was, though it was more. Yes, I needed the money. I was between jobs, and the in-between kept growing longer and hungrier. In the old days, between jobs, I'd have just gone out and found another job, which usually meant another totally different line of work. But now I was an actor. Except I wasn't acting, so I was an unemployed actor, and I needed the money. And remember, bootlegging was terribly remunerative, and not so terribly looked-down upon. But beyond the need to survive—which existed —the fact is I didn't go out and look for a legitimate job. I bootlegged. I probably bootlegged for the sheer hell of it, for the thrill. It was exciting, just as Dad's gambling was exciting, his association with Joe Adonis and Al Capone, and mine with Shorty Hines and Yellow Charleston. Acting didn't make me childish. I was a child, basically, and I sought out childish pleasures.

The customer at the Algonquin said to me one day, "I have a friend in the Roosevelt Hotel. Can you deliver six bottles to him tomorrow night?"

I did, and the friend said to me when I brought them up, "Bootleg stuff?"

"What else?"

He made a small face, so I grinned and said, "I make a practice to take a drink first, to show the customer I can live through it." I poured myself a drink. "Bottoms up." I tossed it down, and didn't fall over dead.

So he tossed some down, and he made another small face. "You look like a nice guy," he said, "How'd you like a good drink of gin?"

"I'd love it."

He went back into a closet and came out with one of those Imperial quarts of Gordon's Gin, in the frosted bottles.

I slugged down a glass and I smacked my lips. "Delicious," I agreed.

"If you can ever get me this stuff," he said, "I'll give you $5 a bottle."

Actually, the whole drinking bit is a farce. After the first drink, the palate is usually so numbed, you can't tell the difference between Ambassador's and rotgut, or Gordon's Imperial and my gin. The whiskey connoisseur is pulling your leg if he says he can. The first drink, yes. The second, no.

So I went back to our apartment, and I phoned my bottle and label man, over at West 40th.

"Do you have any frosted bottles? The Imperial quarts?"

"Sure. But they're expensive. They sell for $2.00 a dozen."

I'd been buying the routine bottle at $1.40 the dozen.

"Trot 'em up," I said. "I need a dozen."

A few days later I called the guy at the Roosevelt.

"I managed to run into six bottles of that Gordon's you were talking about. You want them?"

He wanted, and I brought and he bought. He took a drink and he smacked his lips. "Man, that's drinking."

Two days later, I'd "managed" to run into six more. Business was good.

So I sailed through my first period of unemployment as an actor—there'd be more, and I'd help them out with more bootlegging—and finally in the summer of 1927 I got a call from my agent to go on over to see Sam Harris, about a part in the touring company of *Chicago*. Harris had me read, and then he said, "I'll give you $125 a week," and we shook hands. No contract. I mention this, because my mother was surprised when I'd told her I'd agreed to do a play for Sam Harris.

"But he's a Jew," she said.

Mother was not a bigot. Far from it. It was just a case of things being the way they were for so long. She was Irish, her forebears were Irish, and lace curtains, straw mats, and back-window awnings or no, Irish and Catholic she'd remain. Which did not make her anti-Protestant or anti-Semitic. It made her Irish Catholic, and it kept her ignorant of other people. A Catholic dealt with Catholics; a Jew with Jews. Just as the sand at Brighton Beach was divided into territories—this for the Jewish families, this for the Catholic, and so on—so too was the world divided, in Mother's mind, and the divisions were very distinct.

I never had a contract with Sam Harris, and he never had one with me. I trusted him to pay me what he said he'd pay me, and he trusted me to do the job he'd hired me for.

Chicago was a very funny, very irreverent play, and I think it would be a very funny play today. It had a smash opening scene—Francine Larrimore, clad in a flimsy chemise, goes ranting across the stage, chasing her married boyfriend, a gun in her hand. "You two-timing no good, etc., etc." She shoots him dead, and the curtain falls with a thud. Sixty explosive seconds, what they call today a grabber.

From there on out, the problem is to get her off, via the efforts of a sob-sister newspaper woman. The newspaper woman decides to write the story of the murderess's life. She visits Francine in jail and tells Francine how she's going to win the sympathy of the public. "Let's begin," she says, "with your childhood. Where were you born?"

"I was born in a convent," Francine says, and the audience always fell apart, and we were home free. So was the killer. When the play ends, she had been booked for a long vaudeville tour.

Chicago was a long tour for me, and though we kept getting our laughs—in Chicago, Kansas City, St. Louis, Baltimore, Washington, Boston, and Pittsburgh—I began to get bored.

I'd begun to sense something lacking in my life. It was a vague feeling, undefined, but it bothered me. How exciting can the same stimulus remain? You strut out on stage and you deliver your lines, and you get laughs or applause or a wet eye, and you've done your job, and you've done it well. You do it again the next night, and the next, and after four weeks, you've done it to death. Some actors can keep discovering new ways to do something, new bits, new gestures. They insist they keep the role fresh that way. When they asked her how she managed to be fresh for every performance of the comedy *Marriage Go Round*, Claudette Colbert said, "Why not? You're fresh for breakfast every morning."

But if I have a soft-boiled egg three mornings in a row, I'm sick of soft-boiled eggs. Make 'em hard, or make 'em poached, or better still, change the menu from eggs to waffles. You can't do that with a part. If it's soft-boiled eggs, it remains soft-boiled eggs, no matter how you handle the spoon or the saltcellar.

Bored is the word. Acting can be a big fat bore. It was a new truth, a painful one, and I was groping my way toward it.

The other significant aspect of my life had settled into a stalemate. When Mary and I had reached the romantic stage just about the time I started in *Aloma*, we knew to keep it lighthearted. We were too young, unformed. Now, in 1927, I was a man of twenty-two, and she would soon be twenty-one. If I didn't make an awful lot of money all the time, I at least made a healthy amount most of the time. So did Mary. She'd taken dance lessons when she was four, and by the time she was sixteen, she could dance the usual stage dances of the day as well as any young girl in the country. God had given her a superb body for dancing, tiny and trim, yet softly curved and very feminine. She was perhaps too little to be a big star on the stage—they look for a Carol Channing or a Julie Andrews, big girls with big distinct features—but for a pony chorus in the beginning and then ingenue leads, you could not touch her. When she was sixteen, she applied for a job in the vaudeville revue, *Oh Mary*, no agent, no friend in the business to pass the word, just her lovely figure and bright gaminish face, and her ability to hoof. She got the job, doing the upstate New York circuit, and later down to the Palace. Then she saw an ad in *Variety* for a *George White Scandals*, and went down and again got tapped. This time she received $65 a week in a yellow envelope, doing her tap dance number, a little acrobatics (backbends, up and over), a whirl or two on her toes, and the buck-and-wing softshoe that got audiences of the 1920s.

When our lives converged, we'd continue to date in the same manner as before—Chinese restaurants, speakeasies, dancing at the McAlpin Hotel at 34th and Broadway to Vincent Lopez's band.

But we had done it all before, and if there is a word for such courtship it is comfortable. We'd become comfortable with each other, a very dangerous state to be in. If a guy isn't careful, when he finds his girl comfortable to be with and not just exciting, he is a short step from marriage. Actually, just looking around, I should have known it doesn't have to be so short a step. My brother Ed had begun dating Cooee Conlan eight years before. They still hadn't married, nor were they officially engaged. They had an unofficial understanding, and you knew they'd get married someday, but the day—it turned out—was still quite a way off. Day? Year. Ed and Cooee finally linked up in 1938, nineteen years after Ed had daringly asked for a kiss the first time they'd set eyes on each other.

I took Mary out one night in 1927, and after our date I

got ready to ride her home on the subway before I then returned to Brooklyn. We waited for the subway on the downstairs platform at 42nd Street and Lexington, and a big chain dangled before us to block off a portion of the platform not in use. This was the quiet hour for the subway; they didn't need all the length of platform.

I put my foot on the dangling chain, and I said, "Why don't we get married some day?"

The platform was empty; perhaps it was three or four in the morning, when the trains ran every twenty or thirty minutes. My words echoed in the long cave beneath the city, where millions slept. I felt sad and lonely and a bit vulnerable. I didn't much like the idea of riding the subway all the way to Eastchester and then riding it back alone. She looked up at me, her eyes wistful, and she said, "Let's," and we kissed out on the platform.

Then the train came, and we got on, and the train slowly pulled away from the platform. I could see the chain, receding, swaying ever so slightly, a barrier that had become a link. Mary remembers the chain as well. "It bound our love," she says.

10

We Dance on Ground Glass

Engaged, but not married. Officially engaged. Dad took me to a Bank of Italy branch—now the Bank of America—at 40th and Broadway, with a friend, George Nelson. We went into the vault where Nelson opened his box, and I like to have gone blind.

There must have been two hundred rings lying there, plus another hundred hunks of diamond, and a handful of other stones, rubies, sapphires, emeralds.

"Pick out your ring," Nelson said.

I picked out a modest-sized diamond ring, and I paid for it, and later Mary went down and picked out a ruby ring for me. You realize they were all pawned rings that the owners had never redeemed. I realized. But I didn't blink an eye—except to shut out the glare of all those carats winking at me—and I never felt a qualm. I winked back. I got a ring cheap, and so did Mary, and we never worried about the poor souls who had once owned the rings but couldn't afford the few bucks to get them out of hock.

Worrying about such people and such things was for other people to worry about. Not for me. I was twenty-two years old, but years don't make a man. I remained the laughing Brooklyn boy, immature as a foal. You cannot scrape the environment from the boy. I was what I had to be. This was 1927, the

peak of the Jazz Age, Westbrook Pegler's era of wonderful nonsense, the year Lindbergh flew the Atlantic, Babe Ruth hit his
sixty home runs, and Jolson sang in *The Jazz Singer*. If 1927
was the peak of the Jazz Age, New York was its capital. The
city danced, drank, and debauched. Gang war raged in the Bronx.
Murder, Inc. began to slaughter people on contract in Brooklyn. But the island of Manhattan lay between the fetid waters
of the East River and the murky brown waters of the Hudson,
a floating Eden, a piece of rock candy we all devoured. Jimmy
Walker was our Mayor, in striped pants and black top hat, a
dancing sliver of an Irishman, a darling man with a darling
smile; he wrote song hits and he sang them, the perfect mayor
for this rock-candy city.

I got arrested the one and only time of my life, in 1927, and
loved every minute of it. New York City Hall Room 9 reporters
used to put on an annual show those days, the Inner Circle,
like Washington's Gridiron Dinner, a night of spoof and lam-
poonery, and somehow, between professional jobs, I got roped in
to rehearsing with the boys in a ballroom at the Hotel Astor.
After rehearsal, we would repair to the suite of Harry Moness,
a bigtime lobbyist. Moness' suite had been used by Charles
Evans Hughes on Election Day of 1916. Hughes listened to election returns until midnight and finally said, certain he had won,
"Let's put out the cat and go to bed." The next day California
came in, for Woodrow Wilson, and they put out Hughes.

We'd rehearse and then go up to Moness' suite, where three
bathtubs lay filled with bottles of champagne, and liquor bottles
covered every dressertop, desk, and table. One night I remember
a few of the fellows got bored and decided to line up the
glasses on a huge bedpost to see how many they could knock
off with one swing. Naturally the glasses shattered all over the
floor, and when the last glass had exploded into tiny shards of
crystal, at our feet, we began to dance. I think if I had to seize a
moment and declare it the climax of any period of my life,
this was it, dancing on ground glass in the Presidential Suite of a
New York city hotel, champagne in the bathtubs.

That night one of the reporters, Clarence Worden, with the

Daily News, said, "All right now, let's eat." Worden later became secretary to Jimmy Walker, which is as it should be.

We walked to a Childs' restaurant, and Worden, who was a little guy, hung on the swinging doors and swung himself. Maybe that was the moment I'd seize and freeze for posterity, a grown man swinging on a restaurant door, like a child. Or any moment, that night, those weeks, that year.

A couple of cops walked by, poor guys, like pint-sized Daniels into the lion's den, like Georges Carpentier fed to Jack Dempsey, like cops fed to reporters and a lobbyist and the Senator. Did I say my father was there? He was. We palled around still, more like buddies than father and son. The cops were green, and a little scared, as young cops often are.

"What do you think you're doing, punk?" one of them said to Clarence, swinging back and forth, a giddy moment in a giddy year.

"Having some fun," Clarence said. "Don't bother me."

Having fun was all you needed to say (we thought). Don't bother me was all you wanted (we thought).

But the cop thought different. "Get off there, you punk," he said.

Clarence got off and stared, in mock reproach. "You shouldn't call names." Then he climbed back on his wooden swing.

"I'll run you in," the cop threatened.

"Come on," Clarence said, delighted. "Let's go."

So we all marched to the 47th Street station house, laughing at the wonderful nonsense of it all. We lined up in front of the desk sergeant, and when he asked who the offending party was, we all pressed forward. "Arrest us all," a reporter shouted, and the police obliged.

The desk sergeant began to write it up, on the police blotter, and as he asked our names, he also asked our occupations. I told the cop I was an actor, and he gave me a curled-eyebrow look that said, "Sure. We've seen your kind before."

When it came to Dad, they refused to make an arrest, no matter how hard the old man pleaded. The sergeant said, "Come on, Pop. Out you go. Go on home."

"I demand my rights," Dad insisted. "Arrest me!"

But they wouldn't, and as Dad reluctantly started out, Harry Durkin of the *Telegram*, shouted: "You know who to call, Senator," and Dad, not so drunk he didn't know what he was doing, promptly went to a phone booth and called Jimmy Walker.

Unfortunately the Mayor wasn't home.

So Dad made a second call. He called the Police Commissioner.

Dad woke him, told him what was up, where we were, and hung up.

A few minutes later, the commissioner showed up, still wearing his pajama top.

"Who the hell do you think you are?" he roared at the sergeant. "Get these men out of here."

So they fell all over us apologizing, and when we got outside the old man was beaming. He'd done something big. This was how we measured our moments, in 1927, in New York.

The show went on that spring, at the Astor, and it was called *Off the Record*. Mayor Walker was there, and he said in his brief talk, "You ought to change the name. Call it, *Off the Blotter*."

So we'd broken the unwritten law. Once on the police blotter, always on. Or so it used to be. Now our names had been removed from the otherwise indelible blotter. What we'd done had officially never happened.

Life was gay, life was gorgeous, life was a cabaret, old sot. But soon, very soon, it was to change.

I returned to New York in January of 1928, getting ready for the last leg of the *Chicago* tour, never knowing, of course, that the era had peaked. This had been the crest, in 1927, and now it began to ebb, though we still danced and drank and played on tireless legs. We in the theater should have guessed. *The Jazz Singer* was not an all-sound film—just part—but the writing was on the wall and the subtitles coming off the screen. *The Lights of New York* would open in 1928—all sound—and the legitimate stage began a slow evolution, to its position today as a specialized medium of entertainment. The movies would be the mass medium, until television came along, and then the TV screen would show Christopher Plummer's *Hamlet* to more people than had ever seen it in all the versions in all the hundreds of years since Shakespeare had written it. Even more people, of course, would watch *Bonanza* or a World Series game. We didn't know anything of television then, back in the winter of 1927, the start of 1928, but we might have suspected what movies would do. They would close us down, all over the country. The people knew what was coming their way, movie houses in their neighborhoods, where for a quarter (tops) you could see and hear Fairbanks and Arliss and Warner Baxter, Norma Shearer, Marie Dressler, and Lionel Barrymore and John and Ethel. All of them—just names before, most of them—now around the corner, bigger than life, and talking, singing, laughing, crying.

I passed through New York on my way down to Baltimore, with *Chicago*, and at Grand Central I phoned Mary.

She sounded disconsolate.

"What's wrong, honey?"

"I got fired."

She'd had a run-in with one of the producers of the show she was dancing in, *Manhattan Mary*, with Ed Wynn. If you must know, the producer had tried to climb into her upper berth one night, and naturally she stabbed him in the eye with the spiked heel of her shoe. He took it as an unfriendly act, and she'd received her slip.

"Why don't you come down to Baltimore?" I suggested.

She paused. "Maybe I will. I'll ask Mother."

So she came down a few days after I got to Baltimore, and I found her a room at the Belvedere. It rained the day she got in, and it rained the next day, and on the third rainy morning, I went over to her room, and I said, "It's raining again. Let's get married."

"That's not a bad idea," she said.

So we got married. The sun's been out ever since.

11

The Bridegroom Thaws Out

It didn't happen quite that fast, but fast enough. I bought Mary's ring, and we lined up a priest, a Father Makassey. On January 19, 1928, we walked down the long dark aisle of the Assumption of the Blessed Virgin Mary Cathedral in Baltimore, and were married, Mary in a blue chiffon cocktail dress, and I in a dark business suit, my hand shaking properly as I put the ring on her finger. Norval Keedwell and his wife, Miriam Sears, stood up for us, and their little girl, Diane, was our flower girl, a darling child.

We jumped into a cab, and drove off, the rain having yielded to a swirling snow, and I stopped off at the Blue Goose to buy three bottles of gin. I also insisted on stopping at a pet store, where I bought my first present for my wife. I came out with a bowl of goldfish.

I handed the bowl to Mary. "Careful," I said. "It slurps." She had to carry it the rest of the road trip.

"Some day," I said to her grandly, on the honeymoon, "I'll buy you solid gold ones. They'll weigh twenty pounds each."

Mary snorted. "And I'll have to carry them around, I suppose."

I had a whole $125 to my name—our name—when the honeymoon began officially that night, with a party in the hotel, for the cast, cold cuts and drink, and I got truly plastered. They had to stick my head out the hotel window, in hopes of sobering me up. All they did was freeze me stiff. By the time Mary pulled me in, my hair had frozen, even my lashes. The party finally broke up, with me lying on a bed, out cold. Very cold.

"What did you do?" a cast member asked Mary, the next day.

"I just waited for him to thaw out," my bride answered, dimpling.

Her wait was punctuated by a series of phone calls, from our parents, wishing us well. Nana Kenny hid her disappointment. She'd much preferred Mary married a security lawyer who'd staked a small claim. Mary has always insisted I was the family favorite, but that is not so. I was, for good reason, that actor bum, and (sometimes) that bum actor, in Nana's mind.

To balance matters, my father was equally disappointed. He figured it was the end of the world for me, getting tied down so young. He also suspected we had to get married. When I'd called to tell my folks the news, my father asked bluntly, "Why, is she pregnant?"

"She'd better not be," I said firmly.

The play moved to Atlantic City, and so did we, playing there a week. Dad came down, to walk on the boardwalk with me, and to buy me a drink, and let me buy him one. The play shifted to Washington, the National Theatre, and the weather dramatically turned. A false spring broke, and the earth opened its dark mouth, and Norval Keedwell introduced me to another of my present-day vices. He said one gorgeous day in Washington, "Let's play a round of golf." I had never held a club in my hand, but—and you'll have to take my word for it (or not, as you see fit)—I made a hole-in-one my first day on the course. I made seventeen other holes in a hundred and forty-one, so you know the magnitude of my luck.

The honeymoon continued, up to Philadelphia and then on to Boston, where Mary and I stayed at the Arlington Hotel, a really old-fashioned establishment, with a sign on our door, EGRESS TO FIRE ESCAPE. In other words, in case of fire, this was the room everybody ran through. We munched cheese and crackers in the hotel room, warming them on a pressing iron at night.

The tour finally ended, and I was again thrown on my resources, which is to say, my agent's ability to get me roles. Mary and I moved in with my folks, on Garfield Place.

We weren't flat broke, let's say almost, except now I had to support her. She could have gone out and let her dancing feet get another job, but she decided she'd rather lean on me than have to stab amorous producers with her spiked heel. A woman has a rough time in this business, especially a good-looking woman. It may seem peaches and cream to the kids back home, wide-eyed over all the glamour, the slinky gowns and furs, the big limousines, the gorgeous homes that come naturally with a girl's stardom, but the cream too often curdles, and the peaches hide a rotten spot inside. There are two worlds for the actor, public and private, and if he is careful and not terribly handsome or glamorous, he can keep the two separate. The two worlds overlap for the beautiful woman, and soon there is no private world, and a Marilyn Monroe is hounded to her death. Others seek escape in pills, bottles, drugs, or a succession of men. Not all, and not even most, but enough to make one pause, out there in Keokuk or Duluth. They may never drape you in ermine, if you marry the hardware clerk and you take on the title of Mrs. Housewife, and not Miss Keokuk, but they are not too likely to drive you into hospitals, your wrist slit (again), your mind muddled by booze or drugs.

So Mary became my wife, a full-time chore for any sane woman, and gave up her career. When she could, she traveled with me; when she couldn't, after the boys were born, she usually didn't, and I called her when I could, except now I wasn't her long-distance Romeo, I was her husband, and as likely as not, I'd say, "How is Barrie's cold?" But Barrie hadn't come along as yet, despite my father's fears.

Later that spring my agent called to say that Sam Harris wanted to see me.

I stuck my head in his door, and Sam said, "What did I pay you last time, kid?"

"Hundred and a quarter."

"Now you're making a hundred fifty. Rehearsals begin Monday."

He told me where, and he told me what play, but I didn't really care. I was back in the groove of working steadily, and I liked it. I was an actor, and it was, without a doubt, my profession, my livelihood, and if Sam Harris said, "Go over to the Lyceum," I went, the same way a plumber goes over to fix your sink. Later, my movie agent Mike Levee, who helped me break a contract with Warner Brothers, warned me, "Bill, when you're out of work, you're no better than the guy on Main Street. And you're worse, if he's working."

I understood then, and I'd understood for some time. Notices don't pay the rent. You can't eat credits. I went over to whatever theater it was, and I met Richard Bennett, one of the great actors of the day, the father of Constance and Joan Bennett, and as nutty as a fruitcake. He was a periodic drinker, except the periods were more like exclamation points. When he'd played the starring role of Tony, in the play *They Knew What They Wanted*, the part Charles Laughton later murdered in the movies, he'd disappear for a few days at a stretch. But beyond the drinking, Bennett had his oddities. Once they traced him to Philadelphia, where he was holed up in a hotel room, with nothing but twenty-nine pairs of shoes. Usually he had more than that. He used to travel with a pet alligator, which he kept in the bathtub. He also had a couple of tiny and very rare Japanese goldfish, no bigger than an eyelash, for which he'd paid $1500. What upset Bennett was spending a whole $2 a year on fishfood.

But he could act.

The play was *The People*, and the opening scene is laid in a graveyard in France, in what is called the Macbeth Trap, the hole in the floor of the stage out of which the witches in *Macbeth* would traditionally arise, and which comes in handy when you need action below the level of the stage floor. Three guys stood in an open grave, digging away, a Negro, a Jew, and an Irishman, with Bennett, the sergeant, in charge of the grave-digging detail, upon the stage, giving us orders. I played the Irishman, naturally, and as the play opens, I climb out and engage Bennett in conversation. Bennett was a tiny man, maybe five-three or four, and I felt foolish, looming over him. You don't

1. My mother.

2. My brother, Ed.

3. My mother in the background looks at her two sons, my brother Edward and me. The two girls are cousins.

4. My Mom and Pop at Riis Park in 1933.

5. Mom and Pop, and, on Pop's left, Agnes Wilson, my mother's sister.

6. Mom and Pop, and on Pop's right, my Aunt Bina, and, on Mom's left, my Aunt Grace. Both of these aunts are my mother's sisters.

7. Three generations of Gargans: My father, my older son, Barrie, and myself.

8. Mother, my younger son, Leslie, and I standing in front of Marion Davies' house, which we had rented when we first went to Beverly Hills.

9. Barrie and Leslie in front of the Davies house. We lived here several years.

10. My dear friend Leslie Howard with my son Leslie, whom we had named after the great English actor.

11. My wife, Mary, and Mother in Hollywood in 1932.

12. The living room of Gertrude Astor's house, which we rented early in my stay in Hollywood. Mary and I are enjoying its living room with Barrie. (*RKO Pictures, Inc.*)

13. This is a classic which shows a group of Russell Markert's Markettes, the predecessors of the Rockettes, who used to dance at the old Paramount Theatre in New York. The third girl from the left is Mary. Russell Markert achieved world-wide fame as director of the Radio City Music Hall Rockettes.

14. Mary on her Pinto pony, Scotch, in 1935.

15. Mary and I whoop it up at the circus party at the Racquet Club in Palm Springs in 1938.

16. My two boys, Leslie (l.) and Barrie, in the uniform of St. John's Military Academy, which they were attending at that time.

17. Bing Crosby and I on a fishing trip.

19. A scene from *Miss Annie Rooney* with Shirley Temple and Guy Kibbee. (*Courtesy of United Artists Corp.*)

18. A photograph taken during my early years in Hollywood.

Some roles that I have played.

20. A shot from *Four Frightened People* with Claudette Colbert, Herbert Marshall, Mary Boland, and myself. (*EMKA, A division of Universal City Studios, Inc.*)

21. Ann Sothern plays Ethel Turp, I am Joe Turp, and Walter Brennan is the postman in this scene from the comedy, *A Call on the President*, which was based on Damon Runyon's famous characters, Joe and Ethel Turp. (© 1939 Loew's Inc. © Renewed 1966 Metro-Goldwyn-Mayer Inc.)

23. In 1932 I played with Joan Crawford in *Rain*, which was shot on location on Catalina Island. *(Courtesy of United Artists Corp.)*

22. Here I am as Mike Hanrahan in *Waterfront at Midnight. (LIN Medallion Picture Corp.)*

24. Carole Lombard and I in a scene from *They Knew What They Wanted*. Charles Laughton, Frank Fay, and Harry Carey all were in this movie version of the Pulitzer Prize-winning play. *(Produced by RKO Radio Pictures Inc.)*

25. Here is a scene with Josephine Hutchinson from *Miracle in the Rain*, which also starred Jane Wyman and Van Johnson. *(Copyright © 1955 by Warner Bros. All Rights Reserved.)*

26. Here is a scene from the screen production of *The Animal Kingdom*. The ladies are (l. to r.) Leni Stengel, Ilka Chase, and Myrna Loy. I am serving as Leslie Howard (r.) and Neil Hamilton look on. My role as Richard Regan won me the Drama Critics' Award for the play and a nomination for an Academy Award for the picture. *(Produced by RKO Radio Pictures Inc.)*

My finest and most popular roles.

27. The first nation-wide network private eye show was *Martin Kane, Private Eye.* It was probably the most popular character I ever played. *(NBC Photo)*

do that to sergeants, and you don't do that to stars. Or so I thought.

The second day of rehearsal I said, "Mr. Bennett, I'm a pretty big guy. Maybe when we're talking, I should stay down in the hole."

Bennett looked me over coldly. "My boy," he said, "when Richard Bennett is on stage, nobody else is on stage."

Well, I thought, it's your funeral. So we played it that way, and Bennett was absolutely right. Somehow he swelled twice his size, and he diminished me to half mine, and you knew who the sergeant was and who the flunky.

Actually, it was a terrible play, and Bennett didn't make it easier by insisting on rewriting it all during the time we were on the road, trying it out. We'd ride from South Bend to Milwaukee, and Bennett would sit up all night on the train, sending his valet and dresser, with handfuls of new pages for me to read. Then by the time the train reached Milwaukee, Bennett would say, "Forget it. Here's a new batch."

Nor did it help Bennett much. One night we started playing, and he blew his lines. I threw him his cue, but he wasn't taking a cue from me. He fell back on the self-esteem that let him think he was the biggest man on any stage, and he began to ad-lib.

"You got a cigarette?" he asked me.

"Yes," I said.

"What kind?"

"Camels."

"Well, I'm not crazy about them, but toss me one."

So I tossed him a cigarette, and a cue or two, but he wouldn't pick it up. Finally, Al Lewis, the co-producer, walked on stage in a dinner jacket, and he said, "Mr. Bennett, your line is—" and he read him his line. Bennett said, "Thank you," (he knew where the money was), and resumed the play.

Even in the sticks, audiences resent a man who does not do his homework, and Bennett sometimes received a cold reception when it came time for his curtain call. This did not make him any more lovable. He would hold up his hand.

"Bring me a chair," he would say. "Keep the curtain up." He would sit and tell the audience what he thought of it. "You're a bunch of fools," he would say. "You don't know good theater when you see it. You've been sitting on your hands all night. You didn't laugh when you should have laughed. You're disgraceful." And he'd go on for ten minutes like that. Years before, when he'd done *They Knew What They Wanted*, the producers fretted about Bennett, and warned him not to engage the audience in any post-curtain tirades. But they neglected to put it in the contract, so Bennett ignored the warning when he felt miffed. He felt miffed often, apparently. Still, he was a great actor. Though not great enough that *The People* could make it. It folded, on the road.

Mike Connolly lined up more work. Not a lucrative job, but work. I took it, second lead with a stock company in Cleveland, doing a couple of plays produced by Pat McCoy, a very successful stock producer in the Midwest. We went on in the Playhouse, opposite the old Hollanden Hotel in Cleveland, and the first show was a melodrama starring Clark Silvernail. You think I've invented these names, but I haven't; look them up. Silvernail had a magnificent deep voice, and was a hell of an actor. He played the safecracker in our melodrama, and I was his assistant, and after a week, we'd flopped so badly we decided to drop that play and try a comedy, *Not Herbert*. But *Not Herbert* didn't do a bit better, and we got ready to call it quits. The company had run out of money, and I had the stubborn notion that *Not Herbert* would be a smash elsewhere. So I phoned Mother and asked her to lend me $1500. She wired the money, and I moved the company to Chicago. I stayed at the Bismarck Hotel, and we picked up a few actors. Once again we did the melodrama first. One of the guys we hired was a florist when he wasn't acting, a man named Opal Schultz. Schultz had one line. He played a cop and he came in when I was jimmying the safe, and he said, "Stick 'em up!"

Except he had a lisp, and every night he lisped, "Stick 'em up!" I would fall over laughing, and so would the audience at the theater on Van Buren, right where the elevator goes around on the city's South Side. It wasn't enough, however, to draw 600 flies, much less 600 people, which was capacity. We got fair notices, but the theater was so far from the beaten track, nobody came. At the end of the first week, my $1500 disappearing, I asked the actors to take half salary. They did, after some grumbling, and we went into the second week, with *Not Herbert*, my ace in the hole, but still nobody came. After a Saturday matinee, I went back to the Bismarck, but they'd put a plug in my door.

"What's wrong?" I asked the manager.

"A little matter of your bill," he said. "You're two weeks behind," which was perfect, because I'd been there only two weeks.

"I'll straighten it out," I said. "We'll have a good house tonight."

"I'm sure you will," the manager said. "But you don't get in your room until you give me some money."

I gave him twenty-five dollars, every cent I had, and he let me go upstairs. I grabbed the clothes out of my trunk, put on two or three each of shirts, socks and suits, and left the near-empty trunk. I went out the back elevator, and to the theater where we had a fair Saturday night (it didn't rain), and when it was over, I said to Kathleen Mulqueen, a very fine stock actress in our company, "Now where do I stay?"

"I've been staying at Mrs. Quirk's boardinghouse," she said. "I can probably get you in."

Mrs. Quirk's, on the north side of town, was one of Chicago's two famous boardinghouses for actors. It was at Mrs. Quirk's in 1919 that Equity was founded, at a meeting headed up by Grant Stewart and other actors of the time. Mrs. Woodruff's house on the south side was the other lodging used by actors. Legitimate actors, if that is what you could call us, used Mrs. Quirk's; vaudeville people, musical comedy people, and some legitimates stayed at Mrs. Woodruff's. Elliott Nugent and his wife Norma Lee used to stay at Woodruff's.

So I moved to Mrs. Quirk's, while hoping to recoup a piece of the debacle. The boardinghouse kept my personal expenses down to nothing. You paid $18 a week, all in. All three meals. A breakfast until noon, a supper at 6 P.M., and a midnight snack laid out on the huge dining-room table around which fourteen could sit. A hatrack stood near the door, and inside its base tiny bottles of homebrew squatted in ice. You bought them for 25¢ a bottle, and signed a book. You settled at the end of the week.

Though the place was nominally run by Mrs. Quirk, the real manager was the cook, Percy, a 300-pound Negro woman who walked on pigeon toes with a sailor's gait. Percy ran the place. What a cook, and what a woman! Later, when I was in Chicago on tour with *The War Song*, Mary came with me, and we stayed at the Hotel Davis. Mary was pregnant, and in the middle of a freezing winter's night, Mary woke and decided, as pregnant women will, that what she really wanted was a dish of fresh strawberries.

"I will give anything in the world," she said, "for some strawberries."

"Forget it," I said, half asleep.

"I can't," she said, sitting up in bed. "I have a craving."

"So crave. It's winter, in Chicago."

"I know," she said, "but if you loved me—"

I got up. I looked at my watch. Two A.M. I put on my clothes. I walked two blocks to Percy's door. I knocked.

Pretty soon I heard her. "Who is it?" she asked.

I told her. "I'm sorry to wake you," I said. "My wife is pregnant, and she'd like some fresh strawberries. You wouldn't happen to know where I could get some?"

The door opened, and her big moon face beamed out. "You wait there, honey child," she said, "I just happen to have some." She went back and came to the door again, with a small box of beautiful round luscious fresh strawberries. I thanked her, and walked back, and Mary ate them all, every single one.

"I knew you loved me," she said, luxuriating, and promptly fell asleep.

I caught a cold.

We got used to staying at Mrs. Quirk's, or, later when Mrs. Quirk died, Percy's. This time, with my two stock turkeys, I didn't stay long. Chicago did not respond to my first venture into production, with Mother's money, and finally Kathleen Mulqueen, who knew everybody, borrowed money from a friend, Jack Donahue, a fine dancer and musical actor, appearing in Chicago in *Sunny* with Marilyn Miller at the time. We all went home on the Erie Railroad, sitting up the entire thirty-three hours to New York.

Yes, the era had crested. Perhaps those were the first hints, in Cleveland and in Chicago, where people did not exactly flock to our modest stock offerings. But you still couldn't prove it. In the summer of 1928, Sam Harris called me in again. This time it was to play in *The War Song*, a comedy-drama starring George Jessel playing a Jewish conscript in the World War, wondering why he has been called into a war he feels nothing for. We opened in September, at the National Theatre, at 41st and Seventh Avenue, with a corking cast. Clara Langsner played Jessel's mother; Raymond Guion, (before he'd changed his name to Gene Raymond), was also in it, and I had a reasonably good role as one of the privates. It was an odd play, with half of the last act done in German. Jessel is taken prisoner by the Germans, and he goes off muttering, crying, mumbling. One German says to the other (in German), "What is he doing?"

And the other says, "He is praying."

We went on the road, and I struck up with Ray Guion one of the deepest friendships of my life. Ray's mother was a real stage mother, a woman who made up her mind that her son would make it big in the entertainment world. She sent him to fencing school; she had him learn French, play the piano, attend concerts, visit art galleries, and become a well-rounded person who could slip into any sort of role asked of him. Unlike many stars pushed by a parent, Ray managed to remain singularly unneurotic, a man's man who just as quickly gave up the evening concert when a poker game needed a fifth hand. Besides his other activities, Gene, today, is a general in the Air Force Reserve.

My friendship with George Jessel also began with *The War Song*, and George and I have known many moments together since. I recall walking crosstown in New York with George one day late in October of 1929, when the newsboys began screaming their Wuxtry. George did a quick little step into a nearby brokerage house door. He came out, face ashen.

"I'm wiped out," he said quietly.

The Stock Market had crashed.

Then a good-looking girl passed by, and George was fine again, a resilient soul and the great romantic of our times. George is the godfather of my first son, Barrie.

Mary spent some weeks with me in Chicago, in 1928, eating her strawberries, and blooming as women do when with child. She returned home near the end of her ninth month, and the show went to Boston. I kept in close touch by phone, and then the ninth month ended, and like many mothers of their first child, Mary waddled serenely into her tenth month, and then some. Naturally I took it all in stride, which is to say I panicked. The brief run in Boston ended, and I came home on a Saturday morning. Mary, meanwhile, had checked into a hotel near Parkwest Hospital.

That Saturday night Mary began to have labor pains, but after a few tremors, they ceased. We slept late Sunday, and after Mass Mary's odd appetite took over.

"What I'd like," she said, "is an old-fashioned."

"You are out of your mind!" I said. "Let's have some food."

"All right," she said. "Then, after lunch, I will have an old-fashioned."

We went downstairs to a drugstore, and had toast, eggs, and coffee, and Mary said, "It's two o'clock. The bar is open. Let's go."

You must understand that Mary never drank old-fashioneds. It never has been her drink. But this was like fresh strawberries in the middle of the night, in winter, in Chicago.

She had an old-fashioned at the hotel bar, and she beamed. "Delicious," she said. "I'll have another."

Our memories diverge at this point. Mary insists she had eleven old-fashioneds. I recall seeing three old-fashioneds disappear into her, perhaps one or two more. Not eleven. But many more than she had ever had in her life. One reason our memories differ is that after the second or third, I called her doctor.

"Are they affecting her?" he asked.

"Not the slightest."

"Don't worry then." But he was worried about the length of her confinement. "When she's finished, take her for a ride in a cab up and down Riverside Drive. Those cobblestones might do it. And give her a belt of castor oil."

So I may have missed a few drinks, on the phone. I got Mary away from the bar, poured some castor oil into her, and hailed a cab. We went up and down Riverside Drive, very fast, and Mary said, "Whee! This is fun!"

Then we went back to the hotel, whereupon Mary steered us both to the bar, and she had an old-fashioned. Then she had another, and she turned to me and said, "We'd better get to the hospital, real fast."

Bill—whom we call Barrie because Mary was having a thing about Sir James Barrie, the romantic playwright—came along on Monday, February 25, 1929, a not difficult delivery. But the next morning Mary began to complain of pains in her breasts. She developed milk breast, an excruciating condition that doesn't seem to hit mothers any more, but then was a living hell. Doctors strapped her breasts and fed her grapefruit to dry up the milk, and I sat up with her one night, holding her hand and trying futilely to help her through the pain.

I had earned $250 a week, with *War Song*, and we'd saved a few dollars by the time Barrie was born. It swiftly went down the drain in three weeks, the hospital, the delivery, the nurses around the clock and the medicine. Mary began to recover from her ordeal, and the boy was a strapping lad, but the depression that soon would catch up with the rest of the country, and most of the world, had apparently decided to begin with me. Depressions have a way of beginning in those businesses where the product is not essential for survival. Man *can* live by bread alone. Maybe not well or richly or in any sense, fully, but he can get by. He does not need, for survival, books or magazines or movies or plays. He can do without toys or games. He must have food, shelter, and clothing—the essentials. I am no shrinking violet, but I also know enough to realize the world will little note, nor long remember, my saying, "Mr. Bob. Heap big coconuts!"

So when a depression is about ready to burst fullbloom, it has a tryout on the road. Book sales slump, toys remain on counters, people stop buying trinkets. And nobody goes to the theater. Nobody.

I was out of work nine months. I did pick up some very small jobs. Jessel, who would say the Crash wiped him out, did his best to wipe himself out. He had made a silent film, *The Ghetto*, but his timing was lousy. It came out just as the talkies came in, so Jessel decided in 1929 to remake it into a sound film. He had the story worked over, and he then shot it in a hole-in-the-wall studio at 34th Street and Fifth Avenue. I had a small part, receiving a stage salary, which is not quite a movie salary. The decimal point is in a different spot. Jessel sank $300,000 into the combined versions which he now called *My Mother's Eyes*. In it, George sang (as usual, offkey): "One bright and shining light/ That taught me wrong from right/I found in My Mother's Eyes." The rest of the film wasn't any better, so George was out close to $300,000, and I was again out of work.

As a matter of fact, I picked up other movie parts, beginning around then. Paramount had started to make sound movies out at Astoria, Long Island, and I'd do a day's work here and a day's work there. But that was all.

The weeks stretched into months. The months threatened to become a year. I badgered my agent, I badgered producers, fellow actors, friends, enemies, anybody who might know somebody who was producing a play, and might have a part for me.

I did something else, to break the dispiriting period. Mary and I had moved up to Eastchester, to live with her folks, and help prove Nana was right—I was an actor bum, or a bum actor, or both. Surely I wasn't taking care of her daughter in the manner to which a securities lawyer would have.

And from Eastchester, in the northeast corner of the Bronx, Mary and I used to travel by subway to church in the Bedford area of Brooklyn, where we made a Novena to St. Therese. To make a proper Novena, as this beat-up Catholic understands it, a petitioner must go nine consecutive weeks, not missing a week. Miss one week, and you've blown the Novena.

Mary and I went on Monday nights, an hour and a half on the subway each way, and in the dimness of the church, I kneeled and I prayed for work. That was my petition, to St. Therese, who, I hoped, would carry it straight to the Boss. The weeks crawled by, and I kept kneeling and praying. "I want a job," I prayed. "I don't care what it is. I've got to walk on the stage. Please."

Mondays, for some reason, turned out to be the most difficult night in the week. We'd chosen it because it seemed so inoffensive. The weekend is gone, the new week begins, you have all those days ahead when a producer might call you or your agent or you'd find a million dollars in an abandoned paper bag. Then Mondays turned treacherous. It rained or it snowed, or Mary's folks would have to be out, and we had nobody to leave the baby with. You know. Everything that can happen happened. If I had found the million dollars in the abandoned paper bag, I'd have gotten a hernia from carrying it to the bank, and the bills would turn out counterfeit.

So we prayed. I prayed for a job on the stage, and Mary, to cover the exits, had a slightly different prayer. "Let Bill go to Hollywood," she prayed. Why not? If you can't have a piece of the earth, shoot for the moon. Even then, as 1929 began to run out of sight, and the crash had people jumping from building windows, the motion picture began to promise a bright future for actors. Especially stage actors. The stars of the silent screen, some of them, were washed up, with sound. Matinee idol John Gilbert was through; his voice was too high-pitched. But stage actors who had bellowed their way from barn to hall to balcony had to speak well. Or at least loudly.

I prayed for the stage, a legitimate play, a legitimate part, and Mary prayed for the films. We got neither.

The ninth Monday came and went, and I blessed St. Therese for listening so patiently. Mary and I went home on the subway, together. We had sealed our love with a subway platform chain;

now we tested it those Mondays on the depressing ride through three boroughs and back again.

The next day I left the house, with my usual 12¢ in my pocket. Five cents for the subway downtown (where I would pick up a morning paper left by some other subway rider), five cents for the subway back uptown, and two cents for the evening paper. I ate breakfast at home; I ate supper at home. I had no lunch.

I was pounding the streets of Broadway, that day after the Novena had ended, when I ran into an actor friend, Charlie Wilson. Charlie had also been in *The War Song*.

"Charlie," I said, "do you know anybody who's hiring? I've just got to get a job."

"Yes," he said. "I am. You're hired."

He was directing a vaudeville revue for Max Gordon, a fifteen-minute sketch called *The Family Upstairs*, written by Harry Dell. I had prayed for the stage, and Mary for the movies, and in the early days of the depression, as vaudeville began its death throes, that is where I got a job. You never can tell.

"I'll give you the juvenile role," Charlie said. "You're the young fellow who's going to meet the mother and father of the girl you're in love with."

Max Gordon agreed to pay me $85 a week, for three shows a day back in the Prospect Theatre, where I used to watch vaudeville instead of selling Wesson Oil.

I don't remember much about *The Family Upstairs*. I do know Mary and Barrie and I moved back to Garfield Place—again—because I would be playing in Brooklyn, nine blocks away.

Nine blocks. Nine weeks. Nine for Novena. The magic had worked. Nine is a magic number, three times three, and three is a magic number, too. The magic of prayer, of petitioning God's emissaries, and hearing them answer, here on earth. I was working again. No, the world will again little note what I did on stage at the Prospect, nor do I even remember. There was something about the family I visited trying to impress me. They served stuffed olives, and I said, "What's wrong with unstuffed olives?" and that always got a laugh. Don't ask me why. Maybe it was a touch of reality, in a pretentious world. The depression was marching on, and soon nobody would worry whether olives were stuffed or unstuffed.

The two P.M. show went well the first day, and I rushed back home—nine blocks away—before the second show, and while I was there, the phone rang. It was a director I knew.

"Bill," he said, "I'm having a hell of a job filling a role, and I think you're the guy to do it. Can you get over here right away?" Here was the Longacre Theater on 48th Street, where they were rehearsing. The show was *Headquarters*, and the star the legendary Bill Farnum.

"I can't," I said. "I'm in a vaudeville show—"

"Can't you get out of it? We really need you. They tell me you won't do anything for less than $350 a week—"

Here I was, in a vaudeville skit, at $85 a week.

"—but we can only pay you $275—"

I damn near fainted.

"—but if the show makes it, I can promise you $350 after the first two weeks. And it will make it."

"What's the catch?" I asked. There had to be a catch, other than that I had a job and probably couldn't get out of it.

"We're opening in three days," he said. "In Atlantic City."

"I'll call back," I said. "I can't just walk out on these guys."

I rushed over to the Prospect, and I caught Charlie Wilson. I told him what had happened.

"Good for you," Wilson said. "We'll find somebody. Just stick with us until you have to leave. Give us the three days."

I found Max Gordon and I asked permission to leave the show. I told him why, and he said, "I wish you the best. You'd be a fool not to take the job. We'll get by."

So I would rehearse at the Longacre and then rush back to Brooklyn by subway. I'd play a show and grab the subway back for another rehearsal, and then back for the second show, three times like that, every day for three days. Thank God for the subway! Meanwhile they found somebody to fill my role. I wasn't the only hungry actor in town.

So I plunged into *Headquarters*, and I met a burly open-faced young guy appearing on the New York stage for the first time, Bill Bendix. I played a detective; he was my dumb assistant. We opened to excellent notices, but the director was wrong. Nobody came.

I made my $275 a week, for two weeks, and the show closed.

But now the casting director at Paramount called me, and I began to make more appearances in movies. The work then was more like dramatic television today. You'd work a day or two, or, if you were lucky, a whole week. I began to earn $150 to $200 a week, when I worked, and my friend at Paramount kept me busy. Herbert Hoover kept saying that prosperity was just around the corner, and soon there'd be two chickens in every pot, but very soon the soup lines would be stretching far longer than the lines in front of box offices. Still, I was working, and as 1929 slid by I got a call from my agent, Jenny Jacobs, to go down to the smoking room of the Plymouth Theatre.

"Ask for Leslie Howard," Jenny said. "He's expecting you. He's directing a play, *Out of a Blue Sky*."

I'd heard of Howard, of course. He'd taken Broadway by storm, starring in *Berkeley Square* and *Outward Bound*.

As I clumped down the stairs to the smoking room, another actor was coming up. He was a big guy I'd seen around town and got to know pretty well, a good-looking guy except for his ears. They stuck out like cup handles.

"They don't like me, Bill," Clark Gable said. "It's all yours."

"That's tough," I said softly. I hated to beat actors out of work. I knew what it meant. I went inside, and they hired me, and Clark Gable went out to Hollywood, starred in the West Coast company of *The Last Mile*, and very soon was a big movie star.

Which is how I met Leslie Howard, and my whole life changed. I became not just a hack actor speaking my lines and walking two steps, but a star.

A straight line could be drawn from the Novena to Leslie Howard. You either believe or you don't. I do. I believe the subway pilgrimage to Brooklyn had been purposeful. I believe the lovely Therese had heard my prayer. I believe God had answered my petition. I believe he answers every petition. Later, when I lay in the hospital and wept silently, begging God to hear my petition, I realize now He heard and He answered. He always answers.

Only sometimes He says, "No."

12

Where's Red?

This time God had said Yes.

I don't know why Leslie Howard and I hit it off so well, except that the law of opposites must have been operating. I was big and gruff, a commoner. He was small-boned and fragile, a noble. I was loud and forward; he quiet, reticent. His nose was always buried in a book, mine in the racing form. I was a quick man with a dollar; he was—for want of a kinder word—frugal. One day while rehearsing *Out of a Blue Sky*, I borrowed $3 from Leslie; I'd run out of cash, which is a chronic runout of mine. And I promptly forgot all about it. I didn't have to remember. He reminded me, every other day. So perversely, I decided not to pay him. (I made it up by buying him gifts, picking up the tab when we ate or drank, buying his cigarettes and whatever.) In nearly every way, we were opposites. A great friendship developed.

Perhaps each supplied each what the other lacked—I was the extrovert he may have wanted to be. He surely appeared to be the artist I envied. I had never learned to act, the way a student learns. He had studied it, mastered it, and now as a director, could teach it. Not that he spent much time on any of this; we had one thing in common. Acting, after the initial spell, bored us. We both delighted in the fringe benefits—I in the camaraderie, the cast parties, the money that could buy my happiness. He was, for all the books and learning, a bit of a playboy. Not that he pursued women. They pursued him, and somehow he did not run very fast. There was nothing stuffy about him, nothing pretentious. He was a fun-loving man, as I was, and this bound us. But the attraction that drew us together must have been born in the unconscious. He was that hidden part of me I never could be, and I the secret part of him he could never be. We became nearly inseparable.

Not all at once, of course. Just before I walked into the smoking room, Leslie and his stage manager George Fogel, who was with him in *Outward Bound* and *Berkeley Square*, had squirmed uneasily as Clark Gable read his lines.

Fogel groaned (so I since learned) and Leslie murmured, "I know, I know."

"He won't do," Fogel said. "His ears are too big, his collar doesn't sit properly. He's got no charm."

And Leslie Howard, of impeccable taste, said, "I know. He's impossible."

I walked in, and they—Leslie and Fogel—found me more charming than Clark Gable. Can you imagine? So it had to be something hidden. We clicked.

Out of a Blue Sky was a German play, by Hans Chlomberg, adapted by Leslie. He had collected an impressive cast for his first directorial effort on Broadway—Gregory Ratoff, Warren William, Reginald Owen, Eleanor Terry, Tammany Young, Katherine Wilson. The play itself was an oddity, a precursor of the theater of the absurd, not unlike that other play ahead of its time, Pirandello's *Six Characters in Search of an Author*, except *Six Characters* made it, and *Out of a Blue Sky* failed dismally.

I played a German playreader. What is a German playreader? I don't know. Under the arc lights of an otherwise bare stage, a couple of stagehands are playing poker, while the audience enters the theater. At 8:30, Gregory Ratoff begins to scream at the two stagehands. "Where are the sets? Where are the actors? We're doing *Camille*, and nothing is ready."

One stagehand says, "You're out of your mind. We're not doing *Camille*."

So Ratoff gets the poster, and sure enough, we're supposed to be doing *Camille*.

Ratoff walks into the audience. "Be patient," he says. "Be calm." He, himself, is screaming, the agitated Russian.

I walk on, the German playreader. I introduce myself to Ratoff. I tell him how we can fill the time; I will walk through the theater and the people in the seats will have tales to tell. You build the set, get the stagehands working.

I walk into the audience, and begin to speak to people who get up and tell their stories, who they are, what they do, their wishes and dreams. Soon it turns out the people who speak are related to each other, their stories entwine. And so the drama builds. Our actors are the spectators; all the world is a stage.

That was the play. Its murky message eluded me. My part eluded me. I said earlier I seldom questioned the motivation of a part. I assume the playwright knew what he was doing. Here, I could not assume. A young man from Brooklyn was playing a German playreader, with no German accent. Reginald Owen and I dressed together on opening night, and an hour before the show I confessed my ignorance to Reggie.

"My boy," he said, "I'm in the same position. Why don't you affect my part and I affect yours?"

So in the dressing room he read my lines and I read his, and somehow his reading made my role more intelligible, and mine his. Not totally intelligible. Just more.

The critics were confused. The audiences were confused. People stayed away.

One of the producers was a man named Sal Gretsky, a clothier. After the first week, he came into my dressing room before the Saturday matinee, wearing a huge raccoon coat.

"That's a beautiful coat, Sal," I said.

"Here," he said, unpeeling it. "It's yours, in lieu of two weeks' salary."

"Not on your life. I can't boil it."

The play lasted two weeks at the Booth; Reginald Owen got great reviews; the rest of the play was dismissed. But I was $500 richer. Almost immediately I was signed to play in a

Theatre Guild production, *Roar China!* dealing with the exploitation of China by the West, and directed by Herbert Biberman. Biberman was a nice guy, one of the new wonder boys of the time, and a Method director. You know the Method. The stage directions say: Walk across the room and open a window. Halfway there, you stop, and the puzzled director says, "What's wrong?" "I don't know," the Method actor answers. "I just don't *feel* it." Everything has to be motivated.

I played the gruff American in a China port, knocked overboard and killed after a fight in a sampan. I had to fall in water eighteen inches deep, and then swim underwater until I wound up offstage. I nearly drowned every rehearsal. Especially because Biberman didn't like the way I hit the water. It wasn't realistic enough. He kept harping on it until one day, frustrated by my unmotivated swandive, he said, "I'll show you."

He got into a bathing suit, climbed into the sampan, engaged in the mock fight, and dove off. Except he forgot to take off his glasses. He came up, covered with tar, his shattered glasses dangling from an ear.

"Well," he said, "that's the general idea."

He stopped criticizing my dive after that.

If the acting wasn't so honestly motivated, the set was real enough. The prow of a battleship projected into the audience, which wowed the public. We had a fair hit on our hands.

So life was good to me, those days, for all the harping directors, murky parts, and drownings. I was working and taking it seriously. We all took acting seriously in those days. Especially the young actors. I remember a young fellow, a member of the Group Theatre, who used to stand in the wings and watch us work. I'd brush by on my way to and from the stage, and I'd say brusquely, "Out of my way, son." Later he got a job in *Green Grow the Lilacs*, which later was set to music and became the modern-day wonder, *Oklahoma!* The young actor was Franchot Tone, and he and I became good friends.

So I was busy, brusquely busy, feeling very alive because I was working. Mary and I were thriving, and so was the boy, healthy, handsome, bright. But we still lived in Garfield Place, with my folks, and Mary was not liking it a bit.

"We've got to find a place of our own," she'd say, at night, in our bedroom, the baby's crib between our twin beds. The bedroom was too tiny for the two of us, much less three. Mother and Dad needed the living room; we all shared the kitchen. I felt it was cozy. Mary insisted it was crowded. It was a Mexican stand-off.

"Come on, honey," she'd say. "Let's look, this weekend."

"All right," I'd say, but when the weekend came along, there'd be an extra rehearsal.

"We've got to find a place," she kept saying, at night, and I'd say, "What's wrong with this place?" and she'd say, "It's too small. We need a place of our own."

"It's not too small. We have a place. This room."

"Oh, Bill," she'd snap, "that's nonsense and you know it. We're cramped. I'm cramped. We've got to move."

"Shh," I'd say. "Speak more quietly. You'll wake the folks."

"That does it. I don't want to wake the folks. I want my own place, where we don't have to whisper."

I must have been afraid to make a move. This brownstone, with my parents, served as a home base. And I kept wondering how long could my luck last? If we had a place of our own, with rent of our own, furniture of our own to buy, what would happen if I had another nine months of no work?

Mary came back one day after walking Bill, Jr.—Barrie—and her face was shining.

"I found a place!" she said. "It's a darling apartment, lots of light, close to the subway, not far from here."

I went with her to see it.

It was on Union Street, in Brooklyn, close to the Grand Army Plaza, with all the old statues of war heroes.

It was a one bedroom place, down from the street level, like the superintendent's apartment you find in the basement. It had lots of light, if you stood on tiptoe and looked out the window. That way you could see a piece of the sky. The rent was $75 a month. We took it.

Dark, small, crowded, the crib in the same room once again, and we whispered so as not to wake Barrie. But Mary was right. It was our place. Reluctantly, I loved it. My folks didn't seem to mind our leaving. They had probably just as quietly and as often whispered in their bedroom—when are they going? Communal living is not for most of us. On Union Street, my mother would baby-sit for us, or even Nana Kenny, coming down from Eastchester, and Mary and I would eat out at one of those inexpensive French restaurants you used to find around Broadway, $1.25 for a table d'hote dinner, always with a pint of wine. You couldn't eat it all in one sitting, which made it perfect for me. I'd get halfway through by 7:45 or so, and then walk up the street to the Martin Beck Theatre on West 45th Street, change into my white suit, get knocked off the sampan, drown and swim off. I'd quickly change clothes, and go down and finish my dinner; Mary would be waiting for me, toying with her wineglass. Then I'd rush back for my curtain call.

Life was beautiful, life was kind. We'd begun to socialize with Leslie and Ruth Howard. We'd eat together, laugh together. He'd somehow manage to fumble the check, and I'd pick it up, and call him a tightwad. Just as he and I hit it off, so did Mary and Ruth Howard.

The two girls needed each other, but for reasons different from whatever underlay the affinity between Leslie and me. What they were, these women, were silent sufferers, or not so silent. Leslie never intended to hurt Ruth, but his little peccadilloes, always obvious to everyone, had to offend her. And I, with my immature ways, my reluctance to assume the more sober role of husband, provider, father, and counselor, must have worried Mary at times, though, thank God, she never let on. She let me grow at my own rate, occasionally giving me a sedate little boot in the behind to speed me up.

So life rolled on, the parts rolled in, we prospered, the four of us, and our children.

After *Roar China!*, I landed a part in a short-lived comedy, *She Lived Next to the Firehouse*, with Victor Moore, William Frawley, and Ara Gerald, playing a small-town siren. It was short-lived at the Longacre Theatre on Broadway, that is. A producer decided to chance it in Brooklyn, after we folded, but only if we'd all agree to half salary. Half my usual salary wasn't very much, but you could eat with it, so I said, "Fine," and the producer used me as a lever to get Victor Moore and the others. Moore didn't like it. He was going to be out from $1500 to $750 a week, which was bad enough, but mainly he'd made arrangements to go to Florida, where he'd lie in the sun and enjoy himself the rest of the winter.

We finally talked Victor into it, and we opened in Shubert's Flatbush Theatre, minus our elaborate set of Broadway. The producer, to save more money, had taken away our horses, which had been our saving grace, real-life horses snorting as they tore out of the firehouse on a treadmill. What was a firehouse without horses? Nothing. At least that's what Flatbushers thought, and we were as short-lived in Flatbush. As short-loved, too. Meanwhile, the producer had run out of folding money, though for some reason he had piles of coins. So he paid us all in paper bags, and you should have seen Victor Moore's face when he was handed a huge bagful of nickels, dimes, and quarters.

Then I did another play for the Theatre Guild, *He*, with Tom Powers, Claude Rains, and Violet Kemble-Cooper. Tom Powers played God, and I was a world champion prizefighter, Monsieur Ping. It was another murky play, ahead of its time, but I enjoyed it, and after we played the Guild Theatre in New York in the fall of 1931, we went to Chicago. Our stage manager was George Fogel, and while in Chicago, Fogel received in the mail the script of the next play Leslie Howard would appear in. Leslie wanted George to acquaint himself with it. Fogel would be stage manager once again. The play was *The Animal Kingdom*, by Philip Barry, and after Fogel read it, out in Chicago, he raved so that I finally asked him to let me have a look at it. He gave it to me.

I was staying at the McCormick Hotel, Percy's boardinghouse now out of business. I took the script to the hotel room, and I read it that night, and the more I read, the more excited I got. My eyes began to focus on a single part; the play itself was fine, but every time Red Regan came on, the wisecracking butler who once was a prizefighter, I felt my pulse quicken. Red Regan was me; I was Red Regan. Tough, gruff, wisecracking, common as salt. I began to read the play aloud, in my Chicago hotel room. When I closed the script that night, my palms were wet.

I returned it to George Fogel the next day, and I told how how much I liked it.

"Why don't you read for it when you get back to New York?" he said.

"I just might."

The run soon ended. We returned to New York, and I told Mary about the play.

"You've got one problem," Mary said.

"What problem?"

"Look in the mirror."

I looked. "You're right," I said. My hair had been a pretty good red all my youth, a bright carrot. But now, all of twenty-six years old, it had started to turn white. The red had faded to rust, and the white had begun to take over. Red Regan? The Old Gray Mare was more like it.

So I forgot about it that night. The next morning, a Sunday, as Mary started out of the house, a convertible careened around the corner and smacked right into a lamp post in front of her.

Mary is worldly wise. She eyed the car, she eyed the driver and she heard, in the distance, the wail of a siren.

"Do you have any liquor in the rumble seat?" Mary asked.

The man looked startled. "Why—yes, I do."

She jerked her head. "Get it out of there and into our apartment. That's a cop car."

So Mary, the guy, and I carried a couple of cases of illegal whiskey into our place, and the man went outside, just as the cops arrived. The rest was routine; the police were satisfied, and drove off to a nearby garage to summon a tow truck for the stoved-in car.

Meanwhile the man was terribly grateful. "Here's my card," he said. "If there's anything I can do to pay you back—"

Mary took a look at the card. "There's something you can do. You own a beauty shop. Can you dye my husband's hair red?"

The next morning, at ten A.M., I had my hair dyed for the first, but far from the last, time. I called the theater, where they were reading for *The Animal Kingdom*. I made a date, and with my newly flaming hair, I went over.

I went in and met the producer, Gilbert Miller, and Philip Barry. They seemed delighted to see me (and my hair).

I read.

I got a call a week later. It was Gilbert Miller.

"The best we can offer is $300 a week. Are you interested?"

I swallowed my heart and allowed I was interested.

"Do you know the star, Mr. Howard?" Miller asked.

"Quite well," I said.

"That makes it even better," Miller said. "Good luck."

Leslie was coming in by boat, from England.

I rushed down to the dock.

"Leslie!" I shouted, as he came down the gangplank. "I've got the part! I'm Red Regan!"

He smiled warmly. "You'll be great in it, Bill." Then his face hardened. "By the way, you still owe me three dollars."

We plunged into rehearsal. Reality does not live up to expectation. The play was good, but not great. Something was wrong. What was wrong was young Katharine Hepburn, not quite ready for so tremendous a role. She was obviously talented, she was grand to look at, she was bright—but she was inexperienced, and after six days of rehearsal, Frances Fuller replaced her as the bohemian girl friend, Daisy Sage. Phil Barry, who had been attracted to Hepburn—who wouldn't have been?—was just a mite early in hiring her. Later, of course, Kate skyrocketed to fame in *The Philadelphia Story*, another Barry play.

Still, I savored my part. We opened in Pittsburgh, before an audience of New Yorkers, brought in by Miller on a train, so we could get a more critical reaction.

The audience loved it; they cheered. I had just a few lines in the first act, the rough-hewn butler caught in the middle between

Tom Collier (Leslie Howard) and the society girl he later marries. Lora Baxter played the society girl. I remember one of my lines—I walk on stage and with a smirk I interrupt a wrangle. "Come on everyone! Dinner!" That's all. The audience howled. It happens once in a while, I guess, once in a lifetime with some. This was my first. The part was so well written, so perfectly written, I could do little wrong even if I had gone on cold. I hadn't gone on cold. I had prepared for it. Leslie had helped. So the part took hold. It had a coarseness natural to me, an exuberance, a boisterous quality. Red Regan served drinks to his master and his master's guests, and then Red Regan drank right along with them. Leslie and I had several scenes together, men of opposites—as in life—and very comfortable with each other, as in life.

At Pittsburgh, the audience roared, and we all took our calls. Finally Leslie Howard stood on the stage alone, to a great uproar. But from the back of the house, a man shouted down, "Where's Red?" And the din increased. "Where's Red?" they yelled. "We want Red!" I began to shiver.

Leslie turned and waved to me. We shook hands, and the audience kept applauding. The curtain fell, and this time Leslie disappeared, and when it went up again, there I stood, alone, shivering, the chill prickling my spine.

I went to the hotel. They could have murdered me in my sleep that night. I had had my acting thrill. Nothing had touched it before. Nothing would touch it again, though I would do more difficult parts and perhaps do one or two of them better. But this was the first massive adulation directed at me, and it is sweet. It is also frightening. You are swept up by it, made helpless by it. I heard the sweet thunder all night. Who needed sleep?

The next day, reality intruded. We would rehearse that morning. Opening nights in Pittsburgh, no matter how received, have to be rough. Phil Barry came over. "I'm sorry, Bill," he said. "I'm going to have to clip your part a little. It's too overpowering."

I nodded. He was right. It was overpowering. Barry knew my part best, because he wrote it, and he had written it perfectly.

But that wasn't my fault. Had the other roles been written as well, the butler would not overpower the master and his fiancée who becomes his wife. I was not Leslie Howard's equal on stage, and I knew it. So the problem wasn't mine. But what could I do? I felt bitter. Well, I thought, I had one night. Now when they yelled, Where's Red, I could tell them. He's been toned down a bit. His hair is really white. That's a dye job. Ask his hairdresser.

So I turned away from Barry, but a hand fell on my arm. It was Leslie. "Just a minute," he said. He confronted Barry. "Don't touch Bill's part, Phil. He's not what's wrong with your play." And on that rehearsal stage, Leslie Howard proceeded to go through the play, part by part, line by line, and show Phil Barry just where the flaws lay. "You began writing a man's play, but you ended it for a woman. Now let's rewrite the play away from Daisy Sage. If you take away anybody's lines, take away Daisy's. I want my part strengthened, to meet your original concept. But I don't want Bill's touched. And if you don't do it that way, I don't open in New York."

Barry nodded, and went to work. I lost one line—after consultation with me and Leslie—and we got ready to go to New York. But first Gilbert Miller's business manager approached me.

"You'll have to sign a new contract, Bill," he said. "A run-of-the-play contract."

I hate run-of-the-play contracts, binding you to play the part the whole season, beyond the limit of my enthusiasm.

"Not at the same money," I said.

So we bargained, and I signed for $450 a week, but I signed run-of-the-play. I had to. "Because," said Miller's man, "if you don't, we will replace you before we open in New York." And let's face it, even with the huzzahs, I wasn't going to deliver the same kind of ultimatum Leslie had given Barry. They'd just replace me. Butlers are a dime a dozen.

This is the ugly side of the business. Dear Gilbert Miller. I hate playing a role for a full season, as I had now agreed. It bores me. It turns my talent, however small to begin with, to stone. I go through the paces, a dead man. All I can ask for, when the pressure is put on, is money. It is the actor's only material return. You can't eat curtain calls, especially Pittsburgh ones.

We opened on January 12, 1932, at the Broadhurst, on 44th Street, just west of Broadway, a misty warming Tuesday night in the midst of the black maw of the depression. People flocked to the theater. That night. Every night. Two matinees. It was unbelievable. It was especially unbelievable when you look around you, and you see around the corner on 45th Street Paul Muni, in Elmer Rice's *Counselor-at-Law;* a block away, Noël Coward's *Hay Fever,* with Constance Collier; a few doors distant, *Of Thee I Sing,* with William Gaxton and Victor Moore; and at the New Amsterdam on 42nd Street, *The Band Wagon,* with Fred and Adele Astaire, plus Frank Morgan, Tilly Losch, and Helen Broderick. Katharine Cornell was starring in *The Barretts of Wimpole Street* at the Empire; Helen Hayes was doing Molnar's *The Good Fairy;* Ed Wynn led *The Laugh Parade.* You could have seen, instead of *The Animal Kingdom, Springtime for Henry, Cynara, Reunion in Vienna,* or that giant of the American theatre, O'Neill's *Mourning Becomes Electra,* with its 5:30 curtain, and an intermission (for a full hour) at 7:30, for supper.

But we were the true smash hit. Every night I stood there, at the curtain calls, no longer alone, but that was not because my part had been downgraded. Leslie's had been firmed, and Frances Fuller was marvelous as the bohemian girl, Lora Baxter was splendid as the fiancée-to-be-wife, and Ilka Chase was a perfect snob as the fiancée's sycophant. They roared for all of us, and you thought on some nights, "My God, they will tear the theater down. They will storm the stage, and eat us up." Frightening, and thrilling.

Still, my fame was not that of the matinee idol. That was Leslie's bit. Every day, women would infiltrate the security system and press into his dressing room. Girl reporters would come in to get a story, and come out woozy-eyed, their hair slightly mussed. I'd say to Leslie, when he and Ruth and Mary and I would sup together, "Any good interviews this week?" and he'd say nervously, "Shut up, you fool," his eyes straying to Ruth's, guiltily.

Nor was the play my whole life, even my whole acting life. I managed to sneak off and make a movie for Paramount, out at Astoria, *His Woman*, with a couple of not-bad youngsters, Claudette Colbert and Gary Cooper. Colbert and I worked well together; it was, again, the chemistry of opposites attracting. That one ended, Paramount called me to make another, with Claudette, *Misleading Lady*. They would shoot it at my convenience. So I squeezed that in, as the weeks of *Animal Kingdom* became months. On the *Misleading Lady* set, I came to know the director, Lewis Milestone.

"Could you," Milly asked one day, "do me a favor? I've got a young lady upstairs we're testing for a role in *Cynara?* That's the Ronald Colman movie. Would you play a scene with her, just two minutes or so?"

So I rushed upstairs, and played the part of an Englishman, to one of the most beautiful girls I had ever seen, Helen Twelvetrees. Then I rushed back down, to be the wisecracking reporter of *Misleading Lady*.

Milestone came over to thank me. He had with him a French director who visited the set. The director, Harry D'Arrest, and Milly invited me to dinner and drinks.

"Sorry," I said. "I have to rush home for the play."

"What play?" Milestone asked.

I grinned. "You Hollywood people don't know what's going on. I'm in *The Animal Kingdom*."

Milly's eyes widened. "We've been trying to get seats. Can you help us?"

So I phoned the box office and lined up a couple for that night, and then I rushed home, met Mary and the Howards at a restaurant, where Leslie and I gobbled down our dinner, and then grabbed a cab, or tried to grab one, and ended up running again down Sixth Avenue to the theater, our coattails flying, and Leslie giggling the whole way to the dressing room, girls tittering behind him, hands outstretched. Then we'd perform, hear the engulfing din at the curtain, and race back to a bar where Ruth and Mary had somehow solved the world's problems, or Motherhood's problems, and were on their third cup of coffee.

The next day at the Paramount set, Milestone said, "You're fantastic. You imitate an Englishman, you play a wisecracking reporter, now you are an ex-prizefighter-butler."

"What the hell," I said. "I'm an actor."

"You ever think of going to Hollywood?"

"If the price is right."

Milestone nodded and walked away.

A few days later, the phone in our apartment at Union Street rang.

It was a man from M-G-M. Would I consider appearing in a movie in Hollywood?

"What movie?"

"*Rain.*"

"How much?"

"Fifteen hundred a week."

The price was right.

I told the man I would call back the next day.

Now my run-of-the-play contract posed a problem. I would have to break it, to play in *Rain*. I went up to my old pal, Leslie Howard. "I've got to get my release," I told him. He sympathized. "I'll see what I can do, old man. I'm afraid it will cost you something—"

He went to Gilbert Miller, and then he came back with a long face. "They don't want you to leave."

"But I've got to! It's my one chance to really make money. I want to go to Hollywood!"

He shook his head, wrinkled his nose. "Hollywood," he murmured. "How awful!"

So I wrangled with Miller, and in the end I bought my way out of my contract for $1400. I played Red Regan for the last time on Monday night, May 2, 1932, and the next morning, Mary, Barrie, and I, and a governess we'd hired from the island of Jamaica, named Katherine, got on the train for Hollywood. A week after we arrived, I read that Leslie Howard, star and co-producer—co-producer!!!—of *The Animal Kingdom*, had obtained a leave to go to Hollywood—Hollywood!—to star in an M-G-M film, *Smilin' Through*, with Norma Shearer.

When I saw Leslie again, I roared up to him, "Co-producer! You cheap chiseling Englishman! You'd see what you could do! You're getting part of that $1400, aren't you? You owned a piece of *Animal Kingdom!*"

"Now, old boy," he said, "don't carry on so."

"I'll carry on," I said. I loved the guy! If I hadn't, I'd have slugged him. "I'll get this back from you if it takes ten years." I frothed, I foamed, I roared. He clucked and patted my back and called me old boy.

In Hollywood, I would say to him, when the waiter would bring the check, at the Brown Derby or the Cocoanut Grove, "That's a check, Leslie. A bill. It is what is owed. You invited me. I am your guest. You are a star. Pay it. And don't tip a measly dime. Pull out the green stuff. People are watching you. Nobody knows me. Pick up that check, you cheap chiseling Englishman, or your name will be in the gossip columns tomorrow." And I smiled lovingly.

It took me ten years, but I got it back. Every cent of the $1400.

13

We All Make These Schlemeil Pictures

Hollywood.

Stately palm trees. Blue haze over the hills. Velvety nights. The golden sands of Malibu.

???

They whisked me from the *Chief*, at the Santa Fe station in grubby downtown Los Angeles, through the hot concrete canyons of the city to a hotel, where I changed, and then was whisked across the street to the Brown Derby, to meet the press, and then to the studio, to meet Joan Crawford (eyes so big you could drown in them), and another whisk to Terminal Island, near Long Beach. I was taken by boat to Catalina Island, some twenty-five choppy miles out in the ocean.

I saw nothing of Hollywood except the interior of cabs. No palms, no sands, no hills.

Catalina is a nice enough island today, but then, in 1932, it was a godforsaken hump of land surrounded by sharks. P. K. Wrigley owns the island, and he owned it then. His Chicago Cubs used to conduct spring training on Catalina, not because the southern California climate is so swell in February and March (it's terrible), but because the island offers no perilous temptations to a bored baseball player, unless he is crazy about hunting wild boar. Wild boar are tough little pigs, with tusks. They fear no man. You hunt them by poking into all the places they might be, and hoping your rear is covered. When you rout out a wild boar, he does not run away. He runs at you.

I shot and killed a wild boar one day on Catalina Island, a feat that does me no honor of any sort. When I saw the tough little tusker go down and roll over, his short legs sticking straight out, I walked over to the bushes and upchucked my lunch. I have never fired a gun since. Years later Jack Haley gave me a .45 as a present, with six splendid deadly looking shells, and I took it with shaking hands and placed it in a box, and locked the box, and put the box in a closet and locked the closet. This did me no good. I fretted over that .45 and those six shells. So I unlocked the closet one day and unlocked the box and gave the gun and the shells to Dennis Day. I hate guns.

So Catalina was my version of Hollywood, for ten weeks. I stayed at the Banning House and for a while I roomed with Guy Kibbee, the pink-faced comedian who hogged so many scenes in his day. He hogged the scene at night, as well. He snored. I mean, he *snored*. He whistled, he snorted, he kar-rumphed, he wheezed, he gonked, he whirred, he snored. I moved in with Walter Catlett, more to my liking. Walter was a wonderful actor, a fine comedian, and a man who took little guff from anyone. Walter is probably best remembered for his brawl with Louis Calhern at the Lambs Club one night. Calhern was winding up a two- or three-day binge and just to finish it off right, he decided to belt Catlett with a wild roundhouse swing while Walter was quietly drinking at the Lambs bar. Catlett flew through the air and landed under the nearby pool table. The Lambs house committee didn't take to all this fistfighting, so a deputation was assigned to walk Louis Calhern around the block a few times to sober him up, while another deputation knelt to revive poor Walter.

Naturally, just as Calhern finished his walk and returned to the Lambs bar, Catlett had woozily climbed to his feet and resumed his stance, right next to Louis. Walter rubbed his jaw, and Louis, instantly solicitous, asked: "What happened to you?"

"Somebody socked me," Walter said.

Calhern thought for a moment. Then it dawned. "I socked you," he said brightly, whereupon Catlett hauled off and knocked Calhern under the pool table.

The house committee clucked for a few minutes, and then Walter was told to put Louis to bed upstairs, and take away his clothes. Calhern would be locked in for twenty-four hours.

So Walter put Louis to bed, took away his clothes, locked the door, and tiptoed out. But he felt sorry for his pal, Calhern, and so for twelve or fourteen of those twenty-four hours, Walter sat outside Louis' room, with a bottle of whiskey and a straw. He slipped the straw through the keyhole, and Louis sucked down whiskey until he felt totally cured. That's friendship.

Over the years, Walter Catlett remained an obdurate man. And an honest man, who pulled no punches in and out of fights.

We all had dinner one night at Catalina, Joan Crawford, Walter Huston, Beulah Bondi, L. B. Mayer, Catlett, Lewis Milestone, and myself. I sat next to Miss Crawford, with Catlett on her other side.

She turned her huge eyes on me, and began to ask how I had liked her in *Dancing Daughters*, a recent picture she had made.

"I'm sorry, Miss Crawford," I said. "I haven't seen *Dancing Daughters*."

She nodded gravely and wondered what I thought of her in such-and-such, the picture before that.

"I haven't seen that one either."

"How about such-and-such?"

And I had to say, "Miss Crawford, I've never seen you on the screen in my life."

She turned to Walter Catlett and started telling Walter how she intended to play Sadie Thompson, the naughty heroine of *Rain*. Catlett had previewed the dinner with a couple of belts of Chicken Cock rye in our room, and after Miss Crawford had gone on for a while, Walter leaned over.

"Listen, fishcake," Catlett said. "When Jeanne Eagels died, *Rain* died with her."

It was the last time we all dined together, though I got to like Joan Crawford, a solid pro and a fine person, and to this day I'm still apologizing for my and Catlett's rudeness.

This was my first big film, and my first Hollywood film, big or small. I didn't like it. Moviemaking is not my dish of tea. Later I would get used to shooting a piece of the action here, and a piece there, never beginning at the beginning or ending with the end, but jumping all over the place at the director's whim. Even then, I never liked it. In *Rain*, I was confused by it. It was, and is, too slow. You never get the initial thrill of confronting a live audience for the first time, in a new play, a new part, a new town. The strangeness and fear and exultation of doing a new thing, and doing it as an entity, is lacking. This is a new experience, all right, but it is piecemeal. Before we ever shot a scene, Milestone would call in a bevy of cartoonists and they would sketch the scene. Then the actors would be blocked in with the cameras, and we would begin rehearsing.

The movie did have one superior scene, and a very tough one to shoot. It took place at night, in the rain (pipes overhead pumped salt water from the ocean down on us), and the electricians and cable carriers were in constant danger from electric shock. In the scene, I try to convince Sadie Thompson—Crawford—to go home, to leave the island. I tell her to meet me on the mainland, and we'll get married. We walk around the porch of a circular house, and the cameras follow us in a complete circle, which was what made the scene difficult. Milestone wanted it in one continuous take. We began one night at nine, and we finally satisfied Milly on the fifteenth take, at four the next morning. Then we discovered at the next day's rushes there was a scratch on the entire negative. Two days later we shot it again, and this time we got it on the fifth take. The scene exhausted close to a thousand feet of film, as opposed to not quite a hundred feet for an ordinary scene. And it exhausted a couple of actors—Crawford and me.

Mary and Barrie visited me one day at Catalina. The trip

to Catalina by boat is often a wild ride, but I doubt that Barrie would have minded. He'd already had his thrill.

He and his governess, Katherine, had gone off to a little girl's party the first week he was in Hollywood (Mary had rented us a small place in the Hollywood Hills), and on the way back from the party, a squad of local police descended on the little blond boy and his maid.

"That is the Lindbergh baby," one cop said, and everybody swore it had to be. The Lindbergh baby had been kidnapped in March of 1932; by May the entire country was being scoured for the missing child.

So Barrie and Katherine were sped to a police precinct, and Barrie, all three years of him, was plopped on the sergeant's desk.

"Who are you?" he was asked.

And true to the tradition of the criminal code, the kid wouldn't talk. In fact, what he said was, "I won't talk."

Naturally it was all straightened out (he wasn't the Lindbergh baby, and Katherine was not his kidnapper), but Mary and I had an odd yearning. "Wouldn't it have been good if he had been?" Mary said, much later, and I nodded. Because, you see, they found the Lindbergh baby dead a few days after our ridiculous episode.

Mary and Barrie came over to Catalina, and if they had thought all the disasters were out of the way, they soon found how wrong they were. They almost didn't make it across. They came on a speedboat, with Harry Ruby, the songwriter, and in the middle of the channel a squall sprang up. A squall is a Southern California word for typhoon. The captain of the speedboat became sick, and disappeared below. Harry Ruby is a tall, cadaverous, very funny man who looks not funny but extremely doleful. With his partner Bert Kalmar, Harry has written some of the zingiest tunes of our time—including *Three Little Words*, which became the title of the movie made about Harry and Bert—but what Harry would rather have been is a major-league second baseman. Harry always assumes the worst, as frustrated second basemen will. During the squall, he took off his expensive wristwatch and strapped it to Mary's wrist. "Here," he whispered, "you keep it." He knew he was going to drown, and he figured Mary wouldn't. Maybe he figured she wouldn't drown because she is an exceptional swimmer; more likely he knew it because they had lashed her to the deck. This way she couldn't drown; she would float on the surface and be eaten by sharks.

The boat finally made it to Catalina, after four hours. It is ordinarily a two-hour trip. Mary staggered off, and Walter Catlett figured she was drunk, and gave her a shot of rye, as hair of the dog. Mary says it saved her life. I don't remember what happened to Harry Ruby's watch. I like to think Mary returned it.

Mary has a way with natural disasters. In March of 1933, when she was nearly six months pregnant with our second son, the last good-sized earthquake to hit Southern California began to shiver. Mary was in the process of putting on her perfume, a $95-an-ounce bottle of Caron Sweetpea, given her by Tom Mix. We had this place in the Hollywood Hills, where all the houses were built of straw like the little piggie's before the big bad wolf blew it down. The floor began to tremble, and she thought: My God, labor pains so early?

I was downstairs, in the billiard room. When I went Hollywood, I went the whole way. Billiard room and all. I lined up a left-handed shot, young Barrie—four years old—by my side, getting an education in the important matters of life, when the table started to twitch. I rubbed my eyes, and thought, My God, DTs so early? and resumed my stance. I saw Mary coming downstairs, holding an open bottle of perfume in her hand. She waved frantically to me, and I waved good-naturedly back, and resumed my stance again. Then I realized it was an earthquake (I have remained a quick study all these years), and I grabbed Barrie and started outside. The chandeliers bounced, the stairs rolled like a funhouse floor at Coney Island, and Mary was knocked on her cute bottom once more.

Nothing really happened, other than that. We had tremors every fifteen minutes for an hour and a half or so, but nothing serious. A few cracks appeared in the streets. In Long Beach, down the coast, the quake hit much harder, splitting streets wide open, toppling buildings, and killing several people. But we had nothing like that, and Mary got to her feet, and stared at her hand in triumph.

"I didn't spill a drop," she said, and she continued dabbing on her perfume.

"At ninety-five dollars an ounce, you'd better not," I growled.

That was after *Rain*. We were veteran Hollywoodites. I had seen my first palms. Idiotic-looking trees. I had seen the sand of Malibu. No different from Coney Island. It still got inside the sandwiches.

Rain finally ended. It was a terrible film, shot much too slowly. Walter Huston, a really great actor when controlled, had badly overacted, but you couldn't blame him. The film otherwise crawled. Still, at $1500 a week, for ten weeks, I couldn't complain. Nor did I.

During my shooting of *Rain*, RKO had got in touch. The studio wanted to film *Animal Kingdom*, with Leslie and myself in our original roles. Was I interested? You bet. I signed a contract with RKO, without reading the small print, and when *Rain* ended, I got a script in the mail. It wasn't *Animal Kingdom*. It wasn't really anything. They called it *The Sport Parade*, and Joel McCrea and I were to play a couple of newspapermen, real buddies, who somehow turn to wrestling. A girl—Marian Marsh—comes between us, and we become unfriendly rivals. At the end, all is well again. Today, it would be high camp. Boy meets boy; boy loses boy; boy gets boy.

I read the script and I went over to RKO, to the office of Dudley Murphy, who would direct *The Sport Parade*.

I held the script and looked down at Murphy. "This script is from RKO to Gargan," I said, "and now it's from Gargan to RKO." I threw it on his desk. "You can take your contract and give me a one-way ticket to New York."

Murphy grinned. "Come on, Bill," he said. "We all have to make these schlemeil pictures once in a while. What do you want to do, waste time around here?"

So I made *The Sport Parade*, and quickly discovered that

schlemeil pictures didn't come along just every once in a while. My very next film was *Sweepings*, where I nearly held my own in the mugging department with Lionel Barrymore, and where I had another run-in with a moviemaker, this time director John Cromwell.

Cromwell had been a fine young actor; now he had decided to make this odd film about the debris behind a department store. I played a rich fat kid, spendthrift, spoiled, a terrible part, ill-written, empty. One scene had me falling in love with the girl, and kissing a bear rug on the floor, in ecstasy.

"Ridiculous," I said to Cromwell. "I can't do it."

"You'll do it," he said.

I went to the studio head.

"You miscast me," I said.

"That's for us to decide," he said. "*We* tell *you* what to do."

I went back to the set. "All right," I said, "tell me what it's all about. I don't understand the scene."

Cromwell sighed. "It's very simple."

"So explain it simply."

He explained, with a ten-minute monologue, the motivation, the premise behind the scene, how the picture had been built block by block (*blockhead by blockhead*, I thought), and when Cromwell had finished, he said, "Now do you get it?"

"No. Neither do you. It's all double talk. I'll play it as well as I can." And I did, and somehow it wasn't godawful. Just plain awful.

Sweepings was so bad a movie that Hollywood, in its wisdom, made another version of it a few years later, under the title, *Three Sons*. I had the honor of appearing in the second version as well. This time, however, I did not kiss the bear rug.

Schlemeil pictures, one after the other, the kind you see today on the late late show. In the middle of either *The Sport Parade*, or *Sweepings*, or some other piece of debris, a New York newspaperman, Ward Morehouse, let it leak that I had won the New York Drama Critics' Award, for my portrayal of Red Regan. We celebrated, Mary and I, and Leslie and Ruth, and I even picked up the check. But it made me think. Here I was, making three times as much money as I made on Broadway, doing mediocre things, and there I had been on Broadway, winning an award over some of the best actors in the world. You pay for the schlemeil pictures, somehow.

But we finally did make *Animal Kingdom*, and Hollywood turned beautiful. The material was the same solid comedy-drama Philip Barry had written; the players, I think, were stronger. We still had Ilka Chase, but now we added silver-blonde Ann Harding, as the bohemian girl friend, and a young woman with upswept eyes who had made an early career of playing Oriental vamps. Her name was, and is, Myrna Loy. She played Cecilia, the society girl who marries Howard and makes his life miserable. There is an intimacy to *Animal Kingdom* enhanced by the closeup camera. The story flowed onto film like syrup. Leslie and I had one grand scene, a long drunken scene in which Red Regan tries very hard to tell his master, Tom Collier, he wants to quit, but he can't tell him the reason (Regan is fed up with the snotty ways of Collier's wife), and Collier has to fire Regan, because his wife has ordered him to. Neither, naturally, can quite get to the point. It is amusing and a bit touching. But it is an entity, seven or eight minutes in two people's lives, not a few-second closeup, a half-minute long shot, a ninety-second medium shot, and so on, ten or twelve little bits to be sewed together later to make one big bit. Hollywood at that time refused to face the psychological fact that the whole is greater than the sum of its parts. This time we forced the facing. Leslie Howard suggested all three cameras operate simultaneously, and we do the scene in one take. He looked at me.

"How about it, old chap?"

"Duck soup," I said.

So the director, Ned Griffith, went along, and we rolled. It was old times, the Broadhurst Theatre, the two of us on stage, and nobody to wave a hand and yell, "Cut!" We did the scene, and when it was over—one take—the director said, "It looks fine here. How do you feel, Leslie?" and Leslie said, "It seemed fine here. How about it, Bill?" and I said, "Fine by me," and that was that. A scene can be successfully shot in one take if

the actors are willing to work a little, and the director is willing
to chance it.

The flavor of playing-making continued. They premiered *Animal Kingdom* at the newly built Center Theatre in Manhattan
—where once I'd sunned myself and eyed *Vanities* girls lying
about half dressed—and when the film ended, the actors made
small curtain speeches. The critics loved the film; I honestly
think it was a better movie than a play. The audiences loved it.
In 1933, with theater-seat prices deflated to rockbottom, we set
a box-office gross that remained a record for years.

It straightened my thinking. Yes, there's lots of mediocrity.
But the good thing does come along, once in a while. And I
couldn't forget such stage epics as *Aloma* or *The Greatest Thing
in the World* (Motherhood!). Bad taste is predominant, in all
places and at all times. I had not come to Hollywood to change
the direction of an art medium. I came out, for the money, for
the ease, for the fun. I had a billiard table, and I bought the
first car I ever owned, a Ford, which Mary drove first, because
she got a license before me. Then we switched to long lean
Packards, and finally to a Cadillac. I took up golf, and I even
played polo. Polo! The kid from Brooklyn on a polo pony on
grass so smooth you could have skated on it.

The country was hip deep in the depression. Hoover's prosperity had remained beyond the next corner. The banks teetered
when they didn't totter. Mary and I were as scared as anyone.
We had managed to stash away $16,000 by the end of 1932,
half in a California bank vault, and half in a joint checking
account. But when we heard the banks were going to be closed
down, we did what so many others did. We removed our money.

"Here," I said to Mary, handing her $8000. She stuffed it into
a shoe. I stuffed my $8000 into a shoe. It made for uncomfortable
walking, but we knew right where our money was. It was right
there, pressing against a bunion.

Everybody was afraid. The nation teetered as much as the
banks, edging close to the brink of revolution. Fear gnawed at
every heart, like cancer of the spirit. And not just here. The
breathing space between the World War (we had not yet assigned

it a roman number) and the next one was starting to end. Japan overran Manchuria, but that would not appease the warlords. Hitler became the German chancellor—elected by the people!—and immediately began to warn the world what he would do for poor downtrodden Germany. Poverty ran unchecked across every border and down through every race. By the millions they died of starvation in India.

Jimmy Walker, that darling dancing songwriting leprechaun of a man, was forced to resign his post as mayor of the world's greatest city; graft was the kindest thing they said about him. (I liked Jimmy, liked him all his life. What he was, mainly, was weak. Aren't we all?) The Lindbergh baby was kidnapped from his crib, and the ransom money paid, even though the kidnapper had already slain the infant and left him to rot in an unmarked hole in the earth. An anarchist in Miami raised a gun and fired it at President-elect Franklin D. Roosevelt, but the bullet was deflected, and instead hit the Mayor of Chicago, who was with Roosevelt at the time.

But man is also splendid, for all the flaws. The bullet was deflected because a woman sprang at the assassin and grabbed his arm. The woman risked her life without hesitation, without thought. She did what people today don't do. She involved herself.

This was the world of the early 1930s, a desperate time in a shrinking globe. Seventeen million Americans were out of work; men huddled in hobo jungles; white men lynched black.

But I played polo on grass as smooth as glass. Life was sweet, and I danced on.

Our son, Leslie, was born on June 28, 1933, in St. Vincent's Hospital. Two children. Two boys. Healthy. Mary was healthy. Mary was beautiful. So were we all, and so were the palm trees, the velvety nights, the hills, the ocean, the sand, the sky.

My brother Ed had arrived in Hollywood in January of 1933, to start his movie career. He set up bachelor digs on North McCadden, in Hollywood, and went to work. He made *David Harum*, and then began his specialty, playing dumb Irish cops. He'd learned to swing a policeman's club by watching an Irish cop on 4th Avenue in Brooklyn; it became his mark. He moved from one cop part to another, until Western Costume always knew to have a uniform ready, from the cap right down to the motorcycle puttees.

Mary and I, meanwhile, had moved from our house of straw in the Hollywood Hills to an apartment on Cherokee Avenue in Hollywood itself. It was the first of a series of moves. From Cherokee we sped over to North Ogden Drive, where we rented a hillside house, and then we found a furnished house at 1515 North Laurel during Christmas of 1933, a two-story, four bedroom, four-bath house with a nursery, and a beautiful garden in the back. But it wasn't Beverly Hills, where we wanted to be, so we very soon rented the house of Marion Davies' mother at 727 North Bedford Drive, five bedrooms, five baths, English Tudor, servants' quarters, the works, all for $200 a month. We got to know Marion Davies, a woman comfortable as an old shoe (provided you weren't walking around on $8000), and we got to know William Randolph Hearst when we visited the two of them at Hearst's beach house. He was very austere, worried about Marion's drinking. Drinking bothered Hearst. When you visited the beach house, or the castle up at San Simeon, your luggage was immediately ransacked, to make sure you had no bottles with you. A single drink was served before dinner, and that was all. When you left, if you'd come with a bottle, it was back in your suitcase.

But renting houses was not the Hollywood way, and the lovely actress Mary Boland, whom we'd known back on Broadway, kept after Mary to buy a place of our own. Finally, in 1937, Mary Boland told my Mary to meet her over on North Palm Drive, in Beverly Hills. Jean Harlow had just died, and her house was up for sale, all seventeen rooms, high vaulted ceilings of natural rough beams, a true Spanish house, magnificently built, beautifully cared for, with lawn and trees and flowers. The price —for those days—was a whopping $27,000, but Mary said Yes, and I said Yes, and we moved in to 512 North Palm Drive, where we'd live for the next quarter century.

There was a catch to the place (other than an odd-looking

lemon tree that would not die and would not flourish, and become my special charge). Rubberneck tourists kept tramping through the gardens, looking for a piece of Miss Harlow, a relic, something. One day the doorbell rang, and Mary answered, and a man in a white suit stood outside.

"I'd like to speak with Miss Harlow," he said politely.

"Oh," Mary said, "I'm awfully sorry. Miss Harlow is dead."

He waved a hand impatiently. "That's her body. I'm interested in her spirit. I'm here to speak with her spirit."

"You can't come in," Mary said.

"Why not? I won't bother you. I just want to speak with her briefly."

"You can't," Mary said. "She's in conference with Napoleon." She shoved the kook out, but he persisted. He kept coming back, even taking to climbing trees, to shimmy onto the roof and out onto our balconies, peering in, for a chance sighting of Jean Harlow's spirit. We finally called the police, and they quietly threw him out of town. But people still rubber-necked their way across the grounds; we tried to ignore them.

That too is Hollywood.

14

Dad's in the Back Room, Dying

In between all the moving about, I kept busy, turning out pictures, schlemeil and otherwise. In 1933, you could have seen me—unless you were lucky—in such epics as *Lucky Devils, Emergency Call, Headline Shooter,* and *Aggie Appleby Maker of Men.*

Aggie Appleby Maker of Men. Grown men, receiving bloated salaries, worked long hours and sweaty weeks to produce *Aggie Appleby Maker of Men.* How real is any place that turns out a product called *Aggie Appleby Maker of Men?*

Never mind. *Aggie Appleby* was no worse than most of the pictures cranked out in 1933. But that just makes the reality of Hollywood more and more open to suspicion. The banks tottered in 1933, but in Hollywood, values tottered more. And still totter. All is not gold that glitters. Especially in Hollywood. Here, it is chrome. It is neon. It is tinsel. How real can any place be where you stroll outside on Christmas morning in sunburst sports shirt and shorts, and wish your neighbor Merry Christmas while he waters his lawn, dried up by too much hot sun? The rest of the country would shiver in February, while the hills of California turned pale green, and then the fields of wild mustard painted them golden. The sky was light blue and as high as heaven; on a clear day you could see *Aggie Appleby Maker of Men,* or some other schlemeil picture. And it was always a clear day. What fun is it when you can plan a picnic any day from May 1 to November 1, and you know it won't rain? Where's the challenge?

What kind of reality is it—and where's the challenge?—for an actor to get a check every week, job or no job? My contract with RKO paid me $750 a week, every week. So in between jobs, we would pile onto the *Chief* and click-clack through the desert and on to Chicago, forty-eight hours away, a porter shining your shoes, a dining-room steward flickering away the tiniest dot of dust from the immaculate tablecloths, and the steward in the bar making his ice cubes ring a merry tune in that long tall drink.

Nana and Pop Kenny would come out, to look after the kids, and we would have fun. From Chicago, we'd take the *Twentieth Century Limited* to New York, and we'd see my folks, see some plays, see some friends. Then we'd wend our way back, click-clacking along the rails of America.

The film jobs flew by. I no longer recall them all. Fortunately. Some I do. Even some good ones. RKO loaned me to Paramount, and I appeared in *The Story of Temple Drake*, a loosely made version of William Faulkner's *Sanctuary*—a grim, sordid, excellent film, with Miriam Hopkins as the obsessed girl, and Jack La Rue as Trigger, the movie counterpart of Faulkner's Popeye. I played the lawyer, Benbow. The film did not make much money; it was too downbeat. But it was a solid job. I also remember some bad ones. One of the worst was a Cecil B. De Mille film, *Four Frightened People*, which we quickly retitled Four Scared Actors. But I didn't mind. This was shot in Honolulu, so Mary and I made merry, Hawaiian style.

In 1934 I made another film with Leslie Howard, *British Agent*, and with that glorious creamy beauty, Kay Francis. During the shooting, Leslie gave his wife, Ruth, a diamond pin for their anniversary. "Where'd you steal it?" I wanted to know. "You couldn't have bought it, you cheap, chiseling Englishman."

"Careful, old boy. I'll make you pay me the three dollars you owe me."

Leslie played a lot of polo. He'd spend tens of thousands of dollars on a polo pony. Then he'd tip the stable boy a dime. We played with Walt Disney, Will Rogers, Frank Borzage, Big Boy Williams.

Once Leslie wanted to send four ponies to England. He'd be going back, to make *The Scarlet Pimpernel* in London, and he wanted his ponies handy. But Ruth, usually the cool head in face of crisis, couldn't arrange the loading in Leslie's absence, so she wired him to come to New York himself. The ponies had left California and gone through the Panama Canal to New York, where now they had to be unloaded and then reloaded onto a ship for England. We speeded up the finish of *British Agent*, and Leslie packed his things for the train trip to New York, and then the leisurely crossing on the *Majestic*. When he was about to leave, he said to me, "Why don't you come to England with me?"

At the time I felt Hollywood couldn't get along without me, so I nixed the idea. But he persisted. "At least come to New York with me." And when he added: "At my expense," I knew he really wanted my company. Actually, he had another reason. Leslie had been gassed in the war, and his breathing, slightly impaired, left him mildly claustrophobic. The small room on the *Chief* would depress him. With company he wouldn't mind so much.

"All right," I said. "Just to New York."

I packed one small suitcase, so I'd have to return right away, and they could open up Hollywood again. We trained across and checked in to the Carlyle, and Leslie immediately began to nag at me to go the rest of the way.

"No," I said flatly. "I can't. No time. No clothes. No passport."

He scoffed. "An American boy, a Brooklyn boy—and you let minor matters stymie you. You ought to be ashamed."

To make a long story not quite so long, I called Dad who knew a man in Washington who sent me to the Treasury Building in downtown New York, and I picked up my passport in one afternoon.

We went. When word got out that Leslie was sailing, we had to battle through 3000 female fans, clamoring for his autograph, a piece of his clothing, a touch of his arm, his face. He struggled against the tide, and then blissfully yielded to it. We dragged him up the gangplank.

"Can't help it," he panted, to Ruth. Then to me, he gloated: "They don't seem to know you're alive, old boy."

I had problems of my own. Yes, I now had a passport, and some money, but I really did not have any clothes. Mary, with foresight, was fairly well fixed. All I had was that small suitcase. So on the ship, tied up at the pier, with a good half hour to go, I looked over the rail down at the crowd of well-wishers below. I searched for an honest face. I finally found one.

I yelled down to the man. "Do me a favor?"

He nodded.

"Catch?" I held up my keys.

He shrugged, and nodded.

I threw the keys. He caught them.

"Got a pencil?"

"Yes."

I waited for him to dig it out, and a piece of paper—he was honest and a walking stationery store, and I am a lucky Irishman—and then I yelled down:

"Mail the keys to Kenny, care of William Gargan—that's me —727 North Bedford Drive, Beverly Hills."

The man scribbled it down.

"Send an airmail letter, special, same address. Tell them to send my trunk—these are the keys—with my clothes to Leslie Howard, in England. With this address." I rattled off Leslie's address; he scribbled it all down.

Four weeks later, the trunk arrived at Leslie's, with my clothes.

Which didn't get me very well dressed on the ship. So I went about looking for more honest men. Mainly, men my own size. I figured it would be duck soup; I'd hit up a man, my size, for the loan of a shirt and jacket. I walked the decks, the corridors, the salons, the dining rooms. No luck. Tall enough, but too skinny; broad enough, and six inches too short. Stylish Stouts and Extra Longs. But no Gargan 38s.

Discouraged, I went into the barber shop. I had a haircut

and a shave, and when I got out of the chair, to tip the barber,
I noticed he and I were eye-to-eye. I looked him over; they'd
cut him from the same cookie-cutter.

"I'll buy your shirts," I said to the barber. I told him why.

"Not buy," he said. "You can borrow them."

He even loaned me a tux. I was the best-fitted man on ship.
Robert Sherwood, the dramatist, was on board. We all dined
together. Sherwood and Leslie knew each other; they were dicker-
ing over Leslie's appearing in a play Sherwood had just written,
The Petrified Forest. Sherwood had a copy of the play with
him. He gave it to me to read.

That night I read *The Petrified Forest,* now an American
classic. The next morning I said to Sherwood, "I want to do
Duke Mantee for you." Duke Mantee is the escaped killer who
terrorizes a cafe full of people out on the Arizona desert.

Sherwood seemed pleased. "Would you?" he asked.

"You got a boy."

We left it at that. I told Sherwood I'd be back in Hollywood
fairly soon; we'd conclude an actual deal then. In any event, we'd
all have to wait on Leslie finishing his movie, *The Scarlet
Pimpernel.* He was the star and the big name, and he would
again be co-producing, probably just to cheat me out of my
pay.

So we partied our way across, landing at Southampton, I
finally relaxing enough to get ready for a brief vacation. I didn't
realize how brief it almost was. An Exchequer official in striped
pants boarded the ship at Southampton before we debarked and
came up to me. "Is your name Gargan?" he asked.

"That's right," I said, secretly flattered.

"The actor?"

"That's right," I said. "Want my autograph?"

"Hardly," he sniffed. "I want the money you owe my government."

The Gargan they wanted—it turned out—was my brother Ed.
Ed had been in London a couple of years before, to appear
in the stage musical, *Good News.* Ed got into a verbal scrape
with the authorities, who thought he owed the income-tax pay-

ment for his work over there. Ed, who always had a mildly loose attitude toward money and managed to spend it all even when he couldn't find chewing gum, thought otherwise and left in a huff. Without paying. So the word filtered down to English customs that an actor named Gargan would not be allowed to set foot on the tight little isle (and after Leslie, I knew why they call it "tight").

The Exchequer man sniffed and blustered and hemmed, but finally he believed I was Bill, not Ed, Gargan, and Leslie immediately took me sightseeing. On Downing Street, we were again besieged by autograph seekers. This time they came at me. Nobody paid any attention to Leslie.

"You don't seem very big in London, kid," I said.

I began to enjoy my stay. Which I knew I wouldn't really enjoy because I didn't much like not working, and I didn't have the cash to sustain a long vacation.

But God must watch over indigent Irishmen. I was in London one day when the theatrical agents, Linnett, Dunphy, and O'Brien, contacted me.

Was I available to make a movie while in London?

I was.

The deal was signed the next day, and I made *Things Are Looking Up*, with that very fine comedienne, Cicely Courtneidge, for Alexander Korda of Gaumont-British.

Meanwhile, in the mail had arrived an offer from Warner Brothers, a seven-year contract which would pay me $40,000 the first year, $60,000 the second, and with increments soon have me at and over $1500 a week.

The Warners contract posed a dilemma. If I signed it, there'd be no Duke Mantee part, no *Petrified Forest* on Broadway. If I didn't, I'd do the play, and with a Duke Mantee part under my belt, I felt true stardom, huge stardom might be just ahead. Even if it wasn't, I could still go back to RKO, and more epics like *Aggie Appleby Maker of Men*. Worse yet, I might be loaned out to make another *Four Frightened People*. Not that Warners was promising me only Alfred Lunt roles. Far from it. But they were offering me a fat cushion of money. It was a case of Warners bird in the hand, versus a Broadway role, and maybe real stardom in the bush.

I'd actually come very close to that kind of stardom. Right after *Animal Kingdom*, Merriam Cooper, one of the top men at RKO, called to congratulate me. "I'm going to tear up your contract," he said, "and write you a new one. We'll make a *big* star out of you."

I stopped off at church on the way home that night, murmured a word of gratitude and hurried to tell Mary. That night Cooper had a heart attack and was forced to quit working. He was replaced by David Selznick, who had no memo to tear up my contract and make me a big star, and that was that.

I rushed through *Things Are Looking Up*, wondering if they were. I really wanted to do the play. I didn't expect Bob Sherwood to wait forever for me. But the holdup—now—was Leslie. I finished my film. He kept sauntering through his.

"Come on," I'd growl to him. "Speed it up."

"Can't, old boy," he said. But he did try.

I got ready to go back with Mary, but at the last minute Gaumont-British decided they needed retakes, so I kissed Mary goodbye, and stayed on another three weeks, fretting now that Leslie would finish before me, rush off to New York, and they'd decide to go into production with another Duke Mantee. It worked out that way, but in a different order. I finished the retakes, and Leslie still hadn't completed *Scarlet Pimpernel*. I took the *Berengaria* to New York, and the first night I was in Manhattan, I ran into Bob Sherwood, which isn't too difficult. He stood 6'8".

"I can't wait much longer," Sherwood said. And I said, thinking of Warners, "I can't wait much longer, either." When two weeks went by, and Leslie still hadn't returned, I reluctantly told Bob I'd have to accept the Warner contract or risk losing it.

I went back to Hollywood. Sherwood found a young man who'd been in a couple of films and plays as a pretty boy, and decided to let him grow a two days' growth of beard and be his own ugly self. Which is how Humphrey Bogart began his stardom. Actually, Bogie came out to Hollywood shortly before

Petrified Forest opened, and we got to know each other quite
well. One day he also had a Warners contract thrust at him.

"Should I sign it, Bill?" he asked.

"Please," I said. "I beg of you. If you have to, get down
on your hands and knees and crawl back to New York. You'll
be a big star. Then come out, and sign for $100,000."

Which is swell advice, except it doesn't solve the problem of
last month's gas bill. Bogie signed at considerably less than
$100,000, went to Broadway, where he was an instant smash,
and Warners had a great star dirt cheap.

They also had me.

Everybody should—at least once—work for Warner Brothers.
It is like, except more painful, sleeping on beds of nails; it is
like, except more persistent, the Chinese water torture, dropping
a drop of water on your head every five seconds for seven years.
It is like—well, you get the idea.

No, I wasn't headed for big stardom. I was making junk.
I had a name in Hollywood—King of the Bs. King of the B
picture, the cheap little shove-em-out-on-celluloid; who-cares-what-
they're-like-films. Bill Gargan, King of the Bs.

I made seven films for Warners that first year. You cannot
make seven good films in one year. Today, you can barely make
seven good one-minute television commercials in one year.

It was a seven-year contract, but it started to come apart the
first year. It went on for slightly over two years, mainly because
I managed to get loaned out to Paramount, to appear in *The
Milky Way*, directed by that funny man, Leo McCarey. I again
played a prizefighter, flattened ignominiously by Harold Lloyd,
playing a meek milkman. There haven't been many funnier films
than this McCarey job; everything was in his hands, and he
never made a mistake. Adolphe Menjou played the fast-talking
fight manager, to perfection; Lionel Stander was—superbly—the
gravel-voiced trainer. Not only did I get knocked cold by Lloyd
(three times), I also was kicked unconscious by a horse. All in
fun. And all very funny.

And all very leisurely, which was the best part of it. McCarey
took nine months to shoot the film, which is more like it. True,

it gets long and dull and boring, creeping along day after day, but McCarey was a brilliant man, a great and inventive director, and he made it a most pleasant stay. Actually, anything would have been pleasant after seven Warner Brothers movies in a row. And frankly, I didn't really work for nine months. I hid a lot of the time. The rule was, when I was free, I was supposed to go back to Burbank, and report to my keeper, put on another cop's uniform, or a newspaper reporter's slouch hat, and memorize a few lines that didn't change from one B-movie to the next. The word got out that I had actually finished working on *The Milky Way*, and Warners would call me and say, "We hear you're not shooting." I said I certainly was shooting, hung up, and raced over to McCarey who cooperated beautifully. He'd call Warners and tell them he needed me for another take, or a retake, or some dubbing of dialogue or whatever would do the trick. And I'd check in briefly, and then go out to Palm Springs, or play some golf or tennis, or ride horses.

Even *The Milky Way* finally ended, and I had to return. One factor kept me sane. The greatest bunch of actors—as people—worked out of the Warners factory—Jimmy Cagney, Pat O'Brien, Allen Jenkins, Frank McHugh, Horace McMahon, a fun-loving crew. We'd all finish our respective drudgery, and then we'd repair, usually, to Pat O'Brien's dressing room, and we'd begin letting down, relaxing. The camaraderie helped restore my sense of self. I was King of the Bs at Warners, but somehow I picked up another name during the social hour. The boys began to call me "the Big G." Big Gargan. I am only slightly ashamed to admit I enjoy hearing myself called the Big G. I even referred to myself as the Big G on more than one occasion.

The socializing in a dressing room often extended from there, perhaps to the Masquers, and then to one of our houses. One night, after a tough day before the camera, we had our cocktails in Pat O'Brien's dressing room, and then we started out for the Masquers, and I said, "How about dinner at my house tonight?" and everybody said, "Swell," so I called the house.

On this particular night, I picked the wrong house. I had forgotten that Mary and I had hired—just that day—a new chauffeur, cook, and general housekeeper, a Negro named Arthur Baker. He'd worked for Jack Haley and helped raise Jack's daughter, and now that we were in at 512 North Palm Drive, it was apparent we needed somebody to take care of the house. Thus, Arthur Baker, gray-haired, distinguished, a college graduate, and a great man.

Arthur answered the phone, when I called, and I said, "We'll be eleven for dinner," and then I realized it was his first night on the job, which was a hell of a way to break him in.

"What time, sir?" he asked quietly.

"Well," I said, mildly embarrassed, "I'd like it at 8:15." It was now six.

"Very good, sir," he said. And he hung up.

We got home, and he had the ice out, and the bar open, and we proceeded to have a few drinks. At 8:15 I went into the kitchen, to see how the poor guy was making out. He had a half-pint bottle out—his own—and he was pouring himself a shot. "Heart medicine, Mr. Gargan," he said. "Heart medicine." He downed the shot and then he said, "My apologies. I've had some difficulty finding the cooking utensils, and the oven is a bit strange. We'll be delayed some."

"That's all right," I said, figuring an hour, an hour and a half delay, and knowing it was my fault, not his.

Fifteen minutes later we sat down, the table lit by candle, the food served impeccably, and cooked like—well, like Mama Pinsky might have cooked had she ever been to New Orleans.

This was my true introduction to Arthur Baker. A short while later he brought into the house a friend, Connie Williams, to look after the boys, and Mary and I often looked at each other the next few years, wondering how we'd ever got along without Arthur Baker and Connie Williams.

Still, this didn't make my stay at Warners any easier; nothing could have remedied that. I told my agent Mike Levee I just had to have my release, and the two of us began a campaign to harass Warners until they'd let me go willingly. I wouldn't answer my phone when the casting office called. I was outspoken to people in the industry in my criticism of Warners.

I complained about the films I made and the films other Warner actors made. Finally—two weeks after my second year under contract—I received my liberty.

Mary and I went dancing that night at the Clover Club, to celebrate. And who was there? Jack and Ann Warner. Ann Warner came over.

"How come you're so happy?" she asked me.

"I just broke my contract," I said.

"With whom?"

"With him," jerking my thumb at Jack.

Whereupon we all celebrated, and Jack Warner said later that happy night, "How about going to Europe, the four of us?" That was Jack, always unpredictable.

With help in the house, and a gardener hired to come in every month, we could afford to play, afford to go to Europe or to Hawaii when the urge hit. When the boys were older, we sent them off to school. They attended St. John's Military Academy grade school, and then Bellarmine College Prep, in San Jose, a Jesuit boarding school. We had the money for it; we had the money for nearly everything. It flowed in, and it flowed out. But the clouds had begun to gather, on the world's horizon and on ours.

They'd been gathering on ours for some time. It was a perfectly ordinary warm August day, in 1935, when I heard it on the radio. Will Rogers was dead, at Point Barrow, Alaska (I had no idea where that was, until then), with Wiley Post, in a plane crash. As warm and funny and fine a man as I knew, and a hell of a polo player.

That same summer I sent my folks some money for their annual vacation to Miami. Dad now liked to go to Miami in summer; it was an idiosyncrasy. The place was empty, deserted, and dirt cheap, in summer. So they went, with our blessings. We saw them shortly after they got back, at 103 Garfield Place; they were happy, their noses peeling from too much sunburn. Other than that, nothing had changed. The single tree that grows in Brooklyn grew outside, in the back, where every summer as a youth I had tried to plant corn, and once succeeded.

The corn grew so high it covered the first floor windows. We cut it down late in August and boiled it, and let me tell you, that was pretty lousy corn.

The folks seemed fine.

"Keep in touch," we said.

"Keep in touch," they said.

We did keep in touch. Mary and I got to New York again in the spring of 1936, on a press junket, publicity for a movie, and we checked into the Essex House. I called the folks at Garfield Place.

Mother answered in a faraway voice.

"What's wrong?" I asked.

"I haven't seen you in ten years," she said. Her voice rambled, faded; sentences begun ended in splinters.

"How's Dad?"

"How's Dad? He's in the back room, dying. That's how he is. Where have you been all these years?"

I dashed over. Mother sat in the parlor, used only for marriages or wakes or special occasions. She was irrational. I did not know it, but she had had a small stroke. Small areas of her brain had been blotted out; gaps broke her thoughts, her memories. Dad was not in the back room. He was in a hospital. He'd been taken, bleeding, a few days earlier.

I rushed over to Manhattan General Hospital, on 19th Street. I still had on the smoked glasses of the Hollywood actor; the white corridors looked dim. I saw Dad; he lay unconscious. Even with the glasses, he was white. The sunburn hadn't lasted. I met the surgeon. He wanted to operate immediately. It was the bladder. He was afraid it was cancerous. We talked in that dim-white corridor, and then the doctor looked at the card in his hand, and at my smoked glasses.

"You're William Gargan, the actor?" he said.

"That's right."

"The price will be $2500, in advance."

I told him to hold off. I wanted to consult another man. The surgeon shook his head. "We ought to hurry," he said.

I called my father's friend, Clarence Worden, the gay little man who had swung on the Childs' restaurant swinging door. Worden knew everybody.

"Who is the best cancer man in the city?" I asked.

He said he'd check and call right back. He did. It was a man named McCarthy, at Postgraduate Hospital. McCarthy lived at the Waldorf Towers.

I called. Dr. McCarthy told me to move Dad to Postgraduate. I did. McCarthy saw him.

"Don't operate," he said. "Don't let anybody put him through a major operation. It's cancer and an operation would probably be fatal."

I believed him.

"What do I owe you?"

"You look like a nice kid. How's $25?"

The other doctor sent me a bill for $650. I sent him $250 and told him to sue me for the rest. He never did.

I asked McCarthy what I should do for the old man.

"Give him a steak and a scotch and soda. When he's feeling stronger, we'll perform a cystoscopy—go in through the penis and catheterize the bladder."

Then he looked carefully at me. "And you, kid, take these two pills and get some sleep."

I got some sleep, and I saw Mother the next day. She was worse. I put her in the hospital where they told me it was a stroke. Ed—who also lived on the Coast, making movies; doing small roles, cop roles and the like—came in, just in case.

A week later, they catheterized Dad's bladder, and a week after that, he walked out of the hospital. Mother improved quickly; the blood vessels in her brain healed. She became rational again. I have a hunch about these things, and probably so do a lot of you. A man and wife for thirty or forty years, like Mom and Dad, become a single person, Siamese twins. You can't separate one without injuring the other. When Dad became ill, Mom had to, as well.

Out of the hospital, they were well again, but weak. I knew I couldn't kid myself. They were old. You cannot set time aside.

They came out to the Coast, to recuperate, and rented an apartment on North McCadden, next to Ed.

Dad had a good six or seven months, not fully recovered, but not bad. He even joined in one of the more fun-filled days of those years. A priest had asked a few of us to put on a benefit for a church in Highland Park. The benefit conflicted with a party we were throwing—for Mom and Dad, for the O'Briens, Pat and Eloise, for Frank McHugh, Wally Ford, Wheeler and Woolsey, and a half-dozen other fine partying friends. We just moved up the hour of the party. The old man made a gallon of martinis and a gallon of manhattans and a gallon of something I swear was a mixture of the two—a manhattan, a martini.

We drank it all down and chartered a bus, and took everyone to church in Highland Park. Pat O'Brien emceed the show, and we went on. We raised maybe a thousand dollars for the church, minor-league stuff so far as charity goes. But it didn't matter how big or little, a church charity or a Broadway play, or a film like *The Sport Parade* or one like *Animal Kingdom*. When you were on, you were on. It didn't matter we'd been partying before the church benefit—we were professionals, doing a job. You went on, and all else slipped away, the pressure of job, the depressing atmosphere of Warner Brothers, or any studio, the banality of the script, the lack of imagination of the director, the stinginess of the producer, even the knowledge that your father had just months to live—all of it disappeared, when you were on. It had to. You have a job to do, weave a little spell, toss a sprinkle of magic on some uplifted faces out in the black pit, people you never saw, never knew, people who had the same and probably worse banality and loneliness to contend with, and who'd come together to be released. So whether it was a two-million-dollar movie, or a small benefit in a church in Highland Park, California, you were on, totally on.

We finished and got back on the bus and resumed the party all over again. What clouds on whose horizon?

I personally work a little better with a few drinks in me. I never drank on the movie set (except at the end of a working day), but I find it helps in the work I do these days. If I land in a new city, and I'm whisked off to lunch where I am expected to speak, without a chance to relax, to feel my surroundings and my audience, I am dull, not alive. I need the opportunity to relax, to feel the situation. A drink helps me relax, helps me warm to the strange city, the strange faces.

My friend Frank Morgan had been the great exponent of a little lubricant in the system. I guested a few times on his Maxwell House radio hour. He wouldn't think of going on without three old-fashioneds (and he wasn't even pregnant). It charged him with energy, and it relaxed him. They say it is false energy you get from the bottle, and undoubtedly false courage. But some reality is too real, too terrible to be borne, so we seek our escape. I can't change the reality, so I change myself. I take a snifter, and the strange faces that loom up become friendly faces. I lie to myself this way, but such delusion may be necessary. It is the old Eugene O'Neill theme; take away man's illusions, and you kill his hopes, and eventually kill him.

It became true of Dad. He had his good six or seven months, and then his cancerous bladder began to bleed again. We rushed him to Hollywood Presbyterian Hospital. Again, the surgeons said, "Don't operate. Just catheterize, through the penis. It's too far gone. You'll kill him if you open him up."

I paid most of the hospital bill, and Ed, out of his more modest movie pay, the remainder. I was still under contract with Warner Brothers, though getting closer and closer to that day we'd both mutually call it off. The $1500 a week came in handy. After meeting each week's bill at the hospital, I got back a handful of change. Dad was in the hospital fourteen months. We made it as comfortable as we could. We had help. The race track at Santa Anita had just opened, and Dad used to study the races in the paper.

"I can beat them," he said to me one day.

I called a bookie friend and told him to accept bets from my father, eight a day, but only $1 a race. Not a cent more. Therapy I'd give him, but not a blank check.

So Dad began to play the races again. Color returned to his cheeks. Now when I saw him, he was propped up in bed, no longer supine. His eyes shone. Scratch sheets lay all over the bed.

One day I got a call from the bookie.

"Jeez," he said. "That old man of yours. He's a wizard. He's $400 into me already."

"How's he doing it?"

"Playing the favorite in the third hole."

Good. He couldn't go broke too quickly that way. Or so I thought.

Dad began to look simply marvelous. His spirits rose. He began to enjoy the flat hospital fare. He was back in the saddle.

I'd keep tab on how he was doing, with the bookie, every few weeks or so.

The $400 mounted, to $600, to $800, to $900.

Then one day, quite a while after Dad had checked in, the bookie called. He sounded terrible. "I thought I'd let you know. He blew it."

The bookie had forgotten the instructions. The old man had bet the bundle.

I rushed over to the hospital.

"How come?" I asked.

"Aw," he said, "I figured if I hit a hot one, I'd be able to take care of the whole hospital bill."

He was ashamed of himself. And dejected.

"You want me to start you all over again?" I asked.

He shook his head. He lay flat. That ended the gambling. That ended the dream, the illusion. Pretty soon he began to deteriorate. One night I left Dad at eleven, and went home. The phone was ringing when I walked in.

"He's gone," the doctor said.

The papers said he died of a lingering illness. But it had a name. Cancer.

When the funeral was over, Mother said, "I want to go back to Brooklyn, Bill." Back in Brooklyn, her relations wanted to know how she possibly could have left California, for the crowded drab city. "My sweetheart was gone," she said, "and I didn't want to stay any longer." I think she wanted to go home to die. She became, at times, irrational again. Fluid had begun to fill her chest cavity, the edema of a failing heart. Mary and I flew in to see her when we could, which was often, but not often enough. We were building a house in Palm Springs; it was becoming the thing to do. Palm Springs was "in," the gentile Grossinger's.

One day in 1937, I got a call. Mother had had another stroke. I took the *Chief* to Chicago, and flew to Newark. I taxied in, but Tom Wilson met me and said, "She died in her sleep, Billy."

We held services at St. Francis Xavier's parochial school, and the Franciscan Brother Eugene, my old principal, dismissed school for Mother's funeral. Over 2500 people came to the funeral. I felt a great sense of loss, though I had felt more for my father. I emulated him; I took a lot from him, and made it mine. But I mourned my sweet mother, who probably would have liked a punch-clock existence, but Dad never permitted it, and she went along with whatever he wanted. She never held back.

Before they closed my mother's casket, I asked to be alone with her. She was never without money. I put a couple of quarters in the casket, and I murmured, "If you ever need change, you've got it, darling." She lay there in an offwhite gown, her blue-gray hair a soft crown. God will be enchanted with her, I thought. I kissed her cheek.

The undertaker, Thomas Dunnigan, said, "There'll be the hearse and twelve to fifteen limousines, and we will proceed slowly from the church to Holy Cross Cemetery—" and that is when I interrupted him.

"Pardon me, Mr. Dunnigan. She was a spirited woman. Go like hell."

We sped from church to cemetery.

I hope this does not offend you. It is how I feel about funerals. If you believe in the Resurrection—and I do—then you do not grieve unduly over the loss of loved flesh. The spirit has risen. So we swagger through wakes, boisterous and laughing and merry. (Then we go home, and weep.)

Every morning, to this day, I say a prayer for my parents, God love them. I love them.

But the funeral is a ritual. It helps purge grief. If it swells grief, somebody has done a lousy job. When Frank Morgan died suddenly in 1949, the merriest man I ever knew, I rode to the cemetery with Spencer Tracy and Ralph Bellamy, and we laughed all the way out. In a way, it was a joke on Frank. We'd palled together quite a bit, and whenever he'd hear me talk about my boyhood in Brooklyn, he'd say, "I wouldn't be caught dead in Brooklyn." Which is where they caught him, dead. They buried him at Evergreen Cemetery, thirty-six blocks from where I was raised.

So Spence and Ralph and I talked about this and we talked about other things, and we laughed all the way out. Nothing wrong with that. Frank would have wanted it. He was a laughing man, in a world that needs laughter almost as much as it needs peace. Maybe more. At the graveside, a minister from a way out faith asked us all to hold a rose. He delivered a way-out prayer about birds and bees and flowers, and he did it badly. The guy was a bad actor, and if there was anything Frank Morgan couldn't stand, it was a bad actor.

We were all shaking now, with laughter held in. Spencer Tracy was nearly doubled over, tense, hugging himself to keep still. We all dropped our roses. I threw mine. Frank undoubtedly would have caught it, except he probably was trying to fight his way out of the casket to tell off that way-out minister.

So that is how I feel about funerals. If they are to honor someone's life, let them be like their life. Spence and Ralph and I told jokes all the way back from Frank's grave. Not as good as Frank's jokes, but we figured he'd forgive us. We weren't bad actors.

15

Beaten Out by a Spittoon

One afternoon in the late thirties, I wandered into a movie house on Wilshire Boulevard, where they usually showed those artsy films I have trouble understanding. This one I understood, though for the life of me I cannot recall its title or what it was about. But I remember the director. His name was Garson Kanin, and when I came home that evening, I said excitedly to Mary, "I saw a great film. A guy named Garson Kanin made it."

To Hollywood actors, the director is king. Not even a great director can make a bad film good, but a great director can make a good film better. And a bad director can annihilate the best story in the world and the best acting.

"You should have seen the things this guy did," I said to Mary.

"You sound like a fan magazine," she said.

"That's how I feel."

"Write him a letter. Maybe he'll send you an autographed picture."

Damned if I didn't. I'd never written a fan letter in my life. I sat down and wrote to Kanin, care of the studio, and told him what I thought of his picture. And I forgot all about it. (He never sent me an autographed picture.)

Meanwhile, even without Warners, my career went along swimmingly. I made film after film, forgettable mementos—*The Crime of Dr. Hallet, The Devil's Party, She Asked For It, The Crowd Roars, Women in the Wind*. Once in a while, a pretty good one, like *Joe and Ethel Turp Call on the President*, a Damon Runyon story, with Ann Sothern, and good enough it really should have been turned into a series, and eventually into a television series. It still should be. But mainly they were pictures I could do in my sleep. Today that is what they are good for, sleep. You see them on the late late *late* show; they are the industry's answer to insomnia. People sometimes wonder why there are so many terribly old, and oldly terrible, movies on television. Television swallows material like growing boys swallow their food, uncaring of the taste just so long as there's lots. But television producers could fill this maw with something better than the usual nightly sleeping pill.

It's cheaper. That's why.

Draw the line at 1948. On films made before 1948, actors do not cut into television royalties on the showing of the movie. The Actors' Guild finally got tough enough, and now if a film was produced after 1948, we actors get a slice of the money paid by television for the right to screen that film. Actually, once I got tough enough, or lucky enough, or something enough. At RKO in 1933, actors were forced to accept a big cut in salary, because of the depression; I was among them. We held a meeting, to determine whether we'd accept the terms dicated to us by RKO's bigwigs—a 50 percent cut in pay—but the meeting itself was just a gesture. One actor got up and said, for all of us, "It's still better than driving a cab in Brooklyn." We signed at the half-pay terms. But I balked at one clause in my new contract. It said, in effect, I would relinquish all rights to any further compensation in the event my movies would ever be sold to television. Everybody else signed, because —we all thought—television was the same as science fiction. It just wouldn't happen in our lifetime. I didn't. Not because I had a crystal ball. I just hated giving anything away to the moguls that ran Hollywood. They surely didn't need my charity.

So I crossed out the television clause, and now if anybody does *Animal Kingdom* on television, I'll get my cut.

Actually, I should have had a glimmer that television was going to be more than a pipedream. While I was at RKO, I'd been asked one day to stand in front of a newfangled thing RCA had hammered together—they called it a television camera —and chat with John Barrymore, while the camera whirred and a tiny receiving set showed us as we talked. Still, if that set and camera were forerunners of mass entertainment, then my name was Aggie Appleby. The camera was as big as a kitchen, and twice as hot as the worst leaky oven you ever cooked with. You just knew this thing would never get off the ground. So nobody really took television seriously as a new source of acting income. A little radio, maybe, but television? Science fiction. Pipedream.

I made my films, and lived my pleasant life, chasing the next laugh, and finding it more often than not. The boys, Barrie and Leslie, grew older, sturdier, tougher. Barrie, the older boy, kept things to himself, a seemingly pliable youngster, and easy to get along with. Leslie—a chip off the old blockhead—developed a strong will, a refusal to bend to my own strong will. Besides, he was always too smart for me. He'd say something, and I'd run to the dictionary to find out what it meant, so I could have a snappy comeback a week later.

But they both were grand, and healthy. They also were ordinarily obstreperous. Mary would try to discipline them, with little luck, and I'd get a call from her during the day. "When you get home," she'd whisper, because the little monsters might be listening, "pull a Barrymore. Okay?"

"Okay."

So I'd get home, not having the slightest idea what they'd done, but knowing they'd bugged Mary, and I'd put on my bellowing best style.

"How can you behave like that?" I roared, one foot inside the door. "What right do you have to upset your mother like that? I want you to shape up, both of you, right now! Now—tell me exactly what you did, and no nonsense."

They assumed I knew and was trying to pin a lie on them, so they told the truth, to the letter. This kept them in line. Slightly.

Later, Barrie would go to the University of San Francisco, and Leslie would get into Notre Dame, and then manage to muff a registration deadline in his sophomore year, shift to Santa Monica City College, and end up at UCLA, a wandering minstrel, not much impressed by the Mikado's rules and regulations.

Mary—my Mary—got brighter, prettier, and lovelier. And I kept playing. Polo could not fill every hour of my leisure time (which was the problem of life), nor could golf, though they tried. I took up tennis, which quickly became another obsession. One day Mary said she'd like me to meet a man she'd run into; she thought the two of us would hit it off.

"Does he play tennis?" I asked.

"Nope. He rides." Riding was Mary's obsession.

So a bit reluctantly I met Travis Rogers, in Palm Springs, and another long friendship began to bud. Trav in those days owned a place called The Stables, where he had horses for hire and for sale, and where upstairs he held a Thursday night dance every week, a typical cowboy hoedown that made the whole neighborhood shake. For a spell, I joined in partnership with Trav, but our main connection was friendly, not business. Trav and I formed a ride that every year used to travel the mission trail, resurrecting a piece of old Spanish history in California and combining it with visits into the lovely old missions that dot the state from San Diego on up to Monterey. I rode a horse named Gigolo, a big palomino stallion, and pretty soon I was as obsessed with riding as was Mary. Trav also got me to take up roping and tying calves, and he and I held contests to see who could rope, wrestle, and tie down a calf first. I remember I finally tied a calf in five seconds; Trav never quite cut that mark. We'd make a $500 bet each year, to see who'd set the fastest time; one year I'd win, the next year he'd win, though, of course, neither of us ever paid the other. Trav and I both bought ranches in the Palm Springs area in the late 1930s, and it was at the old Rogers ranch—now the Palm

Springs Ranch Club—that he and I founded the Mink and
Manure Club to raise funds for the building of the first hospital
in the desert area. But mainly, Trav Rogers and I rode, which
was just another form of pleasure, another game I played.

I played other games. I took up handball, at the old Butler
club on top of the Equitable Building, playing with Pat O'Brien,
Jack Benny, Allen Jenkins, Jack Haley, and the club director,
Dave Butler, a fat guy who moved on the handball court with
the grace of a Babe Ruth on the ball field. And speaking of
ball fields, we moved en masse to Gilmore Field, next to the
Farmer's Market, to watch the Hollywood Stars play the Los
Angeles Angels, in the Pacific Coast League. Naturally we rooted
for the Stars; naturally the Angels kept beating them.

Del Mar opened its track above San Diego, and we all made
this new pilgrimage, a charming intimate track—where the turf
meets the surf, as the ads say—owned for a spell by Bing Crosby
and Pat O'Brien, among others. We made the local circuit,
Santa Anita, Hollywood Park, Del Mar, even down to Caliente,
in Tijuana.

Mary and I also saw much of Ed and Cooee, who finally
made it to the altar. Though it took some doing. Early in
1938, Ed wanted finally to make their unofficial engagement
more official, but he was having trouble getting a ring onto
her finger. Ed had one of Mother's diamonds which he intended to have set in an engagement ring. But Ed, true to his
ways, had recently hocked the stone and didn't have the funds to
redeem it. So he wrote to Cooee: "The rains won't let up. I
can't get down the hill to get the stone set." Finally, a friend
and character actor Chester Clute—Chet Clute—came to the
rescue. He advanced Ed the money, and Ed got the stone out
of hock, and mailed the ring from the Burbank airport. In
April, Ed and Cooee were officially engaged, and Mary and I
looked at each other, figuring another nineteen years would go
by before it went any further. So we were caught unaware, and
unavailable, when Ed and Cooee suddenly decided to get married. Mary and I were sailing on Frank Morgan's yacht, and on
Sunday afternoon, July 10, 1938, Ed and Cooee were wed at

Blessed Sacrament Church, the Reverend Cornelius McCoy, S.J., officiating. Fortunately Barrie and Leslie were there, both in their St. John's Military Academy uniforms.

The newlyweds skipped down the coast to Laguna Beach for their honeymoon, where Cooee proved she was a true Gargan. She stayed out in the sun too long, and the honeymoon had to be cut short because of Cooee's fierce sunburn.

Yes, we all played. And the clouds grew blacker, closer. Hitler turned into a mad dog, ravening a continent. On the other side, the tiny warlords began to slice up southeastern Asia. The United States was too large an island, figuratively, to worry about the mad dog or the samurai swords, but the island would shrink, and quickly. America Firsters gathered in Chicago, and Bunders in New York's Yorkville; you couldn't go to a party without somebody saying, "But all he's doing is trying to get some breathing space for the poor German people. *Lebensraum*." When you heard *lebensraum*—living space—you probably had a Nazi in your midst.

Not that I listened to that talk, or cared much. Sure the clouds grew black. But I kept finding the silver linings.

My agent, Sam Jaffe, called one day and invited me to have lunch with RKO bigwigs getting ready to make a film. I had been on loan to Metro, working with Robert Young in a horse-racing film, *Sporting Blood*, and I knocked off early and traipsed over to the RKO casting office. A door opened, and a little guy came bounding in.

"Bill Gargan," he said, sticking out a hand. "I'm Garson Kanin. You'll never know how thrilled I was by your letter. I want to thank you."

"Don't thank me," I said. "You deserved every word of it." Now where's my autographed picture?

"We're making *They Knew What They Wanted*," Kanin went on. "I'm directing it. I want you to play Joe."

You'll find *They Knew What They Wanted*, Sidney Howard's Pulitzer Prize play, in nearly every anthology of the best of the American theater. Richard Bennett, Pauline Lord, and Glenn Anders—as Joe—had made it a memorable production. Now, it

would be a movie. A middle-aged grape rancher named Tony—
as Italian as his name—becomes bored with his material success;
he wants a wife and children. But he is middle-aged, a pudgy
little guy, Italian, and afraid. He advertises for a wife, but when
it comes to sending her his picture, he substitutes a snap of his
much younger foreman, a very American guy named Joe. The
girl comes out, marries Tony, and has a brief affair with Joe.
It is a solid triangle, and a picture of a slice of American
life—the first generation immigrant buffeted by the natives. The
story had humor, pathos, drama, tragedy.

The part of Joe had no relation with anything I had ever
done. A foreman of a grape ranch; a smiling fornicator who
steals his boss's wife (and never gives up feeling sorry for the
boss), a radical who argues politics with the local padre.

Kanin wanted me to be Joe.

"That's fine with me," I said.

"There's a catch," Kanin said.

Here we go again.

"The girl has to approve."

"Who's the girl?"

"Carole Lombard."

I'd once met Lombard, a delectable blonde with the vocabulary of a coal miner.

Lombard soon traipsed in, trailing furs, snakes of beads clutching her throat.

She came over to me and smiled a toothy smile.

"You'll make a charming Joe, you great big beautiful hunk
of flesh," she said. She gave me a fat kiss. No wonder Clark
Gable swooned.

We were in business.

Charles Laughton was Tony. Years later, Mary and I socialized
with Laughton and his wife, Elsa Lanchester, in England, and off
the set Laughton could be pleasant company.

On the set, he was the most difficult man I've ever worked
with. An inveterate scene stealer, not at all subtle, without any
of the charm of Barrymore (or his talent), he was a grubby
man who fought and clawed for every inch of celluloid. He'd

once played Captain Bligh; now he kept playing Bligh. He'd become a tyrant.

On the set, while we were not shooting, he spent his time knocking the United States. Pretty soon we'd all developed a good-sized dislike for Fat Charles.

But the shooting was worse. In an early scene, Tony, the rancher, has me write a letter to the girl. He stands behind me, and tells me what to write; I have to rewrite Tony to make it English and to make it romantic. The camera is up fairly close, on both of us, and as I would look down to start to write, or as I would say something, Laughton—behind me—would begin to writhe, his heavy face hanging over my shoulder like a full moon. Every line I'd speak, every time I'd bend to work on the letter, he'd growl, grimace, wipe his nose, lick his blubbery lips; he'd grovel, rub his hands, do everything but have a fit.

Finally, he had his fit as well.

So did Garson Kanin.

Kanin took it for a while, slowly burning while Laughton fiddled. He was a fine director, perhaps the best I ever worked with, showing me how to play a role both sympathetic and unsympathetic, a wife-stealer you could like, and I just placed myself in his hands. But Laughton needed no direction (Charles knew best); Laughton would take no direction (from an American!). The letter-writing scene dragged on, until Kanin's patience finally snapped and he began to let Laughton have it. Naturally Laughton answered back; it turned into a great roaring donnybrook. I crawled up a rope ladder and sat on the flies, a perch where the camera usually sat. I pondered my immediate future. No silver linings. Below me, the director and the high-priced star were equally adamant. Kanin wanted Laughton to desist; Laughton intended to act his way and nobody else's. Well, I thought, there goes the best role I'd had in years. Out the window.

Nor was Kanin alone in his scathing criticism of Laughton. Carole Lombard picked up the slack every time Kanin took time for a breath. What she said could not be printed, except in a

Norman Mailer novel or a LeRoi Jones play. Suffice to say she was in rare form. Lombard even well-done was juicy enough.

Kanin finally called shooting off for the day.

The next day we started it again, and so did Laughton start it again. The grimacing. Kanin gave him another tongue-lashing, but when he saw it was to little avail, he finally said to me, "Stick around tonight. We'll shoot your stuff all by yourself."

So the company finally broke; Charles wiped his nose a few times, spat out some nonsense about America, and went home, presumably on the *Bounty*. I stuck around; so did Kanin and a camera crew.

The next day, during lunch, we all wandered over to a screening room, to view the latest rushes. The rushes are the uncut, unedited films of the day before. And there I was, big as life, writing the letter. No Laughton grimaces, over my shoulder.

The lights went up, and Laughton spoke up from a front-row seat. "When was that scene taken, Mr. Kanin?"

"After you went home, Captain."

Laughton got up. He walked from the screening room and onto the stage. He gathered up his jacket. "I am through with this film, Mr. Kanin." He took a few steps, and then he paused. Perhaps he expected Kanin to invite him back, to apologize.

Kanin instead followed him. "Your hat, Captain," he said.

Lombard followed them both, putting on display her amazing vocabulary.

Laughton was shocked by the reaction. He bellowed back. Now Kanin dropped the hostile act. He began to speak earnestly to Laughton. Laughton appeared adamant; finally we all went home again. Early.

The next day, not knowing what lay ahead, I got to the set, despondent. But Fat Charles was there, rubbing his hands, licking his lips, whining, wheedling. We made the picture; he never threatened to walk off again. But Kanin never could convince Laughton that it was a film we were making, and not a nose-wiping contest.

And so a good movie might have been a great movie, but wasn't. Laughton knocked us out of the box. Lombard was something to dream about. She turned on the humor, she turned on the pathos, she played wanton lover and tearful wife. She did it all with zest, and men fell in love with her all over the set, and when the film came out, all over the world. Then, two years later, all of thirty-three years old, this talented, beautiful woman who was as real as a kitchen stool and as glamorous as any movie star that has ever lived, climbed into a plane on a press junket, and died in the ensuing flaming wreckage.

I was nominated for an Academy Award, as Best Supporting Actor. Which means people in the industry thought I was one of the five best actors in my category, that year. I cherish the honor. I didn't win. Walter Brennan won, in *The Westerner*, a film in which he spent most of his time spitting into a cuspidor. Whenever I saw Brennan after that—we were and are good friends— I'd growl at him, "Beaten by a lousy spittoon," and he'd cackle with glee.

But there wasn't too much glee, by the time the Academy Awards were made in 1941. The mad dog had overrun Poland, briefly lay slobbering at the borders of the Lowlands, and then plunged across, to conquer the bewildered French. In Spain, the Loyalists had been crushed by an Army general named Franco who split the loyalties of American Catholics. Russia, that enigma, had signed a non-aggression treaty with Germany, shopping to buy time before she, too, would lie like meat before the ravening dog. (Meanwhile, the Russians kept their trigger fingers loose by slaughtering helpless Finns.)

So in 1941, when Walter Brennan won and I didn't, the world —again—little noted or long remembered. In Asia, the warlords plotted, a cunning people sent peace envoys to America, just as they were warming up their planes at home. The clouds thundered closer together, blacker, and on December 7, 1941, they crashed over the Pacific. We were at war.

I began work on another film, appropriately titled, *I Wake Up Screaming*.

16

This Is the Army???

Early in the war I contacted USO and asked to be assigned to a troupe to entertain our fighting men. USO told me to sit tight; they'd find a spot for me. So I made more movies. Real gems. Significant. *Miss Annie Rooney. Song of the Sarong.*

The kids grew. We prospered. The war dragged on, a million miles away, men dying in steaming jungles, on the sandy wastes of North Africa, on the bloody beaches of Tarawa and Makin.

Not that I wasn't doing my duty. The ranch Mary and I had bought in San Jacinto—in the Palm Springs area—had a patch reserved for use as a Victory Garden. The federal government would tell ranchers and farmers what it needed, and you'd suddenly find you weren't just a cattle rancher any more, but a tenderer of radishes. Originally, the 70-acre spread had been a real working ranch; we had twenty-five head of white-faced cattle and a field of alfalfa for fodder. Now we raised radishes, Belgian endive, tomatoes, and lettuce. On one acre of sandy loam, we grew watermelon; nothing else would have thrived in that sort of loose soil. We grew more watermelons than we could handle, great big 50-pounders. I gave melons away; I packed them into a trailer and drove to the studio and left them with a sign: HELP YOURSELF. Coyotes came at night (on the ranch, not at the studio) and ate melons. We still couldn't get rid of them all.

When I say "we," I mean not only Mary and me. Arthur

Baker practically ran the ranch; the kids were pretty much grown by now, so Arthur had time on his hands. Besides, he loved working the ranch. He milked the cows himself, made the butter. He tidied up the redwood ranchhouse (which was a mere ninety years old, and tilted like its age).

Ours was not the only ranch in the vicinity. Trav Rogers had his ranch; Frank Morgan had a nearby ranch; so did another friend, Bill Jones.

When the war broke out, the federal government got more and more into the act, and pretty soon we ranchers were becoming specialists. Trav raised horses; Frank Morgan raised Black Angus and Poland China hogs; Jones had cattle and alfalfa; gradually I became a hog rancher. Arthur Baker and I wired and fenced the spread, and we bought a herd of some forty to fifty hogs, nearly all sows with a couple of boars thrown in to keep things hopping.

Just about the time we'd finished fencing the hogs, complete with electric wire, the USO gave me a call. They were putting a group together; I would head it. I couldn't have asked for a grander troupe: Paulette Goddard, a delightful traveling companion; Keenan Wynn, Ed's son, a very funny man in his own right, and a man who could play a drunk as well as anybody in the world (he had trained well for it); and a prominent accordionist named Andy Arcari, who'd once played in the Philadelphia Symphony. Our liaison officer and public-relations man was Paul Zimmerman, today the sports editor of the Los Angeles *Times*.

Before I could leave, I had to hire a hog herdsman; the hogs had become a full-time job for one man, and Arthur Baker had the rest of the ranch to oversee. I had picked up a rule of thumb on hog-raising from a book on animal husbandry: "You keep a hog over five months, five weeks, five days, and five hours, and you're losing money." In other words, raise your hogs and sell them fast—while they're young—five months or so. Hogs are very prolific.

So I hired a man who said he knew all about hogs, and I impressed upon him the need to unload hogs while they're young and before you're overrun with them, and he nodded and said, "Yup," and that was that. You took what help you could find during the war. Besides, the hog herdsman said he truly loved hogs, which seemed to me a big plus.

I was gone slightly over six months. When I got back to the ranch, to check things out, I had to fight my way in. Hogs were all over. They'd eaten all the vegetables; they'd trampled the flowers they hadn't eaten. They met you at the gate, and you had to wade through hogs all the way to the kitchen door. They took over the walkway, stood rump to snout along the gravel road; they owned the joint. Maybe there were 350 hogs in all. My hog herdsman had loved the hogs too much. He just didn't have the heart to sell them. I fired him (when I could make myself understood over the squealing squalling din), and I called a trucker in San Jacinto and had the hogs out of there and to market in two hours.

The sight, however, must have haunted me. For two years I couldn't eat pork. Today, when I do eat pork, I often break out. I have developed an allergy to pig. Don't ask me why.

So I am not too sure—today—which was more hectic, the home front or the overseas front.

Our troupe—Goddard, Wynn, Arcari, Paul Zimmerman, and I —assembled in New York in February of 1943, for our briefing. Briefing meant typhoid shots, tetanus shots, smallpox vaccination, malaria pills. I felt like a punchboard. Briefing meant papers to fill out. Because I was in charge, I had the most papers. An Army officer explained how serious it all was.

"Here is your money," he said. He handed me $2500 in cash. "You will pay every member of the troupe $10 a day. You will keep a record of all expenses."

He meant all expenses: every meal, every tip, every newspaper, Paulette's lipstick, Andy's packs of gum, everything.

"Where are we going, pal?" I asked him.

"You'll know when you get there."

I wore a major's insignia. I wanted to know why.

"In case of capture," he said, "you will be treated better. They don't kill majors."

28. Paulette Goddard and I doing our routine for the troops.

29. Keenan Wynn and I indulging in a skit. (U.S Air Force Photo)

My wartime trip to the CBI theater of operations.

31. Paulette and I resting in India during our trip.

0. I study the terrain of the area e are going to.

32. My talk to a speech class of laryngectomees at the National Hospital for Speech Disorders in New York in 1962 that really started me on my present work. (American Cancer Society)

33. An address to the members of the New Haven Lost Chord Club. (American Cancer Society)

34. In 1963 I had the honor of meeting with President John F. Kennedy while in Washington helping to kick off the annual Cancer Crusade.

35. A real thrill for Mary and me, our audience with Pope Pius XII. (G. *Felici*)

36. I introduce two cured cancer persons, Mrs. Alice Holton (l.) and Miss Linda Turnipseed, to President Lyndon B. Johnson at the beginning of the Cancer Crusade in 1966.

37. A scene from *The Best Man* with Gene Raymond. It was during the run of *The Best Man* that I found I had cancer. (*Millar of Hollywood*)

38. Jimmy Doolittle presents me with the Criss Award while V. J. Skutt, Chairman of the Board of Mutual of Omaha, and Dr. Charles Mayo look on. *(Mutual of Omaha)*

One of the proudest moments in my life.

39. The best moment of all. *(LIFE Photograph by Lee Johnson © Time Inc.)*

40. The whole family helps celebrate the Criss Award. Front row (l. to r.), my brother Ed's wife Cooee, Margaret Kenny, Mary's aunt, my son Leslie, Connie and Joe Kenny, Mary's brother and his wife; back row, Tracey Anne and William III, my son Barrie's children, Barrie, and his wife, Kay. (Mutual of Omaha)

Among those there were:

41. Bob Hope and Casey Stengel. (Mutual of Omaha)

42. Eloise and Pat O'Brien. (Mutual of Omaha)

43. Veronique and Gregory Peck. (Mutual of Omaha)

44. Ray Bolger. (Mutual of Omaha)

45. Despite everything, I'm still able to enjoy life. (*Mutual of Omaha*)

"Thanks, pal."

We broke in our act at a camp on Long Island, to iron out the edges. Paulette was the cheesecake, and the big hit. Keenan set up an old burlesque routine, he played the dirty doctor, Paulette the sexy nurse, and Andy and I straight men. I emceed the show, did a monologue; Andy played the accordion. A simple show. Somehow the boys liked it.

One day at noon we got orders to leave for Miami that evening. The usual routine those days was to use Miami for embarkation to the Far East. I wandered over to the 21 Club on 52nd Street where I knew the bartender. I told him I was probably going to the Far East, and he hauled out two bottles of scotch. "If you run into Gene Markey, give him these," he said. "He's in New Delhi."

So began my other true role in the war. I was a bookkeeper for our troupe, and now I was a messenger boy. We got to Miami and reported to our rooms at the Floridian Hotel. One minute later, Paulette came bouncing downstairs.

"This is insanity," she said. "Call that a room? It's a closet with a naked light bulb. I demand it be changed."

The officer in charge smiled faintly. "This is the Army, Miss Goddard."

It became the refrain. At first I rejected it.

I picked up the phone and very grandly called the Roney Plaza. I identified myself. "I'd like a suite for myself, for Miss Paulette Goddard, Mr. Keenan Wynn, and Mr. Andy Arcari. Immediately."

"What year?" the clerk said.

So we stayed at the Floridian. I roomed with a fat guy who snored better than Guy Kibbee. He'd been there for weeks, on alert. This meant he couldn't leave the hotel. He was waiting for orders. I took to running up cigarettes, booze, food, anything to keep him from getting more stir crazy.

But we enjoyed ourselves, Paulette, Keenan, Andy, and I. We ate at the Roney Plaza, drank champagne with supper, and saw the shows at night. We were told how tough it would be to find any good whiskey once we left the States, so we made up for future losses. It was a lovely war. So far.

"Do you want to be paid?" I asked them.

"No," they said. "We've got plenty of money."

I marked it all down, in the book the Army provided. I paid for everything out of the $2500 cash. A thousand dollars disappeared in the five days we were in Miami. Paulette was off my hands most of the time. She'd latched onto a general who was squiring her around. One night she said, "I know where we're going."

"Where?"

"Over the Hump. China-Burma-India."

So I called Mary, and told her, and she said, "Bill and Mary Morrow are here. Bill's brother is in New Delhi. Look him up, if you can."

I marked it down.

Before we left Miami, we had another series of briefings. I met Father John Hughes, a Maryknoll priest, who said to me, "Bill, there's a Maryknoller in China, a Father Pearson. They'll know where he is when you get to Kunming. The Catholic USO on Madison Avenue in New York has taken up a collection, to send him vestments, hosts, and wine. I'd like you to bring them to him."

"A pleasure, Father."

Two bottles of scotch, a kid to look up in New Delhi, reversible vestments, 3000 hosts, and two bottles of wine, for a missionary priest in China. I started to resemble Ringling Brothers, between cities.

At five one morning, a sergeant banged on my door. "This is it!" he sang out. He came in, to make sure I'd heard. I'd have heard him back home in Beverly Hills.

I got dressed. The guy I roomed with looked up weakly when I got ready to go. "Send help," he said. For all I know he's still in that hotel room, snoring away his life.

We flew out on a DC-4, sealed orders in our hands. They read: The CBI Theatre. China-Burma-India. The Hump. Surprise!

The States drifted away behind me; we began to move south

before we moved west, all for the purpose of going east. This is the Army. We stopped at Port-au-Prince, Haiti; we stopped for a layover in Georgetown, the capital of British Guiana. Georgetown was plush. We stayed at the general's quarters, twenty servants waiting on us hand and foot, and more scotch flowing than I'd ever seen. This is the Army? So much for the rumor about no whiskey to be had.

We practiced our show on the plane. Those who weren't airsick applauded. The others stayed sick. We went down the coast to Natal, for two days, and then we headed for Ascension Island, a British dot halfway between South America and Africa. It is a long push for a DC-4, so I took a sleeping pill and woke up six hours later, to find everyone peeping out the blackout curtains. I peeped with them. One propeller stood straight up, dead.

"What do we do?" I asked the captain.

"Nothing. We're past the point of no return. We fly on three engines."

"Any problems?"

"Only if we run out of fuel."

"Then?"

"We throw things out of the plane. If that doesn't work, we jump."

THIS IS THE ARMY!

We landed (phew!) at Ascension, hours late. They repaired the plane and we flew to the Gold Coast of Africa, primitive huts, thatched roofs, natives sitting by the water, fishing. We billeted at Accra, on the coast, for two days. A captain named Carleton Young, a radio announcer who'd done some acting— he was in Archibald McLeish's radio drama, *The Fall of the City* —ran special services at Accra. He took us to our tents. I noticed a box sticking out from under my cot. I looked under. Three cases of scotch. Under each of the four cots in the room, three cases of scotch.

Young worked hard for that whiskey. He knew the ambassador of one of the smaller African countries down the coast, and he also knew that the ambassador was a teetotaler. The scotch was the ambassador's embassy allowance, for which he had no use. So

Young went down in a fleet of small boats, and brought back the scotch. He bought them for $23 a case. Water is dearer.

"Can I buy a case?" I asked.

"Not a chance. I need it for the boys stuck here." The encampment at Accra was fairly big.

We had a party the night before we were to leave. I made sure Captain Young had two drinks for every one of mine. Finally he passed out. I tucked him in. A sergeant came through at four A.M., and we got ready to fly out. "Just take one of those cases to the plane," I said. The sergeant looked at Young's silver bars; he looked at my gold maple leaf. "Right, Major," he said.

I left $23 in an envelope, with a note: *Dear Carleton. Just so we can toast you wherever you may be. Thanks for agreeing to sell me the case last night. You are a prince. Remember me to the ambassador.*

We flew to Maiduguri in Nigeria, for more shots. The typhoid shot in New York and in Miami had no effect. Three was the charm. I walked toward the plane, and I fell as if shot dead. I came to on the plane with a raging fever. I thought I would die. Then I thought I wouldn't and prayed I would. Khartoum was a blur of pain and fever; I looked down and saw the Nile; it looked like green bile. Ethiopia is a long green carpet; green made me nauseous. I was well by the time we hit Aden, Arabia. We had strict orders in Aden; never travel in a single car or jeep or truck. Always at least two.

"Why?"

"One jeep, alone, will be stopped by hordes of natives. In two minutes, the jeep will be gone, motor, wheels, everything. The natives sell the parts, back to the motor pool. Two jeeps, they leave alone."

We traveled in tandem. Except for Keenan. Rules were not made for Keenan. He'd find a motorcycle and tear off for town. He was a wild man, on a cycle. Nobody stopped him. Nobody could. He had reason for being a wild man, on this trip. Either in Aden, or at Masirah, or Agra, someplace along the line, he got his draft orders. Report at once to your induction board. He ripped off a choice reply, and kept on going, with us. We refueled at

Masirah Island, in the Arabian Sea, and flew on to Karachi, today the capital of Pakistan, before heading for Agra. I saw the Taj Mahal from the air; it looks better on a postcard. Sandbags covered the marble statuary, the jewels had been removed, to protect it in case of bombing. We went on to New Delhi. We'd been gone eight or nine days all together. I felt like a pogo stick.

At New Delhi we checked into the Imperial Hotel, a magnificent establishment in the new city. Each of us had a private suite; I had twelve or fifteen servants. Maybe more. One guy ran my tub, one shined my shoes, another cleaned the bathroom, one laid out my clothes, another scrubbed the floor. It was beautiful, sybaritic, slothful. We spent money in town, and relaxed. I looked up Bill Morrow's brother. Bill Morrow had written the Jack Benny radio show and the Crosby radio show. I called the kid brother and invited him over for a drink.

"We're not allowed in the Imperial," he said.

"Why not?"

"It's for officers."

"Well, I'm an officer, and I'm ordering you over here."

"Can I bring a buddy?"

"You can bring the whole platoon."

He brought a buddy, and while they were drinking with me, I phoned Gene Markey. Gene was the Navy commandant. We'd have a party.

So Gene walked in, and immediately stiffened. "What are these enlisted men doing here?"

"Drinking," I said. "Join us. You know Bill Morrow? This is his brother. And his buddy."

Markey unbent slightly, but not much, so when it came time for me to give him the scotch the bartender at the 21 had put in my charge, I shortchanged Gene by one bottle. He thanked me, stiffly, and went off. Paulette, Keenan, and Andy joined us, and with the two GIs, we polished off the other bottle.

We flew on to Chabua, jumping off spot for planes going over the Hump to Kunming, China, and very likely the world's largest hotel at the time. Because conditions for crossing the Hump were at best doubtful, a continual backup of men formed at Chabua,

often as many as 25,000 men, waiting to go up and over, or else
just arriving back down. An Air Force captain from Red Bluff,
California, ran this sprawling hotel. Naturally his previous civilian
experience well qualified him for the job. He'd been a farmer.
Actually, he probably was the best hotel manager in the whole
world, a man who made do. Take the way he fed his complement.
He did this by a combination of confiscation and accommoda-
tion. He'd made an arrangement with the mess sergeant of the
train that brought troops into the area. The mess sergeant always
would appropriate from quartermaster three times as much food
as he needed, under the theory that he never really knew how
many troops he'd have on board. But the mess sergeant also
knew not to have any food left over; you always have to justify
yourself to the quartermaster. So as the train neared Chabua on
each trip, the sergeant would dump off the excess food and supplies at a siding just before climbing the final knoll into Chabua.
Had anybody ever asked him, he would have said he had to
jettison the stuff; otherwise the train never would have made the
hill.

Meanwhile, our hotel manager-farmer-Air Force captain would
send out a cadre from his hotel-encampment and pick up whatever lay alongside the tracks. What lay alongside the tracks was
usually a mountain of canned hams, Spam, C rations, K rations,
tomato juice, sacks of potatoes, beans, sugar, flour, frozen meats,
the works.

But the hotel manager could also go the gourmet route as
well. At Chabua, after the show one night, we asked him for a
steak.

"Why not?" he said. He got one of his soldiers to shoot a
sacred cow. Who am I to look a gift filet in the mouth.

We barbecued the filets. They curled up like hot leather; they
tasted like leather. That's gourmet-cooking? That's what you get,
Gargan, knocking off sacred cows. Later I ran into Merrill's
Marauders; they told stories of traveling through India on open
trains. They took rifle practice by shooting sacred cows. But then,
the Marauders took practice by shooting each other as well. When

they got bored, they'd practice drawing; one Texas boy managed to have his hand shot off. This is the Army.

We did three or four shows at Chabua, and then received orders to fly out, over the Hump. But before we boarded the plane, more orders came in, scrubbing us from the flight. The plane took off, without us, and never was heard from again.

Finally we got a C-26, with bucket seats. Paul Zimmerman, our public relations colonel, told us to put on all our clothes.

"Even so," he warned, "you won't be warm."

We took off and began to fly straight up. We sucked on oxygen tubes, to replace the thinning air. It got cold. At 16,000 feet we flew over Japanese airfields, all lit up. We were in a narrow pass in the Himalayas, the wind a cat-o'-nine-tails; Zeroes would need more room to maneuver than this narrow slit in the range, and the wind gusts would be treacherous to any fighter plane. We flew safely on. It got colder. At 23,000 feet I passed out, seconds ahead of Paulette. I came to in ten minutes, my blood properly adjusted, but I felt naked to the cold. At 25,000 feet you could look up and still see snowcapped endless peaks. My ears began to ache. So did Andy's. We flew some 300 miles through the Himalayas, feeling like the original abominable snowmen, and then we broke out of a maze of hills over Kunming, China below.

We were coming down from over 25,000 feet to a city that lay 7000 feet above sea level, so we had to circle and slowly lower for forty-five minutes to acclimate ourselves to the abrupt drop in altitude. The city was lit up like a candle. Back in the States, Pittsburgh would be blacked out. Here, on a raging war front, Kunming blazed with lights. After we landed, we were jeeped to the American Red Cross, for hot chocolate (never a better drink), and taken to our quarters. I asked my number one boy, a polite smiling Chinese, where the men's room was, and he told me, and I took off my jacket, and went. When I came back and put my jacket on, my Parker 51 set was missing. The set had not as yet been marketed; it had been a gift from the Parker people. The next day, while downtown with Paul Zimmerman and Andy Arcari, we stopped in front of what looked like a Chinese hock shop, and there in the window sat my Parker set, on sale for 300,000 Chinese dollars, fifty or sixty American dollars. This is the Army.

We dined with General Claire Chennault, and his beautiful Chinese wife. Chennault had the face of a hem-stitched hawk, a forceful man who conducted a one-sided conversation. We listened.

Then we hopped to Kwelin. I ran into a Father Smith, the chaplain at the base, and I asked where I might find Father Pearson.

"What do you want with him?"

I showed him the hosts. I mentioned the vestments.

"The hosts won't keep much longer," he said. "I'd better keep them. He needs the vestments."

"Well, where is he?"

"Is that all you brought for him?" Father Smith smiled a sweet smile.

"You know I brought something else."

"And what would that be?"

"Two bottles of wine."

"For one bottle I'll tell you where he is."

Flummoxed by the Father. I gave up one bottle. He told.

Meanwhile, I'd let myself be talked into a crap game with General Casey Roberts, and the staff officers of his bomber wing. It was their diversion, gambling. Every day planes took off to fly to Hanoi, unload their bombs on the Japanese, and head back. Some did not make it back. We did a matinee the first day in Kwelin and during my monologue the planes began returning. The general stepped out on the runway, for a good view. We stopped the show. I walked out with him. Together we counted. They all returned. The planes touched ground. Men tumbled out of the planes, and kissed the ground, threw their arms about each other. The planes looked like Swiss cheese; gaping holes from flak riddled the fuselage and wings. Finally the show continued, but you couldn't touch this other for drama.

Still, they liked us. Maybe they liked us because of the other drama. We were artificial, a release from flak and blazing cockpits.

Paulette was wonderful release; the men screamed when they saw her. They hushed when Andy cranked up his concert accordion; they laughed so hard they cried at our foolish burlesque routines. It made the ovation for Red Regan seem insignificant.

In the backroom of the Officers' Club, I shot craps with General Roberts and four or five of his officers. I couldn't lose. Everything I threw turned up winners. I made eight or nine passes in a row. I broke the game, $3000 richer.

"You don't think you're going to get out of China with that money?" Roberts asked.

"I doubt it," I said. "But I'll give it a try."

We flew out, to Choiswan, and had to hold up in the air at the airport. The Japanese had come in a few minutes before, bombing holes in the landing field, raking the P-51s on the ground. As we circled, we could see the repair work. Coolies came out of the surrounding hills, carrying rocks on their heads. They walked in a straight line to the field, dumped the rocks and walked back. Thousands of them, like a trail of ants. In a half hour, we were waved down. At Choiswan, I spoke to the Commandant, who told me where to find Father Pearson.

He turned out to be a strapping man, working in a nearby Chinese village, as Maryknollers do. I gave him the vestments, told him Father Smith had confiscated the hosts because they were going bad, and handed him one bottle of wine.

"One?" he said gently. "I was told two."

"Take it up with Father Smith," I said.

"Oh, that pirate!" he said softly.

I went to Mass, with seventy GIs, in a tiny chapel. One GI passed the hat; I figured General Roberts wouldn't get all the money, no matter what. I put two hundred bucks of it in the hat.

That night we did our show in a little theater covered with pasha leaves. Father Pearson sat in the front row, roaring at our burlesque, even beaming at Paulette's cheesecake. When it was over, he came up to me. "Oh, thank you for the money," he said. "It couldn't have been anyone but you."

"Thank General Roberts and his men," I said.

We got back onto our plane. It was like the road shows of my

early stage life, a night or two, and then the trail. We flew to
Chungking, the airport nestled in hills, the city looking much like
San Francisco. All the time, onto and off planes, I would find a
GI and ask him to carry the case of scotch. I had no idea where
or when it would be drunk, but I felt like saving it for a special
occasion. I hadn't had a drink since New Delhi. My ears bothered me, and so did Andy's, and for all the baths, we were starting
to grow moldy, like old cheese. Our clothes began to smell like
dry rot. But the show had—again—become the target. We went
on, and the job was clear. Sprinkle the magic. Make 'em laugh.
Make 'em listen, make 'em cheer, make 'em whistle, applaud,
ogle, but mainly, make 'em laugh.

We did a show at Chungking in what was called the Broadway
Theatre, 400 seats, a fine public address system. The first night,
Keenan on one side of the theater, I on the other, working our
burlesque routine—selling and giving away things from an apron
basket ("two tickets to last week's show at the Roxy; a toilet
seat; a photograph of Vice-President Truman—if you win both
the toilet seat and the photograph, the seat makes a beautiful
frame"), I saw sitting on the aisle two men I knew. Dick Watts
and Brooks Atkinson, New York drama critics.

"Hold it!" I roared to Keenan.

Both men had been marvelous to me in the old days, on
Broadway, particularly Watts. If I had a walk-on, Watts would
mention how well I walked. If I had a single line, he'd rave over
the delivery. It got to be a gag. No matter what I was in—there
it would be: "The outstanding part was played by William
Gargan, as the butler." Or the gangster, or whatever.

They were with the Office of War Information—OWI—in
Chungking, and when the show was over, they came backstage.
We were all invited to OWI headquarters, but before I went, I
asked a captain to drive me back to my quarters and then to the
OWI. Now I had a reason to crack open the scotch. That is, if
I lived through the drive. The captain's car was a charcoal-
burning jeep; we stopped two or three times while he stoked the
fire. We finally climbed to the hospital where we were billeted,
and I tore open the box of scotch.

"Is that what I think it is?" the captain said.

"It isn't fuel for your jeep," I said.

"I'll give you $2500 American for it."

"You can't give me a quarter for it."

We unpacked it. One bottle had been broken, but the scotch had been absorbed by all the wrappings. The other eleven looked like perfect soldiers. We took six bottles to the OWI mansion— a wooden Victorian palace—and I marched the six soldiers to the mantelpiece. At last I could pay these two men for their hospitality and generosity to a poor ham. I broke my fast with a single drink, the toast delivered by Watts: "To the greatest sonofagun that ever came out of America!" That was me. This was the Army, but to me it was a showcase. It was fun. I was the Big G again, having a ball. This was where the next laugh was.

After breakfast the next morning I said to a sergeant assigned to me, "Take three bottles to Dick Watts. Keep one for yourself. Then pack the last one, with the rest of my things. Make sure Watts get those three bottles." I knew the sergeant could get up to $500 for three bottles of scotch. "I've got your name and number."

"I'll deliver them," he said.

I never knew, of course, whether Watts got the bottles, until one day back in the States I read the *Herald Tribune* and there on the drama page was a piece by Dick, headlined: "Broadway Goes to Chungking," a long rave of our show, with, as usual, special attention to Bill Gargan. The last line was the tipoff: "I want our benefactor to know he cured an awful lot of hangovers the next morning." He'd got the bottles, hair of the dog.

We flew back to Kwelin, having made a complete circle of the bases in China, and General Roberts met me with outstretched hands. I shook his hand; he had a pair of dice in it. "The boys have fresh money," he said. "We want at you."

So they had at me, and I got lucky again, and came close to breaking them again. But my heart wasn't in it. I began to give them all kinds of odds. What kind of war was this where I kept getting rich off the soldiers? I finally got rid of most of the money I'd taken the first time.

We started back, tired, filthy, aching. My ear was inflamed, Andy's was ruptured. Paulette was going on nerve. Keenan was going on all fours.

We flew out of China, over the Hump. I froze again, and my ear burned like a piece of hot ice. We lay over one day at Chabua, and began to work our way down the Stilwell Road, playing in tiny clearings while men with rifles stood guard on the perimeter, just in case. We got our signals crossed the very first day on the Road. We'd planned to fly to one base, but somehow we overshot the mark, and when we landed, three jeeps tore out of the underbrush to meet the plane. An excited officer got out.

"What are you doing here?"

We told him.

"There's a Japanese patrol a mile away." We were taken by jeep to the underbrush where we ate a silent lunch with a small eyeglassed man getting on in years. But General Joe Stilwell was the same vinegary soldier he'd always been. Paulette asked him, "Any chance of getting to the front?"

"You will eat your lunch," General Stilwell said, "and get the hell out."

We gave our show anyway, on the back of a truck, and I caught on to the routine. A plane would zoom by, and the anti-aircraft guns would point at it, until somebody said, "It's ours." Then we would continue. It raises hell with your timing. So the next time I got into a joke and a plane roared overhead, I shouted, "It's ours!" and as everybody relaxed, I polished off the joke. The show must go on. (It was ours.)

We flew from Stilwell's headquarters at Shinbwiyan some forty miles down the Hukwang Valley, where we landed in a clearing just after Merrill's Marauders had cleaned it out. Japanese bodies lay in the broiling sun. The bodies had been piled on logs, with wood piled on top of them, and the whole grisly sandwich set on fire. Every so often you'd hear a pop, as unspent shells in the dead soldiers' cartridge belts would ignite and explode.

We played the Road, we played the hospitals; we saw the Naga headhunters and their beautiful barebreasted wives, and we downed Myitha meat, that tastes like veal, with our rice wine. We reached Ledo, at the end of the Burma Road, where Marco Polo once walked. Goddard's clothing was a mess. "I smell like a polar bear," she wailed. The rest of us smelled worse. We washed with cold water out of rigged-up spigots; we shaved with cold water, which is only slightly preferable to shaving with a lawn mower. We flew from Ledo, finally, to Calcutta, where dead children lay in the streets. The poverty, the starvation of India at the time dwarfed the imagination. The casualties of World War II were minute, compared to the deaths from starvation in India. Women would beg with a starving baby in their arms. If the baby died, the woman would go out in the street and buy another baby; the baby was a gimmick for more money. Life had no value. I met a man from Reuters News agency, and he took me to the Burning Ghats, on the Ganges, where the bodies of yesterday's dead are brought every morning, by truck and trailer. Oil is poured on the bodies and lit. A man wandered about the Ghats, in rags and turban, carrying a staff. Legend had it he had brought his brother there, and when they burned his brother, his mind had snapped. He would not leave; he had become a sort of unofficial caretaker, wandering among the charred bodies. They said he was leprous. Who would get close enough to know?

I went back to Calcutta, to the British-American Club, and fell off the wagon with a long loud thump. We were there a week; I drank to rid the memories of the Ghats; the women in the streets, with those black stick figures in their arms, dying (or even dead) of starvation. This is not why I had come. I had come for laughs, to give them and take them back with me.

We ran into more non-laughs, in the form of a pilot who decided we needed some thrills. The guy was a major, one of those air jockeys you run into once in a while, a pilot who thinks the plane he's flying is his special toy. I guess he wanted to show off for Goddard. I guess he was crazy. I guess I am more sensibly chicken than I ever realized. The major wanted us to go down across the Japanese lines, into an area totally surrounded by Japanese troops, to give our show. Except, of course, we didn't know any of this. A sergeant from Brooklyn tipped me off finally. "I hear you're going to such-and-such," he said, mentioning the town's name. "Yeah," I said. "Another town, another show."

He shook his head. "Some show. You can't get in there. If you do get in, the Japanese will have you surrounded. You'll never get out."

I took this information to Paul Zimmerman, our liaison man, and I added: "I don't mind for myself. But why take chances with Paulette?" (Which makes me very brave, for the records.)

Paul agreed, and went to the major, who came to me in a small fury. "You are in the Air Corps," he said stiffly. "You will take orders from me."

"Hell, no, I won't," I said. "I'm a civilian. I'm only a major if I'm captured." Or if I have to outrank a captain over a case of scotch.

So we didn't fly into that hornets' nest; he found other ways to torture us. He located a storm front, and rode it like the pure air jockey he was. We hit the front, and Goddard went straight up and hit her head on the plane ceiling, and was knocked cold. When we got ready to land, he overshot the field, and roared back to make his pass again. Goddard tottered out and gulped down three-quarters of a tumbler of whiskey. A sergeant on the plane, the steward, said, "They can court-martial me, but I won't fly with that man ever again."

We took Paulette to the local hospital, her nerves like violin strings. We did a show, without her, a poor shadow of a show, even though Keenan put on an extra bit that laid them in the aisles. We needed Paulette. At New Delhi, I checked in to the Inspector-General's office, which was run by Eddie Eagan, the former Rhodes scholar and amateur boxer, and Eagan said he'd look into our air jockey major. (Back in the States a couple of years later I ran into Eddie at Madison Square Garden on a Friday fight night. "The pilot never flew again," Eagan told me. "He turned out to be psycho." And we had the proof.)

At New Delhi, Keenan received another notice from his draft board. This, too, was the Army, a perfect picture of the war, if you had a cockeyed camera, a funhouse mirror. Here was a guy who'd been in Burma, India, China, North Africa—landing on bombed-out airstrips, huddling in clearings while Japanese patrols roamed within miles—and now he was going to have to rush home to meet a draft board, to determine whether he was in shape to be sent to a fighting front.

We celebrated Keenan's notice by going out on the town. By this time the last of the original $2500 was gone. I went to the finance office and asked for more money.

"How much do you need?"

"Another thousand."

"Ask for $2500."

I did, and in a few days, I received a thousand. This is the Army. I paid off Paulette, who had to remain in New Delhi until she felt better. Our show had run its course. Keenan took off, for the States. Andy and I continued flying back the same way we had come. At one port they told Andy—whose ears were worse than mine, and mine were bad enough—he ought not to fly any more.

"Take the boat," they said.

"How long will it take to get home by boat?" Andy asked.

"Ninety days."

"I'd rather be dead."

He almost was dead anyway. He and I. We were in a DC-3 over the southern desert of Iran, when the wheels locked and would not come down. Rather than risk landing with locked wheels at a stone strip, the pilot decided to put her down on the desert. We dumped the gas, covered our heads with blankets, and prayed. I thought: You asked for it, Gargan.

We landed, and it was like landing on a huge pillow. We bounced once, lightly, and came to a halt. Perfect, perfect landing. A truck picked us up, and our return trip continued. We stopped in Cairo for two days, in Casablanca for two days, and then went on to the Azores, so badly fogged in, we were billeted until the weather cleared. As I headed for my billet, I passed a tent and heard inside a familiar voice. It was Keenan. He'd left New Delhi two or three days before us; we'd taken our time; he'd been rushing like crazy. But in typical Army style, we caught up.

But we split up again. The planes from the Azores for Newfoundland were each assigned a different altitude. My pilot flew at 8000 feet. We could see a weather front ahead. We hit it a half hour later, but luck was with us. It opened up, and we went through like a knife through soft butter. We landed, and then a few minutes later, Wynn's plane came in. He'd flown at 6000 feet, and hit the front flush. They carried Wynn off the plane. I heard one man say, "I think he's dead." The man at the other end of the stretcher said, "Naw. He's just out."

Then Keenan came alongside. He opened one eye. "I want my money," he said. So I paid him off, $10 a day for all the days of the tour. "I want you to know," I shouted after him, as they lugged him away, "you were worth every dollar of it!"

The first thing I saw of America was Portland, Maine, blacked out. I never saw a more beautiful sight.

17

"God Called. Pick Out a Contract."

The war marked a dividing line in my life. In America's life, as well. The nation entered the war a confused people. The war was not of our making. Pearl Harbor had been visited on us, and Hitler had sprung across borders uninvited. With the war's end, we had become the acknowledged leader of the world. The time had come to live up to the leadership, to accept the responsibility. If the Depression had not sufficiently buried the Jazz Age, the war had. We had danced all night on broken glass, but the dawn had broke, the ball was over. And our feet hurt. We sang a song in World War II, "When the Lights Go on Again, All Over the World," and the way the song had it, when the lights did go on, all would be good again, fun again, Mom's apple pie again. But it wasn't. The lights went on, but the candles had been blown out.

You didn't have to wait for the war to end, to find out.

I came back from the USO, my ears so swollen Mary called me Dumbo, and we borrowed an apartment in New York from a friend, Eddie Cohen. Under contract to M-G-M at the time, I got ready to make a personal appearance at the M-G-M-owned Capitol Theatre on Broadway, one of those moviehouse-stage show theaters so popular in the 1930s and 1940s.

I went on the first week in June of 1943, and the lights were blacked out, and then a white spotlight swooped down on me,

and the band played, "Coming in on a Wing and a Prayer."
Bill Gargan, fresh from the CBI Theatre, began his act.

I opened by saying, "The last time I was on Broadway was
with Leslie Howard in *The Animal Kingdom*," just to remind
them I began right here, and was really one of the boys. I went
on to a lighthearted patter, but I didn't get much response for
the first few minutes of the show. It improved later, but I fretted
about the opening as the curtain fell. We had five shows to do,
and I wondered what was wrong with the opening lines.

Then I found out.

I stepped out of the theater, and there was the headline.
LESLIE HOWARD KILLED. PLANE SHOT DOWN OVER
BAY OF BISCAY.

I did the five shows, with a stone in my chest. I changed that
first line, and got my laughs, but now I didn't need them or
want them.

And I didn't need the war to end to prove to me the candles
had been blown out.

I went back to Hollywood, after my engagement at the Capitol, and plunged back to work. I made movies, and you couldn't
tell a new one from an old one. *Swing Fever, She Gets Her Man,
The Bells of St. Mary's*—where Bing heard me sing and wondered about my health—*Murder in the Music Hall*. That was my
1944 fare, my return from the Hump.

Still, life was different on the West Coast. Los Angeles had
changed, totally and irrevocably. From all over the country, people poured into the Basin. Bing sang, "Make the San Fernando
Valley Your Home," and the people made it, pushing across the
Hollywood Hills into what once had been old ranchland. Mary
and I had lived in the Valley briefly, renting a house from a
friend, Al St. John. It had a pool. Except Al had had the pool
built on weekends by his friends, instead of by a pool construction outfit, and the pool leaked six inches of water every
day. We had the largest water bill in the Valley.

Freeways sliced into once-lonely acreage; ticky-tack houses
standing cheek-by-jowl uprooted the orange groves; the velvet
went out of the air, and smog sneaked in. A way of life began

to fade. We still went to premieres at Grauman's Chinese, in rented limousines and dripping with borrowed jewelry, smiles pasted on our faces as we neared the kleiglights, but the glamour was disappearing as well. Producers in berets, behind baronial desks, slowly were replaced by hardnosed young men, back from the wars, both real and the bloodier ones on Madison Avenue. A new breed took over Hollywood, and before you made a movie, you checked with your banker in Switzerland to see about the exchange rate in dollars for overseas distribution.

Television sets began to show up in friends' homes, tiny curiosity five-inch screens at first, the picture spoiled by dark gray dots that swirled on a light gray background, and which we all started to call snow. When it didn't snow, you got Indian head patterns, or, even better, hours of blank programming. But it was here, and the coaxial cable began to stretch across the continent to bring New York entertainment into a Beverly Hills home.

Typically, I went backwards in time. When I had been out of work in the late 1920s, the stage dying and movies a vigorous newcomer, I wound up in vaudeville. Now I made my big move, in the face of technology. I hit radio.

With my agent, Ken Dolan, I dreamed up a half-hour mystery package, hired two writers, and cut a couple of records. I played a private dick who solves murders and other crimes in exactly twenty-six minutes, leaving four minutes for commercials and station breaks. We trotted it over to ABC, and the studio liked it well enough, but nobody else did, so we went on without the commercials, on a sustaining basis. Which is to say ABC paid us, while it, and I and my agent looked for sponsors. Sometimes we found one. For a while, the Rainier Brewing Company sponsored the show. When it came time for Rainier to renew, the show's producer suggested I go to San Francisco and meet with the Rainier bosses, ingratiate myself with them. You know me, the perfect ingratiator. I met a man named Humphreys and his Yesmen at a conference, and for the first twenty-five minutes Humphreys ignored me. Finally he said: "Just what do you do for a living, Mr. Gargan?"

"I'm your most expensive salesman," I said. "I do *Murder Will Out.*"

He apologized. "I don't listen to radio," he said.

"Well, we're even," I said. "I don't drink your beer."

Pretty soon we were terminated.

But it kept me busy, with or without sponsors. Radio work was busy work. It was up to you, a sound-effects man, and the microphone, to get it all across. No two-hour delay on a tricky lighting effect or a star who didn't like the way a closeup had been done.

I knew about radio, from first hand. Shortly after I hit Hollywood, under contract to RKO, I had taken over as emcee of the first live coast-to-coast radio show, *Stars Over Hollywood,* one hour a week, where RKO paraded its stars into listeners' homes. We had Mary Pickford, Lionel Barrymore, Leslie Howard, and others, all for free. The thing I remember best about the show was the tons of mail it received. Just for comparisons, Constance Bennett, who was one of movies' biggest stars in those years, was receiving an estimated 5000 letters a week, which nicely matched her $30,000-a-week salary. I was receiving five to ten sacks of mail a week, untold thousands of letters, which nicely matched my salary of $2.98 a week. Not that I let the mail go to my head. One day I opened a sack, and the first letter read: "Why don't you get off the air, you bum!" The others were less flattering. Still, it had its compensation. We did the show from the Cocoanut Grove, where I met Phil Harris, and another friendship developed that has lasted to this day.

So I knew radio, and its busy-ness. Still, it wasn't all that busy. An hour a week, plus rehearsal time, plus an occasional movie, still did not fill up my life. With the war over, and too many people forgetting too quickly, Mary and I took to entertaining World War II wounded. One day we had a bunch of amputees over at 512 North Palm, together with a priest, Father Paul Redmond, who'd gone ashore in the first wave at Guadalcanal, against the orders of his Marine Corps superiors. I'll never forget that Sunday afternoon, with the amputees, men with an arm off, or a leg, or two limbs, or four, men who had been torn apart, literally, yet spiritually had refused to wilt. You never heard such laughter as that afternoon, one-legged men hopping up to help no-legged men, getting the booze, pouring it (if they had arms), passing it. And always laughing.

Physical disability is cruel, but it is not as cruel as spiritual weakness. You can live with one leg, but you can't with no soul. Such a man is an empty shell, the spiritual fire gone out. He is better off dead.

If you truly have a soul, of course, it doesn't really matter what you are or what you do in the physical realm. Around this time, 1945 or so, an actor I'd known for years, a guy who'd been a vaudevillian and later had done bit parts in some of the Warner films I'd made in 1936 and 1937, dropped by to see me.

"Bill," he said, a wide grin on his face, a man absolutely delighted with a decision he'd made, "I'm giving up the theater. I'm giving up show business. I'm going to become a lay brother, in a Jesuit order. I've got a car outside, an old jalopy, and I'm selling it to pay off my debts. But I need another $300. I want to go back East and see my mother in Massachusetts before I join the Order. Can you help me?"

In the Order, of course, he'd be making and, he'd hope, keeping a vow of poverty. Yet it seemed exactly the right path for this man, judging by his grin, the sheer joy inside that obviously possessed him.

"Wait a minute," I said. "This is too big for one person to take on himself. I want to spread this around." Not that $300 was too big; I could do it, and forget it. But here was a man who'd found a new road that seemed absolutely right for him; I wanted a few friends to help him on the road. So I called my old pals from Warners, other actors who'd worked with him, Cagney, O'Brien, Allen Jenkins, Frank McHugh, Horace McMahon, and the six of us chipped in $50 each. And the guy went off.

That was the last I saw or heard of him for years. Then one Thanksgiving, I'd taken the family to the Brown Derby in Hollywood for supper, and on the way home, we neared the Church of the Blessed Sacrament, a Jesuit church on Sunset Boulevard, and I felt my scalp prickle as we got close. I said, "Let's go in here for a minute and say a prayer of thanksgiving." We went inside, and we kneeled, and then as I stood, I saw a monk in a brown cassock, sandals on his feet, his hair gray, but when he looked at me and caught my eye, his face broke into that marvelous grin. It was the same man, the former actor; he opened his arms wide to me, as if to hug me, and I knew that was one of the biggest fifty dollars I ever spent. Spiritual strength, soul—he had them.

I was fortunate to become a member of the Bohemian Club in 1946, and began to spend a part of each summer up at the Grove, 75 miles north of San Francisco. I met Alec Templeton, the blind pianist and entertainer, one summer, and learned more about spiritual strength. Alec and I would go into the shaded groves for long walks.

"Pick out a redwood," he'd say to me, and I'd lead him to one.

He'd put his arms around it, feel its mass. He'd press an ear against a trunk as though he were listening to the sap stirring inside.

"It must be 280–290 feet," he'd say. "The first major branch begins about five feet over my head. It points south." And he'd be right. "God," he'd say fervently, "it must be pretty, its leaves so green."

He'd never seen green. He'd never seen light or shade or height or mass, and yet that night he'd sit at a piano at the Grove and play a love song to that tree. You'd hear all he had sensed.

I knew Alec Templeton well, and I knew George Shearing, the blind pianist, and I knew a man named Graham, up at the Grove, also blind, and none of them ever said, I wish I could see. They saw. Alec Templeton died, in 1963, of cancer. I bet he never whined. I have thought a lot about Alec, and those amputees. I think about them still. It helps me; it helps me help others. I think: "How lucky I am, only losing my voice." So when I face men in hospital beds, beaten, dejected, contemplating suicide, because they have lost their voices, I croak at them: "It could be worse. You could be blind; you could have lost your legs, your arms, both legs and arms. A basket case. All you've lost is your voice, and you can get that back. How about the blind?

Who's going to give them eyes that see?" But more, I can talk to them about soul, about spirit, and how it flames in some men and sputters in others, how God finds His way into one physical wreck of a man and turns that man into a life of great stature, no matter what the physical damage. And how God is cut out of another man's life, because he has permitted his soul to wilt, his spirit to turn to cold ash.

I met another man at the Bohemian Grove one summer. It was a chilly night, and I heard a sound outside my cabin. I stepped outside, and a man said sheepishly, "I've lost my way."

"Come into my camp," I said.

We had a couple of drinks, to warm him up, and we checked his location on the Bohemian map, and then I walked him back to his cabin. We swapped names, but little else. The motto of the Bohemians is, "Weaving Spiders Come Not Here." Bohemians like to help each other, but one way is not by selling insurance policies or used cars to fellow Bohemians while at the Grove or in the San Francisco clubhouse. I told him I was Bill Gargan, and he probably knew I was an actor, though I didn't say, and he said he was Frank Folsom, and he worked for RCA, and if I were in New York, I should give him a ring.

I did look him up. I was in New York in 1949, staying at the New York Athletic Club, and I gave him a ring. He remembered me.

"Come on over for lunch tomorrow," he said instantly, and I did.

Lunch?

I was floated up to the 53rd floor, led by two aides through a maze of hallways, until I got to a door that read: OFFICE OF THE PRESIDENT. I stood there, a barefoot boy from Hollywood, and I said, "Hey, Frank, is this on the level? I figured we'd have lunch, not an orgy."

His English butler whipped up a lake of martinis, and then he introduced me to his luncheon guests of the day, John Coleman of the New York Stock Exchange, Ben Duffy of BBD&O, Tom Sheehy of Chatham Blanket, Victor Zaminsky, president of Union News Company, the big magazine and paperback book distributor, and three or four other guys who formed the boards of directors of half of America's biggest corporations. I was knee deep in tycoons. We dined in a private room, and when we finished, Frank said, "We don't usually make speeches here, but you're a special guest, in from Hollywood, and I think you might want to say a few words."

I took the plunge. "Gentlemen," I said, "I want to apologize, wasting your valuable time. You're looking at an actor out of work. I'm looking for a job in television."

Whereupon Frank Folsom picked up a phone and called downstairs to NBC-TV—which I had thought of as a giant on its own, but in reality was a mere subsidiary of RCA—and he said to Norm Blackburn, vice-president in charge of television and radio, "I've got a guy up here with a good talent. He's an old friend."

I knew Norm. He was an old friend, and in fact I'd been drinking with him the night before. My visit to New York was not totally innocent. Back in Los Angeles, my business manager Noel Singer had said to me one recent day: "Bill, you ought to go into production. You are what I would call a leader of men." Which was a funny line I decided to take seriously. If I could boss Mary around, I could boss anybody. Why not? So I hit New York, trying to peddle my private eye idea.

Now I went down to NBC's television department, a tiny den in the cellar, and when I entered, Blackburn was on the floor in a deep salaam.

"God called," he said. "Pick out a contract."

Actually, I was lunching one day at the Lambs Club and I ran into Mike Kirk of the Kudner Agency. Mike wanted to know if I would be interested in playing a private detective for an NBC television series sponsored by the U. S. Tobacco Company. I jumped at the chance—even though I would, for the sponsor, smoke a pipe on the show. This is known as giving your character class. Which is how *Martin Kane, Private Eye* was born.

As soon as I signed the contract with the Kudner Agency, to do the show, I got on the phone to Beverly Hills, and told Mary to come on East.

"And bring my pressure cooker," I said. "The big one."

"What's the matter?" she said. "Doesn't Macy's carry pressure cookers?"

"Don't be smart," I said. "I want my own, not Macy's."

So Mary came out, on the train, and because I was now a star and part-producer of a new television show, a host of NBC bigwigs, plus members of the press, went down to meet Mary at Grand Central.

Had I thought, I'd have scrubbed the meeting. Here I was, trying to establish the image of a tough private eye, and here was my wife, getting her revenge for years of my bellowing, "Bring this. Bring that. Tote that. Lift this."

She'd strapped all the pots and pans we owned to her luggage. She wore a set of old jeans and a crumpled cowboy hat. She wore her old riding boots. She plaited her hair into two braids, like Judy Canova. And all across the country, on the train, she practiced learning to roll her own cigarettes.

So she got off the train, and NBC's executive suite saw her, and so did the press, and I like to have died. She leaned against a pillar in the terminal, and she broke out her Bull Durham, and casually rolled a smoke.

Finally she looked over at me. "You," she said. "I'm sick and tired of your calls. 'Bring my pots and pans.' Well, I've brought them for the last time." And she scratched a wooden match against her tight jeans, and lit up.

Actually, Mary didn't bring all my pots and pans. She left a few back home, because her father, Pop Kenny, lived with us. So did a Japanese houseboy, a charming bright young man named Haruso (Harpy) Komaru, who attended USC, and kept an eye on Pop and on our two new poodles we'd just got, one of whom we named Martin Kane. The other was Tinker Bell, but Martin Kane was the character. Once when we all were back in Beverly Hills again, Mary and Leslie were in the kitchen, with Mary in one of her better moods, which is to say she was barking at everyone in sight and a few out of. The dog yipped, and Mary whirled. "That's enough out of you, Martin Kane," and the poodle barked a long series of sounds that ended up, "Grrghhhya-ol'-bat."

Leslie stared at Mary; Mary stared at Leslie. They both turned to stare at the dog.

"Did you hear him?" Leslie asked.

Mary nodded sickly.

"He called you an old bat."

Mary nodded. She never insulted that dog again.

That was Martin Kane, the dog. *Martin Kane*, the show, was just as unpredictable. Television is not dull. Maybe to watch, but not to do. Especially live television. Even filmed shows. You shoot a filmed show in four days, one scene right after the other, and yes, you do sit around between scenes, but you'd better eat your lunch then or learn your lines or powder your nose, because that is your leisure time, Buster. If boredom is the key to moviemaking, frenzy is television's. Live shows are ten times more frantic. *Martin Kane* was live.

For a spell, I enjoyed *Martin Kane*, and when I stopped enjoying it, it was not because I had become jaded or exhausted by the pellmell routine. If anything, the frenzy kept me enjoying myself long after the joy ought really to have ended.

Martin Kane, Private Eye had a lot of good things going for it, especially in the beginning. The first detective series on network television and Martin Kane was the first private eye to capture an enormous TV following. Very soon in the game I realized our stories were nothing to rave about. How much well-plotted story line and genuine character development can you accomplish in a half hour? So I made the program a showcase for me. After all, that is what we were selling—Martin Kane. I developed a tongue-in-cheek style, a spoof of the hard boiled private, a way of saying silently, Don't blame *me* for the lousy stories, I didn't write them. And anyway, what's the difference? Relax.

It was nothing staggering, my decision. It made the only sense. Bogart's movie version of Sam Spade applied the same ground rules. We gave the audience a good time, and if all the loose threads were not tied tightly in a half hour, we swept them under the bed. Have fun. And the show, for whatever reason, took hold. It became one of the most popular shows on the air, occasionally rivaling Arthur Godfrey for the number-one spot.

The show had charm, and its charm held together the lunacy, the feeble character development, the limited camera work.

It also had a producer I could not abide. This was TV's early era, bringing entertainment into your living room, and early in that early era, a few people tried to make the casual intimacy of television a kind of sexual intimacy. The sight of pretty women, a touch of deep cleavage, a show of thigh became—to these producers—more important than the content of the show. Our producer was so inclined. He used the show as a vehicle for a flesh parade. The result was we often had pretty, emptyheaded girls on the show, blowing their lines all over the lot.

The show began to slide downhill. In desperation, I began to mug a little more, to cover up the new holes, and the script writers began to write more blatantly. You get into a terrible rut this way. Everybody works harder to undo the damage, and the result is more screeching, more overacting, overwriting, which starts to drive the viewers away, and to get them back you come up with more and more desperate gimmickry.

None of this happened fast, and none of it was that serious that the show was in bad trouble. But the edge was gone, the gloss, the charm. *Martin Kane* lost his warmth.

What was worse, to me, was the embarrassment. I am no prude. Probably the best part I ever did on film was that of Joe, in *They Knew What They Wanted*, a wife-stealer. But this was just sleazy. The girls paraded on, showed their cleavage, muffed their lines, and tittered off.

While in New York, I'd become a member of Cardinal Spellman's Committee of Laiety, an organization of business executives pledged to help raise a million dollars over and above the Cardinal's yearly appeal. I was on the Radio and Television Committee.

I like to think I had also become a friend of Cardinal Spellman's. Each year I'd attend the Cardinal's Christmas party in the grand ballroom of the Waldorf, where the Cardinal sat in his purple robes while youngsters from the Foundling Hospital climbed all over him. These Christmas parties, I think, were the happiest moments in Cardinal Spellman's life; the Foundling

Hospital was especially dear to him. As it was to anyone who ever dropped in. One visit is enough to make you want to go out and pick every available pocket.

Without putting myself on the Cardinal's level, I have always been interested in orphanages and foundling homes, in the children's wards of hospitals. The plight of children affects me more deeply than does the plight of unfortunate adults. The adult, no matter how horrible his fate, *is* grown, *is* mature, *is* more or less used to the buffeting of a sometimes cruel world. The child is not. And the adult, no matter how tragic his condition, how critical, *has* lived; the child has barely begun, and already he is behind the eight ball.

So when I had the privilege of helping raise money for one of the Cardinal's favorite charities, the Foundling Hospital, I was happy to pitch in. And honored to be asked.

What has this to do with *Martin Kane?*

A friend, John Barry, of Midland Trust Company, also was a member of the Committee of Laiety, and one day after a particularly blatant piece of trash, Barry and I were walking on Madison Avenue. We neared the Cardinal's residence, on 51st Street, and Barry said, "Look up there, Bill." I looked, and sticking up from the roof were five TV antennas. Barry said, "They watch your show, Bill," and the message was clear. I was not the only one embarrassed by *Martin Kane.*

So I went down to the studio shortly after, and I said to the producer, "Clean up the mess. Get decent scripts. Cut out the flesh parades. Or get another boy."

The upshot was, they got another boy. Though I owned a piece of the show, I did not own casting privileges, including the lead. After eighty-five weeks, I was canned, which was frankly a moment of pure relief. Who needs $4500 a week?

They replaced me with Lloyd Nolan, and then replaced Nolan with Lee Tracy, and I remember seeing the first show Tracy did, as Martin Kane. I was over at the Stork Club, watching in Sherman Billingsley's upstairs office, and later Lee came in to the club, and I said, "You were sensational, Lee. You hit it on the button." Tracy grinned. "You don't take DiMaggio out of center field when he's doin' good. All I'm doin' is copyin' you."

But you know Lee Tracy. He copies no man for long. Pretty soon he was snapping his fingers, talking out of the side of his mouth, jazzing it up. He was replaced by Mark Stevens, and finally they gave up the ghost and laid poor Martin to rest. Nobody wept.

Not that it was Nolan's fault, or Tracy's, or Stevens'. Or that I had been so good I could not be replaced. It is the public's decision. The public becomes used to a certain person in a certain role. Actors don't deliberately stereotype themselves so much as audiences insist on stereotyping them. In Hollywood, I'd once made a series of Ellery Queen movies, a role originally filled by Ralph Bellamy. Bellamy's Ellery Queen movies grossed far more than did mine. "He's not Ellery Queen," audiences said of me. Now they said of Lloyd, Lee, and Mark: "Hey, *he's* not Martin Kane."

NBC must have felt the same. *I* was Martin Kane. Nobody else. So shortly after I was discharged, I concluded a deal with Sonny Werblin, then of the MCA agency and later president and owner of the New York Jets football team, to do a private eye show for—guess who?—NBC. It was a million-dollar contract over a seven-year spread, with the usual yearly options. *Barry Craig, Private Detective* soon began airing over NBC radio, emanating from New York for a spell, and finally from Hollywood.

So you can see that my relations with NBC were not bad. One producer, yes. The network, no. Frank Folsom remains a true friend. During my *Martin Kane* tenure, he said to me one day, "How'd you like to be a Knight of the Holy Sepulchre?"

I swallowed and said, "Why me?" and he said, "Why not?" and pretty soon I was received as a Knight. The Holy Sepulchre is an Equestrian Order, over nine centuries old, the oldest order outside of the Knights of Gregory, and to a Catholic, membership is a moment and event of highest rank. You do not compare it to winning (or losing) Academy Awards.

I've been asked, less facetiously than my own flip question to

Folsom, why I was invited into the Order. I am not very good at answering.

As I understand it, the Order of the Holy Sepulchre is devoted to charitable works and its members try to live an exemplary life, and by daily routine, your deportment, indicate a love and devotion to the Church. Yet thousands—millions—of other people live equally good and devoted lives. Far better lives. More devoted lives. So far as charity goes, I do the best I can. I've already talked more than I particularly care to about my very insignificant role at the Foundling Hospital. I just happened to be standing next to Frank Folsom when he asked, and you know me when I hear the right cue.

The Order's charity is worldwide in scope, but its special focus is centered on Palestine. When the Israeli army drove the Arabs into the desert after World War II, or the Arabs fled into the desert, whichever, it was the Knights of the Holy Sepulchre that took to feeding the homeless Arab families. Later, it fed uprooted Jews, in the Gaza Strip. Now it is again involved in charity work in the Palestine area. It is one of the few orders in which women participate, and later Mary became a Lady of the Order, and is today a Lady of the Grand Cross. ("It was the only way you could have become a lady," I croaked to her not too long ago. "Aw," she answered sweetly, "if you had another throat, I'd cut it for you.") Other than our audience with Pope Pius in 1956, Mary most cherishes her election to the Holy Sepulchre as a Lady of the Order, and then of the Grand Cross.

So I remain close to Frank Folsom, who has done as much for me as any man on earth. When it was whispered, and I heard, "His Eminence does not approve of *Martin Kane*," Frank Folsom came to my side in a way far more important than had he fired a television producer. He did not interfere with NBC-TV, but he did step in to my life in more direct and valuable ways. One day at the studio I heard he was leaving the next day for Rome, to see the Pope. RCA was building a radio station at the Vatican.

"I'd love to go," I said wistfully.

"Why don't you?" he said.

"Go on," I said. "A million reasons."

"Name two."

"I have to tape a show. Besides I don't have the right clothes—"

Frank set up a recording date at the studio for that night. He sent me a tailor who would slick me up in a full-dress outfit on the spot.

I felt so guilty I decided the least I could do was turn a piece of the trip into a busman's holiday. I called Paris, where Fred Allen and Tallulah Bankhead were readying up a radio show for NBC, and I spoke to the producer, Bud Barry.

"You got a spot on the show for me?"

He must have figured I was kidding, because he said, "Sure. I'll give you three–four minutes. But we're on the day after tomorrow."

"I'll be there."

"I bet."

Tom Sheehy of Chatham Blanket joined us, and we three flew to Paris the next day. I took a cab from the hotel to the theater, tapped Bud Barry on the shoulder and said, "Where's my script?" Fred Allen cooked up a routine for me, we rehearsed it the next day, and did it that night.

Then we planed to Rome, where we stayed at the Excelsior Hotel. My outfit of white tie and tails, resplendently new and perfectly tailored, turned out to be wrong. I needed a black vest, if I wanted any part of an audience with Pius. *Well, Gargan,* I thought, *you blew it.* But Count Galliazi, the Pope's cousin, sent a black vest over, and a limousine, and we were driven to the Pope's summer residence at Castel Gandolfo. We were ushered past a maze of Swiss guards, colorful and stiff as a kid's cardboard cutout, through long hushed hallways, and into an outside office, where we stood and waited. Finally Frank went in, to see His Holiness. Folsom's trip was a business trip. RCA was building the largest radio station in the world, at the Vatican. The minutes ticked by, and Sheehy and I began pacing up and down, looking at our watches. Sheehy would turn to me and say, "You think he'll be much longer?" and

I'd say, "How the hell would I know?" Then we'd pace, and I'd say, "You think he'll be much longer?"

Meanwhile, I'd been coaching myself on what to say. I wouldn't do what so many other friends had done in the past, turn totally mute. I'd speak, all right. Yes, *sir*. I'd tell His Holiness all about me, about Mary, about the children, my work, America, the world—

The door opened, and Frank came out, with Pope Pius. Pius had his arm about Frank. Now he walked over to Sheehy. "I want to thank you for the blankets donated to the American College," he said. His voice and manner were sweet beyond description.

He turned to me. "I understand you're in television, my son."

All right, Gargan. You're on. That's your cue.

"Yes, Your Holiness," I said. Or tried to say. Mainly, I nodded. He said other things, and I said other things. Like, "No, Your Holiness," and, "I think so, Your Holiness." Then he excused himself, and we knelt and kissed his ring, and that was that, my first audience.

We remained at the Vatican a while longer. We were taken to the American College to have lunch, and Bishop O'Connor, in charge of the school, gave us a room in which to change our clothes. Frank Folsom said, "I've changed clothes a lot of times, but never in a bishop's bedroom."

Lunch is solemn. The young novitiates—the future Church leaders in training—are not permitted to look up at the head table (where we sat). Their entire lunch is spent in saying prayers aloud, all through the meal.

But I heard later that one young novitiate stopped and said to the head priest at his table, "Wasn't that Mr. Gargan, who plays Martin Kane?"

"Why, yes," the priest said. "But how did you know?"

"Oh," the novitiate said quickly, "I didn't look up, Father. I just tilted my knife and caught his reflection."

Mary and I had an audience in 1956, when I was in Europe, filming the television series, *The Return of Martin Kane* (old television shows never die; they just become reruns), and while she and I waited in the summer palace, Mary began to chatter.

'What'll I say?"

"Relax."

"Sure. You've gone through this. How about me?"

I took her hand. It was wet. (So was mine.)

We waited in a beautiful room, a dark red carpet on the floor, lovely old paintings on the walls, and an old crucifix on the wall. It was not a totally private audience. Two Army priests were with us, and two Irish nuns, and a Peruvian couple. Again, we'd been told how to behave, what the protocol was. Women did not wear hand gloves. Why, Mary wanted to know? Because, we were told, His Holiness may be Pope, but he is also an Italian gentleman. If a lady becomes nervous and drops her gloves, he will bend and pick them up. It is not that Pius minded picking up gloves for ladies; it is that the ladies later felt mortified that they had somehow demeaned him.

So Many wore long arm gloves, to her shoulder, and a dark mantilla. She looked as lovely as I can remember her. But she was nervous. She also had a special mission. Whenever our friends had come back from an audience, Mary would ask, "What does the Pope's ring look like? The old fisherman's ring?"

And the answer inevitably was, "How should I know? I closed my eyes when I kissed it. I always close my eyes when I kiss."

"I won't close my eyes," she said.

The Pope came in, and walked directly to me. "I remember you, my son," he said. "How is everything in Hollywood?" We spoke for a few minutes, and then he walked to Mary.

She kneeled, and he took her hands. "This must be Mary," he said.

It was nobody else. There she was, on her knees, her eyes wide as saucers, as though toothpicks had propped them open. She kissed the ring, her eyes riveted on it.

The Pope helped her to her feet and he said, "Tell me about your sons?" and Mary did, her eyes wide open, staring at Pius, and at the ring.

Before he left Mary, he took her hands again, and this time

he pressed something into one hand. Instantly, Mary's hand became a claw, tightly balled fist. He went on to the others, and a few minutes later he had finished chatting with each of us. "Would you like a photograph?" he said, and he looked at Mary.

She nodded, eyes wide open.

A photographer came in, and took the picture of all of us, and when I look at the picture today, it all comes back. Each of us, in that room, is looking at the camera, including His Holiness. All, that is, except Mary.

Her eyes are still wide as saucers, with those invisible toothpicks propping them open, and they are staring at the Pope. Never once during the entire audience had she blinked her eyes.

When we were outside, Mary finally opened the hand she'd held clenched into a tight fist since His Holiness had pressed something into it. In her hand was a medal the Pope had given her. She'd gripped it so hard, a tiny pool of blood lay formed in her palm.

"Well," I said, "what does it look like?"

"What look like?"

"The ring."

"What ring?"

"The ring," I said. "The Pope's centuries-old fisherman's ring. *The* ring."

"Oh," she said, snapping out of her daze. "It looks just like any other old green ring."

18

That's the Third Disaster Today

In 1955, I celebrated my fiftieth birthday, if you could call it
a celebration. It is to some men what being thirty is to most
women.

Not so much what it means to you, personally. At fifty I
felt fine. I was fine. But don't look in your address book at
the names of old friends, unless you want to weep. Death and
illness had cut their usual swath, and every year would cut
deeper. One particular kind of death had begun to make an
appearance, center stage, a grinning, obscene killer named Cancer.

Mary and I had danced to Eddy Duchin, for years, In 1951,
Duchin was dead, of cancer. Gertie Lawrence had been the toast
of Broadway when I had broken into show business in *Aloma*.
Gertie died, in 1952, of cancer. Bogart would die, in 1957.
Cancer. General Claire Chennault, that hemstitched, blackeyed,
vivid man, died the next year, of cancer. General Joe Stilwell
was dead, three years after I saw him in Burma. Cancer.

Not always cancer, of course. The boy who had hired me
and Ed to our first movie job—Paul Kelly—and then led such
a checkered life, died on Election Day, 1956. His heart conked
out, and Ed and I spoke on the phone, and mourned Paul.

Nor was all the death restricted to humans. Mary and I have
always had dogs. Mary Boland, the lovely comedienne and warm

friend, gave Mary and me a tiny pekinese in the early 1950s, a beautiful little animal. I know how men feel about pekinese. It is a frowsy devil, the stereotyped dog women clutch when they lie on a divan and eat dipped chocolates.

Well, this one was even more, because he had two crippled legs. I am a sucker for a dog like that. This little beast was no bigger than a quart of milk, a little yipping darling, with his bum legs, and Mary and I loved him.

One Sunday morning, Mary and I went out to go to church and there was the little fellow, dead in the driveway. He had seemed well enough the night before, so I thought for a moment he'd been poisoned, by one of those maniacs you find in every neighborhood, somebody who hates doges, or hates noise, or hates life, or just hates. But then I figured, with those crippled legs, he'd worn himself out.

Ten years later, my son Leslie was sitting with me, and he suddenly looked up and said in a very strained voice, "I got to get this off my conscience. I ran over that peke."

I felt sorry for Leslie, having held it in, all those years. We were closer, for his telling.

But the point isn't Leslie or his conscience. It is death. It starts to become a regular visitor, once you reach a certain age. Fred Allen, with whom I'd done that radio show when Frank Folsom and I went to Rome, died in 1956, and so did Edward Arnold and Bob Burns and Louis Calhern, who had fought that bloody draw with my old sidekick Walter Catlett, at the Lambs. And my other sidekick from *Rain*, pink-cheeked Guy Kibbee, died the same year. And on and on, the list grows. The giants died, Walter Hampden, Ollie Hardy, Erich Von Stroheim, Victor McLaglen; the young ones died, Kay Kendall, Jimmy Dean, Carole Landis, with whom I'd played in *I Wake Up Screaming*; the middle-aged died, Tyrone Power, Errol Flynn.

Mary and I were fine, in what is called the prime of life, particularly by those people who are fifty years old or older. I played a lot of golf, mainly at the Bel-Air Club, and I played a lot of tennis, and a pretty good game at each. My golf would sink into the mid-80s if I kept at it. It is the great game for people who must lose themselves in something. I play less golf today than I would like to, but I get in my rounds. You forget yourself when you play golf (or you play lousy golf). It is essentially a lonely game, for all the alleged camaraderie of the links, the nineteenth hole good-fellowship and the small wagers each side. It is you against the ball, and all else be damned.

In Hollywood you need such an outlet. You probably need it many other places, as well; surely the Madison Avenue boys need it; anybody in an ulcer-making trade needs it, or something like it. Pure perfect escape.

And even with my fun-loving, my life with Mary, and our socializing, I needed escape. Hollywood drills the need right into your heart. And, brother, you'd better take care of it. Or add another name to that long gray list.

So I played golf, rode horses, banged tennis balls, and generally made whoopee. Yes, I worked. (Why else would I need all the escape?) I signed a contract with Ziv Productions to make the television series, *The Return of Martin Kane*, in a studio outside London.

The Return of Martin Kane in a great many ways was better than the original. For one thing, we made it on film, so we had a chance to correct our mistakes. For another, we used a lot of foreign locations, to give the show an authentic quality.

We shot one show on location at Hamlet's castle at Elsinore; the Danes call it Helsingor, north of Copenhagen. The castle had been converted into a military academy, and at first we were denied permission to shoot there. Which naturally didn't deter us. We shot the exterior from a distance, getting good angles of the awesome parapet that ran around the castle, and then we hid our cameras beneath our coats and went in just as any other tourist. Inside, we began to film furiously again, until a guard caught wise and began to give chase. We ran, photographing all the way before the guards caught us and threw us out. But we had our footage. We used what locations we could. When we needed extras, we shot people in the street.

A ferry runs between Denmark and Sweden, and while we were there the people of Sweden were coming to Denmark to buy butter and cheese. We stayed on the ferry, shooting women with their string bags of milk and butter, and their handsome blond children. One day I had my passport stamped nine times, crossing between the two countries.

We shot in Holland, Spain, Italy, England, and Portugal. In Paris we spent a lot of time in a tough Algerian district, getting the kind of footage that made you feel you were at the Casbah. If you didn't look too closely.

When I came back from London after the first season, my income took off like a bird. The films had been released almost immediately—the TV series—and in three months, I made $42,-000. Which made it silly to work much more that year. Mary and I bought a house in Bermuda Dunes, the windiest spot in the United States, three bedrooms, a swimming pool, Spanish style. Bermuda Dunes is actually a lovely place when it doesn't blow. Unfortunately, it always blows.

By this time Mary and I owned a little real estate, and I had managed to buy in on some oil wells in Texas. The deal was arranged by John J. Reynolds, one of my oldest pals. I am not his most famous client. Reynolds buys and sells real estate for the Archdiocese of the City of New York. He's swung a few other big deals. When he was twenty-one, he bought the Merchandise Mart in Chicago for Joe Kennedy, for something like $12,500,000. His commission, poor guy, was a mere $750,000.

He also buys and handles my oil wells. Oil wells in Texas invariably bring a gasp to the listener. I am still in on some of them. The other day I got an income report from one of my wells, the J. C. Stevenson Lease, in Reagan County, Texas. A real gasser. The report read: "Income from oil and gas— $335.50; Expenses—$723.93; Net loss—$388.43." Well, what do you expect when you mix Stevenson and Reagan and Texas. It's harder than mixing oil and water. Actually, some of my wells do better. A few even break even. But I'm very grateful to John.

So life went merrily on. I appeared on television shows in Hollywood, Ford TV, George Gobel. I did radio stints. My income was not what it had been at its peak, but it was good enough, and when I worked, which was often enough, I commanded the kind of salary that makes no sense whatever when you compare my work to, let's say, a college professor's.

I played. Mary didn't play quite as much, but she did have her riding, and once she took up golf. She did it, she says, to surprise me. She took lessons while I was out of town, and one Sunday when I was back, and getting ready to attack the course, she got ready to attack it right alongside.

"Where do you think you're going?" I asked.

"I've got a surprise," she said.

When we got to the first hole, she took a club from my bag. She teed up a ball, addressed it smartly, and then swung. The ball squirted a few feet to her right, and I said, "What in the world are you doing?"

"I'll tell you what I'm doing," she panted, shoving that club back in my bag. "I'm quitting this game."

That was the last time she played. Which was too bad, because she managed to get herself an ulcer late in 1958. It led to another of our periodic small disasters. A whole chain of them.

Our friend, Dr. Louis Martin, examined her on the last day of the year, in 1958, at the hospital, taking X-rays, and then he sent her home. Meanwhile, I went out to play some golf, planning to get home in time to find out how Mary was, and to get ready to celebrate New Year's Eve at the Biltmore Bowl that evening.

I played my round at Bel-Air, and was driving back to Beverly Hills, where everybody drives twenty-five miles an hour, when a lady in a Caddy, going closer to sixty-five, hit me broadside. My Chevy wagon turned over three times. Somewhere in between the first turn and the final, I managed to switch off the ignition key. I was thrown clear of the car, and found myself under a tree. Right next to me was a quart of whiskey, which is the way I like it when disaster strikes. The bottle had sailed out of the front seat with me. I grabbed it and went into a nearby house, where a solicitous neighbor called an ambulance, and I called Dr. Louis Martin's office. I left a message, telling Louis I would be at the hospital. When he got the message from his answering service, he probably thought it was a mistake.

"You must mean *Mrs.* Gargan," he said.

"That didn't sound like a Mrs. to me," the girl said.

So poor Louis had to go over to the hospital a second time for a Gargan. He gave me a pill and sent me home, to join Mary. I called the Biltmore Bowl and canceled out our New Year's Eve, and went to bed.

Except none of our disasters are ever that simple. Unknown to me, as I lay in bed, sinking blissfully into a deep sleep, some fool had thrown a cigarette into the dry brush of Beverly Glen Canyon a whoop and a holler up the road. It whoosed up and began to burn down houses like so many tinder boxes. My son Leslie had rented a house in Beverly Glen, and lived there with a couple of friends. Their house was soon ablaze and the three boys fought the fire, as I lay sleeping. The fire quickly got out of control and they got out just in time before the house was gutted.

The next thing I knew there was a frantic knock on our door and there—soot-stained and dog-tired—stood the three boys. The fire had also unhinged Leslie's mind; he'd been going with a girl for some time, which will unhinge any boy's mind, and the fire finished him off.

Mary got the guest room ready, and I went back to bed. An hour or so later, I was awakened again. This time Leslie was scrubbed and wearing a bathrobe.

"Dad," he said, "I might as well tell you. I'm going to get married."

That did it. I got up on one elbow and surveyed him.

"That's the third disaster today," I said, and I fell back asleep.

Happy New Year. He didn't marry the girl.

The Chevy wagon bore up even better than I did. It had 3000 miles on it when the lady in the Cadillac knocked it hood over tailfin. Today it has over 90,000 miles on it, and it runs like a dream.

Mary's ulcer? We don't permit Mary to cater to such nonsense. My accident knocked her ulcer out of her mind. She had a recurrence, a few years later, but I managed to come down with cancer the same week, so once again she had to forget it. That's what she gets, marrying me. And that's what I get, marrying a hypochondriac.

So that was my life in the middle of this century, and I in the middle of my own century, and the years immediately following. I made the annual summer encampment at Bohemian Grove, where for three weeks we take a holiday from care. As a matter of fact, on the first night, at the Grove, we very ceremoniously burn care. A barge, with a symbolic figure, Care, is burned on the river and sunk. No more care. Then a gloating voice cackles from the trees: "But I'll be back in three weeks to see you all." After the last campfire of the last night of the encampment, we would sing, which always gave me an earache.

Away from the Grove, I palled around with Dennis Day, Gene Raymond, Red Knorp, Walter Bunker, and other long, close friends. Mary and I had become a sort of proxy parent to Dennis Day, not that we were or are that far apart in age. Now he's fifty, and I wonder how he likes it. (He probably likes it fine. Nothing bothers Dennis.)

He used to parade his latest girl friend over to our house, for us to see and cast our vote. We'd give them all thumbs down, until one day he showed up with an absolute doll.

"This one," we said to him, "keep. If you blow this one, don't come back."

So he married this one, and today he and Peggy have ten little Days.

Right smack in the middle of this decade, Randy Hale, my Bohemian buddy, asked me to play in the Joseph Hayes stage thriller, The Desperate Hours, on the West Coast. We would open in San Francisco, move north to Tacoma, Portland and Seattle, and come down to Hollywood.

I had never acted on a West Coast stage. I dove into the work, delighted to be on any stage, and particularly on these Pacific stages.

It is a rousing play. A trio of convicts make a successful prison break, and hole up in the home of a middle-class Terre Haute, Indiana, family. As the police move in, the cons terrorize the family, mother, father, son, daughter. I played the father. That's what I was good for those days. The time had long gone that I played romantic leads to Joan Crawford, Miriam Hopkins, or Carole Lombard. The prime of life, my foot!

We had a fine run, in San Francisco, Tacoma, Portland and Seattle, and then we came down to Hollywood, to open at the Carthay Circle Theatre. We came down, but the set didn't. Or, rather, the second floor of the set didn't.

The set—the middle-class house where the convicts take root—had been chopped into two halves, the first story and the second, and each was placed in a big moving van. The first floor arrived days in advance, as it was scheduled to, but the driver of the second truck managed to get himself arrested up in the wilds of the Oregon coast, and by the time it was straightened out, the set did not get to the theater until ten A.M. of the day we were to open. Ordinarily, it would have taken another twenty-four hours to get it uncrated and built, ready for our clumping feet. We had ten and a half hours to an 8:30 curtain. Actors joined stagehands in carrying sofas and chairs up a newly tacked-together staircase. It became apparent we wouldn't make 8:30, but we wouldn't miss by too much. So we decided to go ahead, and face the moment of decision at curtain time.

At 8:15, with gobs of friends out there, ready to greet us, Randy Hale came up and said, "Well, we won't be ready for another hour and a half or so."

"That's too bad," I said. "What do we do now?"

"What we do, Bill," Randy said, "is you go out and tell them."

"Not me," I said. "You go out. Anybody go out. Let the truck driver go out. Not me."

"They know you, Bill," Randy said. "They'll take it from you."

So I was tapped. I went out and I said, "Ladie and gentlemen. You've heard of the play, *The Desperate Hours?* We're living them." I told them of the race against the clock, which we were losing. "We are the desperate actors. We need another hour, at the least." They groaned, but not too loudly, and I put in a plug for the nearest bars and restaurants. I told them that Chasen's wasn't too far away, and I could vouch for the drinks, if not for the food (Chasen's is one of the finest restaurants in the country), and why not go out, have a quick bite, or a drink or two, and come back. We'll be here.

We opened an hour and a quarter late, and we lost just six people.

So when I recall my triumphs in the theater, I must list that little ab-lib speech to hold a first-night audience at the Carthay Circle.

The play did quite well in Hollywood, and I guess Randy Hale remembered it in 1960, when *The Best Man* came along. He asked me to play the dying ex-President, and I guess I remembered the hectic business of being forced to explain we were still nailing up the set. I didn't really want to do *The Best Man*, and besides, my throat was bothering me. I had a touch of laryngitis. . . .

19

Stop Whispering

. . . I came home from the hospital on November 20, 1960, ten days after my larynx had been removed. Howard Singer, the TV repairman, fixed up my set, and though the first voice I had heard was that of William Gargan, B.C.—before cancer— I soon found comfort in the flickering screen.

I had escaped from the outside world. To the world that inhabits movie houses and theaters, or watches television, and vaguely knew and remembered William Gargan, the Actor, I had disappeared. Not that anybody was asking.

Nor is this different from most actors. I had finished my run and was now between jobs. *The Best Man* had folded, and now I was home, in Beverly Hills, where the chrysanthemums were a riot of color in our garden and the sycamore trees had begun to drop their leaves the size of huge dinner plates. And the lemon tree I kept cutting down, as usual was back in full bloom. All was the same.

Except, of course, between *The Best Man* and my next job, I had found out I had cancer. Not a "lingering illness." Cancer. Not Big C, or Big Casino, or any other fond nickname that manages to avoid the real word. Cancer.

The American Cancer Society today has a campaign it calls, "From a Whisper to a Shout." Let's stop using such euphemisms as "lingering illness." Let's stop whispering about the disease.

Let's call it by its name. It won't smell any more sweet. But it will smell right. Let's stop pretending that if we make believe it isn't there, it will go away. Take it out of the category of moral blemish, take away the stigma of sin. Treat it for what it is—a terrible, often fatal disease that cannot be cured by silence, ignorance, or hushed whispers.

John Wayne did the treatment of cancer a wonderful service, when he refused to listen to his press agents. "You can't admit you have cancer, Duke," they had warned. "It will hurt you at the box office." So John Wayne went out and held a press conference and admitted he'd had cancer. He still makes movies, and his box office has not been harmed.

Which does not mean there still isn't some hushed whispering about most cancer cases. There was about mine. Between Mary and Dr. Miller, I later learned. After the operation was over, Mary admitted her bewilderment to Miller.

"I don't know much about this disease," she said.

"None of us does," Dr. Miller said.

"How long will Bill live?" she asked.

"If one cell escaped when I stabbed that epiglottis," Miller answered, "who knows? Maybe a year."

Mary had to carry that burden all by herself, at least for the first year. I went to Miller often, for periodic examinations, while he searched for the one cell that might have escaped his scalpel. He never found one; he hasn't found one to this day, and I have to think the work he performed on November 10, 1960, was totally successful. Other men and women had gone in for a laryngectomy, and it hasn't worked. A second operation has been performed, and a third, cancer leaping back to life. I have been one of the lucky ones. But then, the odds were with me. We caught my cancer early, and cut it out. Very often, it is as simple as that.

It's easier for me to take a breath today and say, "I'm cured," than it was back at the end of 1960, when I came home to 512 North Palm Drive. I'd had my cancer treated, but I wasn't in much position to cheer. Writing, "Hip, hip, hooray!" on a magic slate isn't quite the same as yelling it.

So began my convalescence at home.

We kept our front door open, just as we had at the hospital, and friends again poured through. Bing Crosby, Eddie Bernard, Charlie Ruggles, Pat O'Brien, Louis Martin, George Murphy, Neil Reagan, Phil and Alice Harris, Gene Raymond, Dennis and Peggy Day; dozens of others, bearing gifts, funny get-well cards, bottles of good cheer, snappy talk. Very early, a week or so later, Pat O'Brien and Wally Ford came over with a bottle of scotch, and because I was still recuperating, they killed it on my behalf.

There were other friends, and other friendship gestures. A friend and Beverly Hills neighbor, Ed Delaney, offered to buy back my Bel-Air Club membership.

"When you're up and around, you'll want to play some golf—"

"When I'm up and around," I scrawled on my magic slate, "I'll need the money." I thanked Ed Delaney for the offer, and he nodded, and a couple of years later, Ed Delaney was dead, of cancer.

Arthur Baker, who by this time was a full-fledged rancher, in Redlands, California, phoned when he heard about my operation. "I'd like to come back and work for you," he said. "Help around the house." But I—through Mary—wouldn't hear of it. Which didn't stop Arthur. He got in touch with Connie Williams, and she popped in one day and announced she was staying. She did, for six months. An angel.

Friendship buoyed me. I remember one night, after the drinks had flowed, and the laughs had followed, mine silent but still rocking inside, Phil Harris had said to Mary, at the door, when they all got ready to leave, "This cat will make it!"

But I was on a teeter-totter. Yes, I knew I'd make it, but I also knew I had no voice, and the second bit of knowledge often overwhelmed the first. People would leave the house, silence would descend over me and through me, and I would go upstairs to my room, and sit before the television set, until I felt tired enough to try sleep. Sleep was difficult. I still inserted the silver tube at night, so I wouldn't suffocate in my sleep. I eventually went to sleep but it was hard. The wall was a comfort, and so were the self-pitying whines: "Why me, God? Why me?" Rough and tough downstairs, the cat who would surely make it, upstairs I wasn't so sure.

I took to praying more often and harder. I would feel ashamed of myself, for failing to have faith enough in God to see me through, and I would murmur the act of contrition concluding with:

I firmly resolve, with the help of Thy grace, to do penance, and to amend my life.

I would firmly resolve.

But my resolution was not so firm as I prayed it would be. The waves of self-revulsion would hit me, the frustration of not seeing immediate progress. If I have a serious sin—and I have many—it is that of vanity. I *knew* I'd be able to talk. I would talk, and quickly, and well. Because I was Bill Gargan. It had to be. Propped by this façade of conceit, of vanity, I began to tackle my pamphlet and the lessons inside. But when I didn't rattle off the Gettysburg Address by the second or third week I was home, the fury would rise in me. You want a definition of frustration? It is feeling furious and being unable to scream.

So I read my blue pamphlet, *Your New Voice*. It said I would be able to speak, but it didn't say when, and it didn't really say for sure. *The going is rough. It isn't easy. The secret is learning to relax.*

But try to relax when the simple fact is, if I slipped in the bathtub and went under the water for a brief second or two, I could drown. Water entering my stoma rushes straight to the lungs. I began to have odd fantasies. Suppose I passed out on the street, and couldn't breathe, and a passerby tried to help. He'd give me mouth-to-mouth resuscitation, which is swell if you want air blown into your stomach. Meanwhile, I'd suffocate.

I would never be able to go swimming again. Swimming was the same as suicide by drowning, no matter how strong your stroke. Water in the stoma is water in the lungs.

So try to relax. I couldn't. And tenseness made everything worse.

Smog hurt my throat and lungs. Other people breathe through

their nose, where tiny hairs in the nostrils catch the impurities. The hairs act as filters. My stoma has no hair.

This was the downtilt of the teeter-totter. Yes, it was pure self-pity, and I knew I ought to have been ashamed of myself. But I would answer myself hotly: Why not? Why not be sorry? I had had cancer. I couldn't speak. Speaking was the weapon of my trade. They could have lopped off a leg, like Herbert Marshall, and I still could have acted. Or an arm. But without my voice, I was without my profession. The silent movies were dead. So, in a sense, was I.

I was out of work, with no prospects. Between jobs? Another euphemism. Out of work. Through. Washed up. Money worries began to nag me. Noel Singer had nicely begun to liquidate our investments and turn them into cash. I was far from broke. But in the old days, if I ever went on a spending jag—an unexpected trip to Europe, a bowl of gold fish when I couldn't afford a glass of water—I knew I'd go out and do a job and have more money than Mary and I could ever really spend. I like to say I spent money as fast I earned it, but when you make $4500 a week, as I did on *Martin Kane*, there is no way you can spend it all. I did not make $4500 a week every week, but a few thousand a week on a movie, a thousand or two thousand on a stage play, two or three thousand a week for a television guest shot—is still a lot of money. So some of it had been socked away, the house, the Bermuda Dunes house, a few stocks, the oil wells, trust funds, savings accounts.

I wasn't broke. But now it would be all outgo. I got out a pencil one day and jotted down my new income. As a totally disabled resident of the State of California, I was entitled to $65 a week. On top of this, I would get $55 in unemployment insurance payments, and on top of that another $127 a month from Social Security. It added up to about $647 a month. This is not the same as $4500 a week.

Yet how serious was it? It did add up to $647, and people do not starve on $647 a month. Over half the working people in America do not make as much.

Nor was I burdened by a huge hospital and doctor bill, as

are so many people just entering convalescence. There was no blood lien on me, thanks to the Motion Picture Relief Fund.

Leon Ames, a member of the board of directors of the MPRF, suggested I go down and apply for a loan. I did, and with Mary, we let it be known I wanted to borrow $2500.

William Kirk, executive director of the Relief Fund, shook his head. "Not borrow," he said. "It's your money." And he handed me not $2500, but $4000. Right there, on the spot. "You need more," he said, "come back."

After Mary and I sold our house on North Palm, I sent the money back. Which was pretty selfish of me. Now I know there's a pretty fair room at the Motion Picture Relief Fund home if I ever need it.

I had begun to eat normally. Hamburgers gradually replaced bowls of farina. I set up a blackboard outside the kitchen. On it I would scrawl: "Do you want me to starve to death? Get out!" And I began to cook again.

Life—basic life— began to take on a normal flavor. I could hide my stoma by putting on a shirt and tie. And who had to take baths, anyway? I began to shower, learning very early how to shield my stoma from the spray while rinsing. I never was that good a swimmer that I would miss swimming. You can talk about missing this or missing that, because of a physical disability, but more often that not, the patient never cared much in the past for what he can't do or eat now. Heart patients who can't use salt with their food suddenly decide what they really crave is a hot pastrami sandwich, though they always hated spicy foods. Diabetics who discover they can't have sugar begin to salivate over the notion of an ice-cream soda, though in the past ice cream gave them hives. So when I whine about never being able to swim, remember I was the guy who hated sand in his sandwiches at Coney Island and who crouched under the boardwalk to avoid a sunburn. I could stay home, in the playroom, and avoid the sun that way, thank you.

Nor could I do much sitting still, in the playroom. The outside world might have lost sight (and sound) of me, but the American Cancer Society knew full well where I was. There is something of a bulldog in the ACS. My intermittent despondency was not unique, and the ACS knew this. Cancer victims, even cured ones, tend to lose a bit of their zest for life. They—we—are even more susceptible to the whisper campaign that cancer is more than an illness. It is an evil, a sin, a stain. Cancer victims are seized by guilt, and because the guilt is senseless, they—we—do not know how to rid it. We become paralyzed. We accept our lot as a sort of cripple, and do not question it, except to whine about it now and then. We turn to the wall. And the ACS tugs us right back away from the wall. It is a tug-of-war, and if you give the ACS just the slightest chance at all, you cannot win. It will win, which in turn means you have to win. If you follow the reasoning.

The phone began to ring a merry tune. The ACS was on the line. Mary spoke to them.

Did Mr. Gargan know about speech lessons, sponsored by the ACS?

"Yes," Mary said. "Bill knows."

Is he going?

"Not yet."

Did he want to make an appointment, with a speech therapist?

"I'll have to ask him—"

Please do. We'll wait.

So the fight is on, the tug-of-war. Fortunately, for me, this wasn't much of a fight. I had my despair, but I had *some* sense. And I had my vanity. Sure I'd be able to speak. Boy, I'd show that therapist. One lesson, and I'd win another elocution contest. I'd met Teckla Tibbs, and she had sold me. (Sent over by the ACS, with Mary pulling the strings.)

I made my first appointment to take speech lessons late in January.

But before the first lesson, I kept on working on my own, right out of the blue pamphlet.

The problem in esophageal speech is getting to be able to belch when and how you want to, making the belch come up where you bounce it off the walls of the esophagus and cause a vibration. This vibrated belch is sound. You are supposed to take the sound and turn it into words via your tongue, lips, teeth, and mouth. Children learn to speak this way, except they get their sound from the larynx. To them, turning the laryngeal sound into words is just as difficult as my new chore. (Admittedly, the larynx is our natural voice box, and even the infant, seconds old, uses it naturally, letting out a healthy cry. I can't cry.)

So I went about my at-home lessons, right out of the book. I was expected to force air into my esophagus by locking my tongue to the roof of my mouth (as you do when you prepare to say the letter K), and then belch up the air. On the wings of that belch, I would articulate the sound into words. Or at least I thought I would.

I swallowed air, to belch it up.

No belch.

I swallowed more air.

No belch.

I drank water, as the book suggested.

No belch.

I shifted to ginger ale, as the book suggested.

No belch.

I kept trying. I kept relaxing (as the book suggested). I kept trying again.

No belch.

But I *did* make some sound.

Violent hiccups.

I read a pamphlet put out by the ILA, the International Laryngectomee Association. It said, "Some laryngectomees take weeks to make the first sound. Others may take as long as a year." I read another pamphlet: "The majority learn to speak, with their esophageal voice."

It might take weeks. It might take a year. Or I might be in the minority that never learns.

It was enough to turn a man to drink. I turned. More water. More ginger ale. Other carbonated drinks.

My stomach began to swell from the fund of gas. I had enough gas to drive to Portland. But not enough to make a simple belch.

One night, Pat O'Brien came over with a bottle of scotch.

He chatted, and we drank, and I relaxed. And from someplace down in my gut, so far down it seemed to come from New Zealand, I felt a passage of air rising.

I opened my mouth.

"Bah!" I said.

My first word!

"You'd be a big man in China," Pat murmured.

Now I began to experiment. I tried beer. I burped. I tried scotch and soda; I burped with finesse. Scotch needs no help from any source. It is a darling drink, all by itself. But the carbonated water gave me renewed gas, and the scotch gave the resultant burp a kind of class I couldn't quite get from beer.

I was on my way.

Not really. What I'd done finally was burped. In retrospect, they weren't really good burps. They surely didn't deserve the honest word "belch." Belch has character and body. Burp, the lesser word and lesser sound, is a frail cousin. I did not truly belch, as yet. I burped. And I burped weakly, badly.

With the burp, I was still unable to articulate the sound into comprehensible words.

I would practice early in the day, standing in front of Mary. A burp would come out, and I'd try to grab it and make it into the sound A as in Day (as the pamphlet suggested).

"Bah," I would say weakly.

"Attaboy," Mary would say. "Come on. You're doing fine."

"Bah."

"Keep it up. That's beautiful, honey. Say it again."

"Uh."

"Beautiful! More!"

I'd say *bah* and *uh*, but not A. Then it would be time to relax, while, unknown to me, Mary would go off to cry. Practice twenty minutes, relax the rest of the hour. Then start the second hour. Do it as many hours as you can.

I often practiced in front of a mirror. The pamphlet says

merrily, "You will soon realize that your appearance is the same when you are speaking as it was before the operation."

My appearance while *not* speaking was also the same.

All this was difficult work. I never knew how many muscles are involved in swallowing, belching, manipulating the tongue, lips, palate, cheeks, throat, teeth. I could burp, but I couldn't really vibrate. Vibrating meant more muscles put into use. I had to turn the burp into a low-pitched continuing sound, more a rumble than anything else. That's what the book said. A rumble. All right, I'd settle for a rumble. Dear God, I'd settle for that breathy, croaky, guttural gibberish of that little tractor driver.

In the middle of December, Mary and I were invited by Teckla Tibbs' secretary to attend a Christmas party sponsored by the Lost Chord Club of Hollywood. The Lost Chord Club is part of the International Laryngectomee Association. I had given up my membership in the Bel-Air Country Club, but I had the ILA and the Lost Chord Club.

The Christmas party was held at Plummer Park, a tiny patch of green on Santa Monica Boulevard, in Hollywood, with a room for use by the public. About twenty laryngectomees and their wives or husbands attended the party. Coffee and cake were served. Each laryngectomee brought a one-dollar present, to swap. Surprisingly, many presents were ash trays. You occasionally find a cured cancer victim who still smokes. I have never smoked since my operation. But then we also have mates. Mary still smokes. All the propaganda in the world has not shaken her out of the habit. The tobacco habit is a vise, or vice, more powerful than common sense.

They had a recording machine at the party. Many of the laryngectomees got up and recorded their speech. I sat and listened. Other than a few burps, I had no speech to record. Most of the laryngectomees spoke badly; a few spoke pretty well. But each gave support to the other; confidence grows when you hear a fellow victim speak. The party was wonderful therapy, for them.

I kept practicing at home, but I hit a standstill. The year

changed numbers, and Mary wished me Happy New Year, and kissed me, and I nodded and scrawled my greeting to her, and kissed her.

About this time, Dr. Miller decided I'd had my crutch—the tube in my stoma—long enough. I no longer needed the suction machine. What little mucus was coughed up, I neatly wiped away from my stoma with a handkerchief. But I still slept with the tube in my stoma. My Linus blanket.

"You can give it up now," he said.

Suppose I can't breathe? I scribbled on my pad.

"You'll breathe," he said.

So I went to bed one night without my tube. I can't say I slept very much. Visions haunted me, purple-faced, bugging-eyed. But I passed the night and someplace before dawn, I fell asleep, deeply. When I woke, I had no tube to remove. True, it had been near my bed all night, just in case. But I hadn't used it. I never used it again. And I slept the next night through.

On a Friday in January, Mary and I, and our new dog, Patrick, drove fifteen minutes to Hollywood, for my first speech lesson.

Dr. Robert Harrington is a tall, ascetic-looking man, with an extraordinary gentleness. His eyes beam out a message— "What can I do for you?" Yet there is nothing supercilious, nothing un masculine about his gentleness. Quietly, he manages to impart total confidence. Dr. Harrington sat behind his desk; I sat across the desk. Between us was a pitcher of water, and a glass.

I knew, from the pamphlet, more or less what to expect. I would again try to force air into my esophagus and back up, and turn the upcoming sound into words.

Dr. Harrington explained it to me, again, and had me try.

I swallowed air. I neither burped nor belched.

He had me try again.

I swallowed more air. Still no belch. Maybe a tiny burp.

He had me drink water.

I burped mildly.

He told me about ginger ale and other carbonated drinks. I nodded and smiled.

He had me relax for a few minutes, and try again.

I swallowed and burped, quietly, off and on, for a half hour. While I worked, Mary got up—eyes wet—and decided she had to walk the dog. I was fairly wise, by this time, to her need to cry, off by herself. Just as she was wise to my occasional weeping, off by myself.

Pretty soon the first lesson was over. It had been no great breakthrough. Nobody would slip me a pocket watch on a street corner. But then, Dr. Harrington seemed pleased. I left, mildly confident.

We drove back and Mary complimented me on my progress. Naturally I had nothing to say. So I burped.

My burps sounded like *bah* or *ah* or *uh*. I found I could be fairly sure of making a sound if I moved about while I talked. I walked and said, "Bah," as my left foot hit the ground. I took two more steps, and said, "Bah."

I gulped, made my bah, and took two steps. It felt comfortable. Talk, step-step. Burp, step-step. Just like *Aloma of the South Seas*. What do you know, I thought, I'm acting again. Wouldn't Arthur Vinton be pleased? I loosened my gait and swung my arms. "Bah," I said. Step. Step. "Bah," step, step.

Take your time, the pamphlet said. Be relaxed. Speak slowly. I followed orders. I followed Dr. Harrington's Friday orders. Within my throat, I felt odd movements. Muscles, long unused, began to stir.

Along about the third lesson, I said, "A," as in day. Quickly I flew into E as in feet, I as in nine, O as in go, U as in you.

Progress. True progress. All the broad vowels, plus a couple of three of the shorter ones. No words, yet. No consonants, except for that B as in Bah. Between the third and fourth lessons, I began to put some of the sounds together, and the consonants started to limp in. I said to Mary one morning, "One-one," and she beamed. "Beautiful," she said. "Try it louder."

Louder? Who needed it any louder? She could hear. I could hear. I repeated, "One-one." She said, "Fine," but she didn't beam. Now what's wrong? "One-one," I repeated. She nodded. "Go on," she said. "Do some more. And do them louder. You're whispering."

I walked away. Here I was progressing like a maniac, like the heroine in *Pygmalion*, and Mary was not satisfied.

I kept practicing, at Dr. Harrington's office, and away. He moved from Hollywood to Long Beach along about the eighth or ninth week of my lessons, and Mary and I went to visit him. I said to the elevator operator, "Six."

Mary beamed. "Beautiful," she said.

But in the office, where I now busily put words together, "One-two . . . Eat egg . . . See us . . ." trying to speak the beginning of each word clearly, and holding the vowel as long as possible, Mary began to fidget. What was wrong? I wondered. At night, now, when the boys came over, for a drink and a conversation, I would drop a word or two into the middle of it, and everybody would slap my back and tell me how well this cat was making it. I'd even learned to say, "Scotch and soda."

So I sat in Dr. Harrington's office, a big grin on my mug, knowing I was setting some sort of world's record for esophageal speech, when Mary spoke up. "Dr. Harrington," she said, "what should I do? Bill won't stop whispering."

Dr. Harrington nodded, his eyes very gentle. He looked across me, to Mary, and he said, very softly, "Why don't you walk out of the room? Turn your back, if he whispers. Don't listen."

I stared at the two of them in amazement. What did they expect? I was just getting started.

Dr. Harrington told me what they—he—expected. Whispering, he said, was a crutch. Yes, I was getting along fine, and quickly. My speech was far more understandable than most. But because it was, I was satisfied to whisper my few words, and hope the listener would strain a little to hear me.

I sat back, dumfounded. I thought of the nightly sessions. Memory came back sharply. People bent toward me when I spoke. It had become automatic. They did not notice it, and I had not, until this moment. They strained. They heard.

Well, what was wrong with that? I had to strain, didn't I? Let them strain.

The lesson ended, and I drove back, stony-faced, with Mary next to me. I had no doubt I'd keep improving, my own way. I was getting on quite well. I whispered a little. Later, I'd speak louder, when I had better control of what I wanted to say. Not for a moment did I believe that Mary would do what Dr. Harrington said. Turn her back. Stop listening. Walk away. It would be cruel, and cruelty was not like Mary.

She looked at me, as we drove. "I'm going to do it," she said softly. "Suppose you're on an airplane someday, all the noise of the jets outside, people talking, a couple of kids running in the aisle, and you need help. Who's going to hear you whisper?"

What airplane? What kind of help? She was talking nonsense.

"Or you're on a noisy street, and you need help," she went on. "Who can hear a whisper?"

"Shut up!" I said.

"I can't hear you," she said. "You'll have to talk louder."

"Shut up!"

"I can't hear you." Her lip seemed to curl. "You. The bellowing Irishman. You could hit every balcony in America."

"Shut up!"

But I guess I whispered it, because she wouldn't.

20

Unaccustomed As I Am to Public Speaking

I had more magic slates than I knew what to do with. People gave them to me as presents. Big ones, little onces, gold-plated ones, ones with pencil and pen attached.

The slate is another crutch. Necessary in the beginning, when your leg is broken, but not so when all you've got is a charley horse. Limp along. Not that I learned this all by myself. I became quite attached to my crutch. I got to write very fast on the slate, and I got along famously well, when I did not feel much like talking. Which was fairly often. Then one day, Mary snatched my slate away from me, and I got the message. You know somebody who needs a couple of dozen partly-used slates?

I spoke. I could say, "Six," to the elevator operator. I could answer the phone and growl, "Yes," when somebody asked if this was Bill Gargan. I couldn't say much more than that, and eventually the other party would get nervous, trying to understand me, and I'd turn the phone over to Mary. I could put a few words together. Take a breath, let it up in a controlled burp, and then speak two or three words. Another breath, another four or five words. The pamphlet suggested reciting poetry. I tried it. I said, "Over the mountains (breath)/Over the plains (breath) /Over the rivers (breath)/Here comes the trains. Phew."

But I never was much for nursery rhymes. I began to try

short passages in Shakespeare. I moved to longer, more difficult ones. I began working on Hamlet's speech to the Players, "Speak the speech, I pray you."

I had to give it up, at first. The letter "p" is one of two sounds a laryngectomee cannot make. Or at least this laryngectomee cannot. "P" comes out as "B." And I cannot aspirate the letter "h." I don't think any laryngectomee can. House is -ouse. How is -ow.

So I went back to simpler stuff. Robert Service served me well. "This is the law of the Yukon/that only the strong shall strive/that surely the Weak shall perish (berish)/and only the Fit survive./Dissolute, damned, and despairful/crippled and palsied and slain,/This is the Will of the Yukon—Lo, how she makes it plain!"

True, it came out—Lo, 'ow she makes it blain. But people are wonderful listeners. They fill in the gaps. You say, "Bob goes the weasel," and they assume you said, "Pop."

I returned to Hamlet's speech, after a week or two. It was ludicrous, a fit of vanity again. "Oh, it offends me to the soul"— I began, and took a breath, and went on—"to hear a robustious —periwig-pated fellow—tear a passion to tatters." It sounded like a schoolchild, learning to recite. I said it in pieces and tatters myself, and the p's were b's; he was a berrywig-bated fellow, tearing a bashun. But I kept on. "It out-Herods Herod." Breath. "Pray you avoid it."

Ludicrous. Wildly hilarious. Out-'erods 'erod, indeed. Bray you avoid it.

But I kept on. If I had a motto, it was *Bray on, McGargan, and damned be 'e who cries.*

I said most of these speeches to my mirror, or to myself, as I walked about, swinging my arms, speaking and step-stepping. I had to speak them to myself, because Mary had meant what she had said.

She had turned her back on me.

She had given me a few days, after Dr. Harrington advised her to stop listening if I insisted on whispering. I guess she wanted me to see for myself whether I could speak louder.

Whether I could or not, I didn't. She didn't turn her back the first time or the second, and I knew she had decided she just couldn't.

One day in February or March of 1961, we were sitting about the table in the playroom, near the garden and I said something to Mary, and she replied, "You're whispering, Bill."

I could answer the phone and carry on a brief conversation. I could go to the store and ask for items on a shelf. I could order a meal in a restaurant. I could say, to anybody at our supper table, "Pass the salt," and they passed it, even if I actually said, "Bass the salt."

What more did she want?

I said, "What do you want?"

"I want you to speak. Not whisper."

"I am speaking."

"No, you're not. You're whispering. You're making everybody bow to you, just to hear you. Who do you think you are, king of the hill?"

I started to answer her, and she bent forward to watch me for a moment. Then she got up and walked away. She went in through the entrance hall to the living room. It is, I said earlier, a huge house, with high Spanish ceilings, where the sound rises and disappears up there with the heavy hand-hewn beams. Well, I thought, if she was going to hide and sulk, I'd turn on the television set, in the playroom. I turned in on. Back in the living room, she turned on the record player and slipped on a few records. We own a gorgeous system, with sound piped all through the house. Her music began to drown out my program.

I got up. I suspected what she had done, but I wasn't sure. I remain, through the years, the same quick study.

I walked into the living room.

"Turn off—the damned thing," I said. I had to gasp to get it all out. The rule is, Relax. I was tense. "How can I hear—my TV show?"

She had her back to me, fussing with the drapes.

"You didn't—answer me."

She did not turn. But she spoke. Her voice was muffled.
"Because you whispered."

"I talked."

She turned. She was crying. "Bill, you're not even talking now. You're whispering. You were the bellowing Irishman. Why don't you bellow now?"

"I—can't." I was panting, sweat pouring down my face and throat.

"You can. You always bellowed. Bellow now."

I turned away. I walked back to the playroom. After a few minutes, I turned off the set and went upstairs and lay down on my bed. Facing the wall.

We went to Dr. Harrington.

"He's still whispering," Mary said.

"Turn your back."

They acted as though I were in another room, another city. This was the man I assumed was so gentle, so kind.

"Very often," he said to Mary, "you'll have to do what appear to be cruel things."

The lesson continued. I tried to speak louder. But I'd become tense. My voice was thin, a quiet croak. We went home, my knuckles white on the steering wheel.

We were silent.

I would begin each morning with a series of exercises. First I'd burp. Bah-bah-bah-bah-bah. Like an actor warming up. Then, A-A-A-A-A. E-E-E-E-E. I-I-I-I-I. O-O-O-O-O. U-U-U-U-U. I will speak . . . Good morning . . . Bacon and eggs . . . Bah-bah-bah-bah-bah . . . I will speak."

We had more and more people over. The nights were filled with laughter. I spoke more and more, and got more and more slaps on the back. The cat was making it. Then, in the middle of a conversation, Mary would look over at me.

"Speak up, honey. I can't hear you."

People would stiffen. You could see their thoughts. What kind of ghoul was this woman? Doing this to a sweet guy like Bill Gargan. Somebody would say loudly, to fill the lull, "That reminds me of the story about . . ." and the conversation would soon continue.

During the day, Mary would sometimes sit with me and talk with me, listen to me and answer me. Other times she would get that look on her face I had come to dread. The lip would stiffen, the face turn into a mask. She would get up and walk to the entranceway of the room.

"I can't hear you," she would say. "Speak up."

"I am speaking up."

"No, you're not. You're whispering. Please, darling. Speak up."

I would answer, try to answer. She would walk farther away. "I still can't hear you. What did you say?"

I would try to make her hear me. But she did not answer; she walked into the living room.

I don't want you to think our marriage was on the rocks. I am a stubborn Irishman, but I knew what she was doing. She was goading me to speak louder. I wasn't really whispering, the way I had been a few weeks before. I just wasn't talking loud enough.

The anger I directed toward her was really anger at myself. I would follow her and clench my fists and try to scream. It wouldn't come out. I was furious with myself. Why couldn't I speak louder?

At night, we lay together, and she murmured how much she loved me, and her face was often wet, in the dark.

We would eat out occasionally, and Mary let me do nearly all the ordering. When a waitress did not understand, I would do what the book said, what Dr. Harrington said. Smile. It relaxes the throat muscles. I'd repeat my order. This time she'd understand. But I noticed she'd bent over, to hear me. I still was "whispering."

The sixteen weeks with Dr. Harrington passed. "You're on your own now," he said, after the sixteenth. "I can't help you any more. You've done splendidly. You've graduated. Now it's up to you to do even better."

Graduated. I thought: Graduated to what? To where? Where was I going?

While hoping to sell our Beverly Hills house, we put it up for rent, and moved out to Bermuda Dunes. On the way to the desert, Mary would have me read the Freeway exit signs and billboards.

"Say, 'Euclid.' "

"Euclid."

"Say, 'Paramount.' "

"Barramount."

"Say, 'Rosemead.' "

"Rosemead."

"Say, 'Wabash . . . General Electric . . . Winstons Taste Good . . . Riverside Freeway . . . Palm Springs.' "

I said them all.

"Say them louder."

Once a week I would drive in, by myself, to collect my unemployment insurance check. I would meet many an actor on line with me. We called it The Green Room.

The routine seldom changed.

The girl would say, "You're looking for work, aren't you?"

I would nod.

"What is your salary demand?"

In the beginning I would write on a sheet of paper. Later, I got to say it.

"One thousand dollars a week." Or, if I was feeling very talented that week, "Two thousand."

Which ended the interview. I got my $55.

I received a check for twenty-six weeks.

One day I got a phone call, from Broderick Crawford.

"How'd you like to work for a week?" he asked.

"I'd love to, but—"

"Come on down to the studio Monday."

So I went down to Ziv Studios, and I appeared in a TV drama, on the show *King of Diamonds*. I played a clown. I worked three days, and I got a check for $1000.

It was wonderful therapy, working, slapping on make-up, meeting a wardrobe call, learning my part (silent). Brod Crawford and Jon Epstein, over at Ziv, gave me a lift when I most wanted and needed it. And the thousand dollars didn't hurt. I didn't collect unemployment that week.

But I did the next week, and for the rest of the year. Nobody else called me. How many clowns are there? I could even see myself doing a part not in pantomime. I could play a monster, with my weird croak of a voice. Except, as Mary would have said, it wasn't loud enough for a good monster.

So Brod Crawford gave me a lift, and then the gloom set in more deeply. I could picture the future, the occasional call. "We need a clown? How about Gargan?"

Or maybe a mute.

No. It was all over, my career. They needed no clowns, no king's jesters, no mutes.

I got another call early in 1961. Not a show biz call. An ACS call. I said there was a bit of bulldog in ACS. Maybe more than a bit.

Unknown to me, while I was moping about, speaking, but not speaking up, a woman in Palm Springs was beating the bushes, looking for a working chairman for the 1961 cancer "crusade" for funds. The woman was, and is, Jinx Ray, the ACS field representative for the desert area, and the search she set into operation would one day sweep me into her net, and from there, change my entire life. I owe lots of people lots of things, doctors, nurses, Teckla Tibbs, friends, actors, strangers, fellow cancer victims, loved ones. Other than my wife, nobody has given me the boost, the support, the feeling that I am a useful, worthwhile, productive human being as has Jinx Ray.

I knew none of what was going on. It began back in January of 1961. The tiny Palm Springs ACS unit had managed to collect $5000 the year before; this year the unit had set an ambitious goal for itself. It would try to collect twice as much. But what was needed was a working chairman, somebody who knew the desert community and its people. Somebody who also was known by the community. Somebody involved in the cancer fight.

Names were kicked around, and rejected. On January 14, 1961,

Jinx Ray—whom I had never met—called a friend of hers, Libby Gardiner, asking for more names. Libby Gardiner had been a staff colleague of Jinx Ray's when they both worked for ACS in Los Angeles. Libby Gardiner asked her husband Al, a long-time Palm Springs businessman. Al said, "Try Bill Gargan."

Libby called Jinx. "Try Bill Gargan." Then she added: "All you have to do is convince him that a brand new door is opening for him. Right now his whole world has crumbled."

Libby Gardiner told Jinx Ray about me, about my cancer, my loss of speech. She built me up, in Jinx Ray's mind, as a man who knew the desert. (She didn't know how I felt about sand blowing about. It's bad enough in one's nostrils; it can be fatal in the stoma.)

"If you can convince him," Libby Gardiner went on, "that he'll be making a meaningful contribution to the cancer battle, you may save him from some desolate moments in the days ahead."

Jinx Ray hesitated about calling me. She didn't know me. But she knew somebody who did. Dr. William Elliott. I'd known Bill Elliott for years. We'd ridden together in the old days, and not too long before, he and I had had breakfast at Trav Rogers' Stables. Now Bill was the local volunteer unit chairman of ACS.

Bill called me on January 15, 1961. He spoke not to me, but to Mary, though I listened on the other phone. He told Mary, and me, about Jinx Ray, and her campaign.

"Tell Mrs. Ray to put the matter into a letter," Mary said. "But I can tell you the answer." She looked at me. I nodded Yes. "He'll accept," Mary said.

The letter arrived. It mentioned, among other things, that the Palm Springs unit would be meeting in March at the Garden Room of the El Mirador Hotel, owned by Ray Ryan. The letter did not ask me to speak; it asked just that I be there.

Mary and I drove to Palm Springs in March, with Patrick, our constant companion. We bustled into the hotel, where we met Jinx Ray, a warm, pretty smiling gal with a personality that could charm birds out of trees, or speech out of mutes.

She didn't ask me to speak that day. She just wanted me to stand up and be seen. I nodded that that was fine with me. So they introduced me, and I got up, and then I took the plunge. I wrestled with my tongue and my throat and my breath. I hadn't spoken more than five or six words in a row with anybody before. I'd had a few brief conversations with Mary, mainly telling her to shut up when she told me to speak up. I practiced poetry in front of a mirror, with nobody around to laugh at my ludicrous attempts. I engaged in tiny—very tiny chitchat with my friends in the social hours of a drinking evening. But these ten or twelve ACS workers were total strangers. I looked down and saw Mary, saw even Patrick, saw Jinx Ray. She smiled at me.

"Unaccustomed as I am to public speaking," I said, and everybody laughed, and I kept right on going, for five minutes. I spoke slowly; I told the volunteers what wonderful work they were doing. I thanked them for asking me to help. I thanked the ACS for helping me. That without the ACS I wouldn't be standing here. I wouldn't be standing, period.

It wasn't much of a speech, and they were friends, even though they were strangers. But it was the first words I'd spoken in public in four months.

Mary and Patrick and I drove back to Bermuda Dunes, a few miles away.

"That was very good," Mary said.

"Thank you."

"Next time speak louder."

That was how I met Jinx Ray, how I became actively involved with the ACS. It wasn't—yet—much of an involvement; we'd traipse across to Palm Springs for meetings with volunteers; we used as a crusade headquarters a house loaned to me by Trav Rogers, on the site of the old Mink and Manure Club, where Trav and I had raised funds for the Desert Hospital. Though the meetings were frequent through 1961, they were brief. My service, if it could be called that, was limited. I couldn't talk that well; I was new at the game. And it all got harder before it got easier.

We moved back into 512 North Palm, the rental season over, and the house still up for sale, but no takers. But we were fortunate. A well known TV writer had just moved from New York and needed a house desperately. We accepted his offer, which was fine, except it left us without a house to live in. Fortunately, we had friends like Walter and Marian Bunker, who put us up at their home in Bel-Air. But we still needed a permanent home, and again we were lucky. Jack and Flo Haley, who owned the Mauretania Apartments where Mary and I had stayed while rehearsing for *The Best Man*, also had a duplex on South Elm Drive, in Beverly Hills. One of the two units was available; did we want it?

"You can have it for $50 a month," Flo Haley said.

"Nothing doing," I said. "You can't cut the price."

So we settled for $75 a month, a nice cheerful apartment. I would miss the playroom, the huge bedroom that had been a porch and was still as airy as the sky, and I would miss that indomitable lemon tree. But we could use the savings. Meanwhile, before we moved—which would not be until after the first of the year, 1962—we had a few months to enjoy the house on Palm Drive. We enjoyed them the way we had always enjoyed them— friends, supper parties, cocktail parties, party parties—though not quite as lavishly as in the past. But we had fun. Laughs. Drinks. Friends.

But after the parties were over and our friends had left, I lay awake asking myself over and over again why this tragedy had struck us. Only God knew, and at that time He wasn't confiding in me. I was sure he would in time, but meanwhile life was pretty rugged while I waited for an answer.

Something was wrong. Not my throat. It felt fine. Dr. Miller checked me out regularly, and I checked out fine. All healed. The first year passed, the year Mary had to sweat out. Now the year was past. The usual rule with cancer victims is—no recurrence in five years, consider yourself cured. One year down, four to go. And every day, in every way (but one), I felt the next four would go on just as well, and even better.

But something was wrong. The evenings were fun; once again I tracked down the next laugh and made it mine. But it was hollow. Jinx Ray got me to agree to serve as California State Crusade Vice-Chairman for the ACS, covering the Southern California area, for 1962. I was learning how ACS operated, how the volunteers worked. But, so far, it wasn't enough. I could speak a little better, but not much. Life, it seemed, was handing me crumbs; maybe more crumbs than it had handed me a few months before, but still crumbs.

The question remained. And it remained unanswered. Why me? I am a beat-up Catholic, but I am a Catholic. Never once in my bleakest moments had I contemplated suicide. My faith prevented it, and I do not mean by faith a bundle of rituals and some sweet palaver. I mean faith. Trust in God. The universe in order, not chaos. We all grow in the same way, legs and arms and brains, the boys straight and sturdy, and the girls slim and fair. The trees are like each other and the flowers like each other; a tulip looks like a tulip and not like a rose, and an ant crawls and does not fly. God's universe. I trust it. It makes sense. It has plan and reason.

One thing puzzled me. It had no plan or reason. None that I could grasp. Why had I been chosen to have my throat cut open, my speech ripped out? Why me? Yes, I know it is Job's question; yes, I know we cannot possibly fathom God's will or His way. But it didn't stop me from asking. Call it self-pity, if you will, and I call it right along with you. But I think there is more than self-pity to the question. Why *me*, God?

Why had this happened to me? Yes, it is vanity. Why does anything happen to anybody? Why is the young man down the street killed in Vietnam defending his country, yet the boy across the way comes back alive and whole. Why him? Why not the other? Why me? Why had God chosen to test Job so terribly, His most faithful servant? Why did Job suffer? Why do the just suffer, and, so often, the wicked flourish? Why *me*?

The question puzzled me and pursued me. It became a nag. It haunted my silent laughter and created my silent tears. Why me, God? Why me?

But God didn't answer.

Yet.

We began the usual round of Christmas parties, 1961. Before one party, just cocktails at our house, Mary said to me, "Honey, why don't you ever tell a story any more?"

I stared at her in amazement. "I can't tell a story."

"Why not?"

Lots of reasons. The voice was a dismal croak. My timing would be shot. Take a breath, speak four or five words; take another breath. And, of course, a few people in the room wouldn't hear, or understand what they heard. I was getting used to people's reactions to my voice. Some people would plaster a fake smile on their face and nod absently as I talked. The nod and the smile indicated they understood what I was saying, but you could see they didn't have the foggiest idea. It is infuriating. You are being lied to. Out of the best of intentions, yes, but you are being lied to. That's one kind of listener, the smiling, nodding liar. The other is equally infuriating, though perhaps more understandable. I would start to talk, and people would understand so well they knew what I was getting ready to say. They would interrupt and finish my word or my sentence, for me. On the stage, we call them cue biters, people who step on your line and hurry to grab the stage themselves.

I suppose it is a kindness. It is, on the surface. Beneath, it is cruelty. Let me wrestle out my words. I don't interrupt you. Yes, it's hard to speak, especially in the beginning. But if you don't let me, I'll never get so it's easy to speak. And, yes, it's hard to listen to me, but please—listen a little harder. Don't be impatient and don't be lazy. I'll get the words out in due time. What's the hurry?

But ordinary speech and telling a story are two different animals. I am impatient with bad story-telling. Most actors are. We have spent our lives learning to read our lines. Not every actor can tell a story well, but an awful lot can. We are the music-makers.

Now my music was a whispered growl, a half-spoken croak.

"I can't tell a story," I said to Mary, again.

"Horsefeathers," she said, and she walked away.

So that party came and went, lots of laughter, more hollow than ever.

We threw a party just before Christmas, buffet for friends and relatives. Mary's brother, Joe Kenny, was in. Ed and Cooee Gargan flew in. Margaret Kenny, Mary's aunt, showed up. Barrie Gargan was in from New York, with his wife, Kathryn. Leslie was there. Friends—Crosby, Wally Bunker, Bohemian buddies, Eddie Bernard, Dr. Louis Martin, who never took a five-cent piece from the time he had helped in diagnosing my illness right on through my operation and recuperation. People. Friends. I loved them all.

The morning of the party, Mary puttered about, getting things ready, and I manned the kitchen. I prepared a turkey, a ham, and a roast beef. I knocked off a few tons of potato salad, the German type with lots of vinegar. In the middle of it all, I said something to Mary, in the other room, and she ignored me. Well, she hadn't heard over the clatter of utensils. No sweat. I repeated what I'd said, and this time I heard her feet walking away.

I had devised a signal to call Mary when my voice didn't get the job done. I would rap my knuckles on whatever wood was handy. I rapped, hard, on the carving board. It meant, Come here, so I can make myself heard.

"I'm busy," she said. "What do you want?" Her feet were silent. She wasn't getting an inch closer.

I took a gulp of air and tried to push out the words. All that came out was one of my early consonant sounds—"Bah-bah." I tried again. All I got out was another weak bah.

I followed her. We would have it out. I was tired of her act. It had become cruel (I thought).

She'd walked into the living room. It is a big room, thirty-five feet long, with picture windows so you can see the olive tree outside, the lawn, and the poinsettias, which were then in full red bloom. In the middle of the room we had our tree, a ceiling scraper.

She'd walked past the tree, to the far end of the room, near the baby grand, which Leslie played; she stood with her back to me, fussing once more with the drapes. I could not see her clearly; the tree stood between us, with its messages on its green boughs. We do not decorate our tree the usual way; we use no ornaments, no tinsel. Just the Christmas cards we receive, as many as we can Scotch tape to the branches, and lights. Nothing else. The tree becomes a warm sermon of love and brotherhood, peace and good will.

It stood between us.

"I don't want you to do that again," I said.

"Talk, then. Even one word."

"I try."

"Not hard enough."

If I had held something in my hand, I would have thrown it at her; I would have sent it crashing through that tree full of love. I wanted to hit out at her.

"I do try hard," I said. I stared at my hands. They were balled into fists. I wanted to belt her one.

"You don't succeed," she said, her voice muffled. "Stop whispering. Talk louder!"

You want another definition of frustration? It is bellowing out your anger, and being told to speak up.

My hands shook, in front of me. My fury was a live thing, inside. She had turned her back to me, her body, dimly seen, stiff as a blade. I wanted to relax (how else could I talk?), but I couldn't. Emotions clashed and smashed inside me. Hate. Anger. (Love.) Fury. Frustration. (Pity.) I felt I was being torn apart. Dear God, I thought, why *me*? Why was this happening to me?

A mist seemed to fill me. I felt confused, harassed, wearied. It had all become mixed together, my question—why me?—and my inability to speak up. I stared at Mary, but all I saw was a tree that must have smelled like all the glorious forests have smelled for centuries, for eons; I thought of Alec Templeton unable to know green or light or dark or even a Christmas card of love. I tried to see Mary, hovering at the drapes, her body stiff, so brittle (it seemed) it would crack. But all I saw was that tree, with its angels, its Santas, its sermons, its Wise Men, its Madonnas, its tiny messages: Peace. Love. Good will.

And I thought—in the midst of fury and pity and hate— what did it matter? I couldn't speak too loud. I couldn't smell. Was that my problem? If it was, what kind of problem was it that reduced me to sniveling sorrow, all directed at myself? Where were those memories of amputees and their laughter, of Alec Templeton playing a love song to a redwood?

I tried to keep my hate. I felt I needed it. It seemed to me to be strength. (It is; it is the strength of weakness.)

"Speak up," Mary said quietly. "For God's sake, speak up!"

I thought: I'll turn my back on her. I'll show her.

I said to her stiff blade of a body, dimly seem through peace and beauty and the wondrous birth of Christ, "Go to hell!" and I started to walk off.

Then I stopped. My voice was in my ears. A different sound. I turned back. Mary stepped around the tree. Her eyes were shining.

"Beautiful!" she whispered. "That was beautiful, darling. Say it again."

I had yelled.

She had wrung it out of me. I don't know how, I don't know why. Maybe some muscle had finally been coaxed into action. But I do know she had done it. She had begged, ranted, swore. She had done everything she could have done. It had been—she told me—the hardest thing she'd ever had to do in her life. She hated herself for doing it. But she knew it had to be done, and she'd done it. I had rejected it—her—for days, weeks, now months. But she wouldn't quit. I don't know how she had the strength for it. Except I think I do know.

"Thank you, darling," I said. "You are a saint."

My voice was full in my ears. It was like diving beneath the ocean and feeling the roar of the water in your ears, or holding a huge seashell to the side of your head, and hearing the ocean's bellow.

I had bellowed. I was, again, the bellowing Irishman. There are prettier sounds. I will not drive Dennis Day out of singing. Olivier need not look to his laurels. But I wouldn't trade them a thing at the moment.

Because more than a muscle had been involved. I sensed it dimly then; I know it fully today. A miracle, of sorts, had taken place. Love had conquered hate. God had conquered doubt. Why *me*? Why *not* me? That was the message, of the tree, of my saintlike Mary, of God.

The party. It went like all other parties, which meant swimmingly. I was talking, a little better in the beginning of the party, using my new voice, but by the time the party had gone on for a few hours, my new voice began to falter a bit. New muscles get tired. So I began to whisper again.

Then somebody said something about somebody named Shaughnessy, and Mary's face brightened, and she said, from across the room, "Oh, Bill, that reminds me of the story you used to tell. You know, that one about Miss Shaughnessy, the 104-year-old virgin. Tell it."

Silence. I heard a cough. Joe Kenny, Mary's brother, looked as though he'd been slapped with a wet flounder. Somebody else began to talk, loudly, over the lull.

I wrestled with a smile (to relax my throat), I took a breath, and forced it down and felt the deep rumble, deeper than a well, begin to crawl back up, vibrating the walls of the esophagus.

"There was this tiny old woman," I began, speaking over the other noise in the room, where the ceilings were as high as a theater balcony, "by the name of O'Shaughnessy. . . ."

I told it. All the way. I never thought of how to tell it. I just told it. The old way. Slow start, a couple of small teaser jokes in the middleground to warm them up, and then a build to the big snapper at the end. A story.

They laughed. They roared. They slapped knees, thighs, backs. Not just mine. Theirs.

"Which reminds me," I said, "of another one."

Keep your Drama Critics awards, your Academy Award nominations. I'll take that one night. And I'll give it to Mary.

She deserved it. Joe Kenny did not understand what had happened. He cornered his sister later, and he said (so Mary has since told me), "What are you doing to Bill? You're torturing him. Of all the unmitigated witches, you take the cake."

She dragged him into a guest bathroom, and she told him what she had done, been doing, would do, if she had to. She would drag sound out of stone, if she had to. She'd surely drag it out of one William Gargan, the so-called bellowing Irishman. And when Joe Kenny came out of that guest bathroom, he was crying. "Bless you," he sobbed. "You are a saint."

What a note. The guy steals my line.

21

"Practice, Man, Practice!"

We moved into Jack and Flo Haley's apartment on April 1, 1962. April Fool's Day. The place needed a painting. Vince D'Acholli, a friend of mine and of Dennis Day's, owns a hardware and paint shop. He sent over the paint, free. I furnished the labor. If there was anything I had plenty of, it was time. And energy.

I painted the whole place. I had to wear a bib over my stoma. The paint fumes made my lungs ache. The bib was my one concession to my illness. When we drove to Bermuda Dunes and ran into a sandstorm, which was often, I'd put on my bib. Now that sand doesn't get into my sandwiches, I saw no need to let it into my throat.

Painting the apartment was swell therapy. But it wasn't enough. I needed something to do, and I needed it badly. What I needed was a job. And no matter how well I painted that apartment, it wouldn't be as a house painter. Not just because the paint fumes hurt my lungs. I was about as good a house painter as I'd been a corn farmer.

Along about this time I received a call from Walter Kennedy, who is today the president of the National Basketball Association. Kennedy was the secretary of a club I belonged to, the Skeeters, founded by Ted Husing back in the early 1950s. The Skeeters were mainly New Yorkers who would traipse across the bridge or through the tunnels to New Jersey, and enjoy a day at the races

at Garden State Park. Toots Shor, Mac Kriendler, and Charlie
Berns, of the 21 Club, were among the original Skeeters. Ike
Levy, Sonny Werblin, Eddie Arcaro, Louis Sobel, Bob Considine,
and Frank Coniff are Skeeters. So am I.

Walter Kennedy's call was a sad one. Ted Husing had died.
Walter wondered whether I would represent the Skeeters at his
funeral, here on the Coast. I said I would, and the next day, as I
got ready to go, I received a phone call, this time from Sanders
Simon, another Skeeter. Sandy is a successful industrialist with
fingers in a dozen pies. He's the kind of guy who kisses ladies'
hands when he meets them or leaves them, and on him it looks
good.

Sandy called from the Beverly Hills Hotel; he was a friend of
Ted Husing's. He'd flown out for the funeral; could we get together?

He picked me up and we went to the funeral, and after, we
repaired to the Polo Lounge of the Beverly Hills Hotel and had
a couple of drinks.

During the course of our drinks and our chat, I mentioned to
him that what I really needed to keep me going was a job. An
honest-to-God job where I worked for somebody, producing something worthwhile.

Sandy Simon helped me get not one job, but two, both with
printing companies. My job was to get new business—which I
did. The jobs made me feel useful, worthwhile, a working stiff
again. I'm grateful to Sandy for his efforts as I am to all the
others who extended themselves in my behalf. But, I felt, this
wasn't why God had taken my speech away. I had a hunch I
knew why.

Because I could speak again, and fairly well, I found myself
making more "unaccustomed as I am to public-speaking" speeches,
for our local ACS unit. And I found myself leaning more on
Jinx Ray. Jinx helped prepare my speeches, brief talks before
local civic and service clubs. Not very well done, I'm afraid,
because I didn't—yet—have a good grasp of my message. I would
ask Jinx to furnish all the data available on the cancer problem
and on the ACS. How many people were struck by cancer;

how many survived; what were the danger signs; how many volunteers were knocking on doors; how much money was needed. Jinx came up with the figures, and I would rely on them, initially, in my early speeches. But even though Jinx's material was infinitely better than my hesitant handling of it, I wasn't very comfortable with the data. For that is what it was: data. Sterile numbers. Statistics. I didn't feel comfortable with them, because they didn't seem to me to be the material that would reach people.

So I told Jinx what I wanted in my fumbling, low-voiced way. "I want people to know how grateful I am to be alive," I said, "after having cancer. I want them to know one of the reasons I'm alive is because of the work done by ACS." This was, after all, the way I had put it the very first time, at the El Mirador Hotel luncheon. "I want to tell people"—and now I was getting down to my answer to all my questions—"I want to tell people that I've decided to dedicate the rest of my life to fighting cancer, because"—breath breath—"because I think my life was spared for that one reason."

Why *not* me?

Somebody had to do it. Somebody had to get out there on the boondocks and say, I've lived through it; it isn't so awful; it could have been worse; look at me, I can talk, I can live. Somebody had to speak to these people from the awful knowledge of the disease, from the awful knowledge of the fear and self-pity and anguish; somebody who knew of the sleepless nights and the hopeless days, the times you try to speak and all you get is a thin trickle of air, a grunt, a moan.

Jinx Ray looked at me. "You've just written your own best speech," she said.

It became the pattern. She wrote it into my next speech; she made it part of any fund-raising letter I sent out; later I suggested that an annual Christmas card—I knew all about Christmas cards, and their message—be used as a fund-raiser. She incorporated into the card what I'd said about dedicating my life to fighting cancer. I had been incapacitated in a special way to help others similarly incapacitated.

My work with ACS began to burgeon. I agreed to serve as California State Crusade vice-chairman—for Southern California —for 1962; meanwhile, I remained Palm Springs Unit crusade chairman, and I added on the job of Honorary Chairman for the desert and Coachella Valley towns in eastern Riverside County for the coming year. All on a volunteer basis, which means without pay. But this is what I wanted to do.

Near the end of April of 1962, I received a call. Because I was speaking pretty well now, the ACS wanted me to speak to a small group of laryngectomees in New York.

The group was part of the National Hospital for Speech Disorders at 61 Irving Place in Gramercy Park. The pieces began to fall together even more. Now I was with the group I understood as well as I've ever understood any group of people I've ever met. And, I hoped, they would understand me. (Today I am on the Board of Directors of the National Hospital for Speech Disorders.)

I went to New York, and spoke, on the morning of May 2, 1962, to fourteen laryngectomees, mostly men, while in the back of the room, a handful of other men and women took notes. I assumed they were doctors, clinicians, and the like, observing the group.

When I began to talk, I could see a change in the faces of the laryngectomees, seated below me. At first they had been stiff, almost hostile. Who was this guy, coming here to con them? Then I began to speak. I told them when I had discovered my cancer, and when my larynx had been removed. Not quite eighteen months ago. Their faces seemed to brighten. You could almost hear them think—"If this guy can talk like this after eighteen months, maybe there's hope for me."

I didn't soft-soap them. I knew better. I'd been there. I told of my own difficulties, and of Mary's perseverance, her turning her back, to make me stop whispering. I told them to put away their slates as soon as possible, to answer the phone, to order meals, to turn away from the wall.

But I kept it light. Maybe I still had some magic to sprinkle. The stories were easy to tell. They all were true. I told of asking my doctor whether I'd ever be able to drink again, I told of the nurse who'd thrown in the booze straight. I told how my first recorded words were scotch and soda. (So maybe all the stories weren't true.)

Then I switched again. Persevere, I told them. There is no other way. They listened, their smiles stilled now. Learn the method, and stick to it, and practice. I told a joke about the well-dressed man carrying a violin onto the New York subway, getting lost, and ending up down in Greenwich Village, where he runs into a bearded beatnik.

"Could you tell me, please," the violinist asks, "how one gets to Carnegie Hall?"

The beatnik eyed him grandly. "Practice, man, practice!" he said.

End of ten-minute speech.

The men and women in the back of the room, taking notes, began to ask questions. I answered them. The meeting ended.

The next day every paper in New York carried the story. The note-takers had been reporters. The story went out over the wires.

I got another call, from the ACS. Would I make another appearance? I would, and again, and again.

I went, and I went again, and I went enthusiastically.

Because I was beginning to get an answer to my question.

You send your petitions to God, and eventually He answers them. He was answering mine.

Why me?

Because somebody had to go out and help these muted cancer victims, as I had been helped. Each of us needs a boost. I like to think I didn't need help, but Dr. Miller had boosted me, and Dr. Harrington, and Mary, and Teckla Tibbs, and Jinx Ray and the whole body of the ACS. Friends had helped me, my sons, my relatives. Strangers wrote me letters, wishing me well and blessing me.

Who knows how much help these other cancer victims had received? Maybe some, maybe none.

Now God helped me, to help them. This is your direction, He

had said, pointing. If you are a music-maker, a sprinkler of magic —He said—make music for these people from whose lives the song is stilled. Sprinkle magic, if you have any left, upon these people who do not lead a fun-seeking life. You're an actor (He said). Act a little. Put on the clown's mask, for real. Make 'em laugh, and make 'em persevere. You won a Drama Critics award (He said); now let's see how good you are. You've never had so huge an audience, so wide a stage. Take it to 'em. He said.

In 1962, I spoke before groups on Long Island, in New York City, in Ohio, Oregon, Arkansas, and California. Service clubs, fund-raising rallies, groups of patients. Nor did I speak only to groups. I would check into a city, where I was scheduled to speak the next noon, at a kickoff luncheon for the annual cancer fund-raising drive, and the elevator operator would say, "I know who you are, Mr. Gargan. I've been reading about you. My father has cancer, and they want to take out his larynx, but he's scared. I wonder if you . . ."

So you go. You sit in a kitchen with a man who's about to have his larynx torn out, if he can summon the will, and he's terribly afraid. You tell him you were afraid, too, and there isn't much any man can do for any other man, at this moment. Yes, it is horrible, terrible, sad, but—you tell the man—God will watch him.

God had watched you, and now you could speak. So could he someday, if he persevered. If he tried. He badly had to want to live and to recover. If he quit on himself, nobody could help him. Then you tell him a story or two, get him laughing a little. You take his name and his phone number and his address, and you promise to call him when he gets out of the hospital, to see how he is getting on. Later, you tell him, we'll meet someplace and have a drink together, a couple of bullfrogs croaking about their operations.

I don't boast about this sort of thing, this one-to-one work, because how many people can you see this way? There are 4400 laryngectomies performed every year; the figure grows by 4 percent every year. Over ten a day. So while I spoke to the father of the elevator operator, nine or ten other men and women were getting ready to roll into operating rooms.

But I have to do it. It is my work, today, my job. If I can get that guy in the dark kitchen to smile once before I leave, to promise he will have the operation, and he will try to speak, I've done my job.

It is acting, once again. You need a different set of lines for each new victim. One of the first laryngectomees I was asked to cheer was a former character actor, a man laid despondent by the loss of his voice and the end of his career. I knew his problem. Because I'd been there, too. I walked into this guy's house, in my jauntiest style, and I grinned down at him, sitting bundled in an old robe in a big old chair, and I growled, "Now, when did they cut *your* throat?"

He slowly began to grin, a smile creased his face, and though I heard no laughter (I couldn't have heard any), his belly, in that old robe, began to heave.

One wisecrack, and he was on his feet.

Others are not as easy. I remember telling writer Jane Ardmore about an early case, a guy so dejected before his operation he looked ready for the river. I went to his hospital room, in Chicago.

"Okay," I snapped, "you want to jump, go ahead. It's your life. I just want to talk to you a few minutes first. I want to tell you, buddy, it could be a lot worse." I thought of those multiple paraplegics; I thought of poor Alec Templeton. "You could be blind, and there's no way out of that. But there is a way out of this, if you aren't too damned lazy to take it." I took a breath, and rolled on; he lay there, listening to me now, no expression on his face. But the glazed look had lifted. "You can learn to talk, I promise you. If you'll work at it. The ACS will send you a speech therapist. In a few months you'll be talking. You won't sound like Cary Grant, but then you don't look like him either."

And the faintest twitch of a grin touched his mouth.

You don't win them all. Some laryngectomees are lazy. They don't want to speak. They don't want to bother. They want to use their illness and their disability as a crutch. I've had laryngectomees write on a pad, "I try to talk. I can't. I can't hold the air. I get sick to my stomach when I try." They do this in front of their wives. They have a good thing going, playing the helpless act.

You talk to these people, you plead with them, you bully them, cajole them, reason with them, pray for them, joke with them. Nothing. Nobody rehabilitates a man but himself. I can help, just as a Teckla Tibbs can help. But you either do it yourself, or it isn't done.

And while I'm at it, yes, I did feel sorry for myself, and I did whine, but I also did tackle those pamphlets and I did go for speech lessons. I felt sorry for myself *at times*. Not always. And now that I've gone beyond that early feeling of helplessness, I don't feel sorry for myself at all.

My faith buoys me. Which is not to say it has not been difficult. One summer two or three years ago at the Bohemian Grove, I remember a very sociable evening, with lots of drinks and good fellowship, and a few of us not going to bed until three or four in the morning. My camp is Aviary Camp; each camp has rows of tents, and in each tent, four beds. My tentmates are Walter Bunker, Howard Vesper, and Red Knorp. So I stumbled by cots on my way to bed, and then at six A.M. it was time to get out of bed again, to attend early Mass. Francis (Red) Knorp and I were the two Catholics in our tent. Red and I very carefully groped our way past the cots of Bunker and Vesper, snoring blissfully, cozy and warm. We trudged to the bus stop where a bus jounced us to the gate, and then, as we always did, we hitched a ride to the little town of Monte Rio a few miles from the Grove. After Mass, we did the reverse, thumbing a ride on the chilly highway, jouncing from the gate back on bus, and then walking through the early morning mist to our tent.

"Knorp," I croaked, looking at the bodies of Bunker and Vesper, still sleeping innocently, over whom and past whom we now had to stumble and grope once more, "wouldn't it be terrible if *they* were right?"

22

One Man's Mouth Against Another Man's Ear

Jinx Ray and I gradually worked out a speech. It had two parts. The first was a personal recitation of my condition, how I handled my recovery, and in detail how I learned to talk. The more real I make this first part, the better chance I have of reaching the cancer victims before me. My presence before them, with a full dossier of the whole cancer bit, acts as proof that a man can come back. I do not minimize the seriousness of their plight, but I do emphasize that faith and determination can go far, plus the assistance of men and women trained to help a patient achieve a high degree of normalcy.

Then I give a once-over lightly rundown of the humorous moments of my life and career. Leave them laughing; take their minds off their troubles for a few moments. Life isn't totally bleak.

I took the speech throughout the country. In 1963, I spoke in the nation's capital; I spoke in Massachusetts, Rhode Island, Connecticut, New Hampshire, Michigan, Louisiana, Missouri, Texas, Arkansas, Nebraska, and California. I went up to Canada.

I helped kick off the annual crusade in Washington, D.C., early in March, and when I finished Dave Powers invited me to the White House. I went to the west gate and was ushered into the cabinet room where I chatted with Dave, and then President Kennedy came in.

"I didn't know until today you'd had cancer," he said. "I'm terribly sorry."

"That's all right," I said. "You've been pretty busy. How's your back?"

"Well," he said, "not so bad lately. But it does kick up now and then. When it does, I have to wear that brace, and . . ." Then he stopped and he said, "Wait a minute. I'm supposed to ask how you are."

So we laughed, and he did ask how I was, and I told him I was fine. He and I spoke for a few minutes until he had to run. He asked me to forgive him because he was pretty busy, and I allowed how I imagined he was, and we shook hands. That was the last time I ever saw the President, though we did keep in touch. Twice he called me. The phone would ring, and the party would ask for me, and then I would hear, "Just a minute. The President wants to speak with you." And he would ask how I was doing.

Actually, I came close to seeing him again. He appointed me to the Committee on the Employment of the Physically Handicapped, with a meeting set for November 23, 1963. Dave Powers called to ask if I was going to be in Washington; I said no, I hadn't planned to, but I'd make sure I was.

On November 22, I was in Seattle, getting ready to go to a ballroom to speak to a group of crusade volunteers when Mary phoned me.

"Isn't it awful?" she said.

"Isn't what awful?"

"Turn on your TV," she said. "The President's been shot."

I turned on my television set, and watched and listened, and then I turned it off and went downstairs. The speech I delivered became in part a tribute to John F. Kennedy. And from the meeting, somehow the volunteers seemed to take on more feeling for what they were doing. My own words took on added meaning. I said to those volunteers: "A cancer volunteer is born the day he or she says, 'I hate cancer! I hate death!'" I looked at my watch. "Since I have been talking to you for six minutes, three people have died of cancer. The ACS knows that cancer can strike any place in the world—that it strikes two out of three families. And, God forbid, but it will strike one out of four in this room."

John F. Kennedy and death and cancer. Death had become less an abstraction, on that November 22, 1963.

After Seattle, I flew east to Providence, Rhode Island, and kicked off another crusade. I had to keep doing it, keep moving fast. Though I felt the greatest affinity for fellow laryngectomees, they are just a tiny fraction of each year's cancer onslaught. Some 300,000 Americans die of cancer every year, and every year the figure goes up. That's 820 people a day, one every two minutes. My speech was now a twenty-minute speech. Ten people died of cancer every time I delivered it. No, I didn't like to rely purely on statistics when I gave a speech. But some facts you could not shrink from.

I began to see a new face of America, just as I had seen a new face the early days I was on the road. Some of the laryngectomees I speak to are illiterate. They can't read or write. You must reach them face to face, or not at all. Still, this isn't a bad way to communicate, one to one. Someone said it centuries ago—the one sure means of communication is one man's mouth pressed up against another man's ear.

Other moments, other confrontations also jar me. I have—perhaps I should say "had"—a few old friends who do not shake hands when we meet. They are afraid of catching my cancer. They remain stubborn relics of the notion that cancer is more than a disease; it is a sin. I excuse their ignorance. But it is hard to call them "friends." Others do not get even that close. They say on the phone, "Let's get together. Let's have dinner some time." If I waited, I'd be a shadow of myself.

But these are minor matters, the exception, not the rule. The rule is a roomful of victims, sitting with gradually interested faces. The rule is a gathering of three hundred people at a crusade kickoff, laughing a lot and crying a little, and getting ready to join in trying to knock this curse out of the box.

During the early days of speechmaking, I suffered a brief setback. Back home, I'd become a very busy person again. Mary and I went everywhere, saw everyone, had everyone over. That was our social busy-ness. I had my ACS busy-ness. I spoke at a county crusade in Los Angeles in 1962 at the Biltmore Hotel Bowl, where my friend Dennis Day sang, "Help just one somebody . . . somewhere," and 500 people cheered and wept. I agreed to co-chair the 1963 California State crusade. I helped organize the first "Fight Cancer" golf tournament in the desert area, at Bermuda Dunes. I was always packing a suitcase, to hop here or there. In 1964, I succumbed to what was now a long-standing plea from National ACS headquarters to join the National staff, no longer strictly as a volunteer. I had resisted for two years. I liked the notion of being a volunteer unpaid worker, no different from the woman down the street who knocks on doors. But the people back in New York wanted to be able to call on me when they wanted, to do what they conceived of as more important chores. All I asked was that I also be permitted to keep working my own beat—the desert area. And so I wore and wear two hats, for ACS.

My pace quickened. In the morning, at home (when I was at home), I'd have a cup of coffee in the kitchen with Mary—almost any drink would give me the necessary fund of gas—and I'd begin to warm up my voice. I'd start belching a little or do a few exercises, and Mary would yell over, "For God's sake, stop shouting at me!"

Things had changed. My voice got stronger and clearer. Oh, once in a while, it seemed to falter in strength. I remember one evening Jinx Ray was over, she and I working on a speech I'd be giving the next day, when my throat muscles got tired, and I couldn't continue. Or so I thought. I rapped my knuckles on the table to signal to Mary—who was out in the kitchen—to bring me a drink of water. But you know Mary. Instead of coming into the room, where I'd then whisper my request, she called back, "I'm busy in here. What do you want?"

I took a big gulp of air, to give her a blast, but all that came out was "wah—wah. . . ."

Tough as nails, Mary bellowed back from the kitchen: "Speak up, Bill! I can't hear you in here."

My face got red, my muscles tensed, but out it came: "*Water,* dammit!"

Mary came in, with a grin on her face, and the glass of water in her hand. She said to Jinx, "He's talking very well tonight, don't you think?"

I was talking very well most nights, most days.

Then I had a rude awakening. In the beginning of my work, I would jot down notes on three-by-five index cards, and make my speeches from these cards. Later, the ACS generously gave me a tape recorder, so I could practice on it and hear just which jokes sounded best and which ones ought to be scrubbed. The first day I tinkered with the recorder—and mind you, this was two or three years after my operation—I spoke into the microphone, "One-one, two-two, testing, testing," studying the sound-level indicator to achieve the proper pitch. Then I turned it from "Record" to "Play," and listened to myself.

Mary was in the room when the tape began to talk back to me, in a stranger's voice. One-one, two-two, the stranger said; the sound was freakish, weird, a croak, a growl, a death rattle in the throat.

That was my voice?

This was my voice!

I had never properly heard it before. In my own ears, it was coming along fine, a little deep, of course, deep as a well, but surely very understandable. Maybe the "p's" were "b's" and the "h's" didn't exist, but that was all.

I stared at Mary.

"That's how I sound?"

"You sound fine," she said.

"But like that?"

"What's wrong with that?"

I felt crushed. Two, three years, and this.

Why hadn't anybody told me? I was a freak, with a freak's voice.

But the time was long gone for self-pity. Just as the tractor driver had made me angry—this was a laryngectomee's voice?— so did my own feedback anger me. This was my voice, eh? It wouldn't be for long. I began to practice even more, do the exercises from the very beginning. I worked on holding my vowels longer, clicking off the consonants more sharply, arching my tongue for the difficult "th" sound. I spoke into the recorder, and listened back. Gradually I heard an improvement. I kept at it. I went in for more exotic exercises. I tried what speech therapists say is impossible for a laryngectomee; I reached for upper and lower pitch. Laryngectomees have one pitch—deep as a well—but I decided to strive for lows and highs within the one pitch. Maybe I don't achieve them, but it gives me a feeling that I am lending expression to what I am saying. And I'm not terribly sure I don't achieve a slight variation of pitch.

But I must have sounded bad enough. Today, when I realize how my voice must sound, it dismays me. But then I have to tell myself the old line—you don't look like Robert Goulet; why should you sound like him? In any event, I never listen to myself any more. I won't win any more elocution contests, but I'm speaking.

Which doesn't mean I still don't resent the sound I make. There's nothing wrong with a little resentment. It acts like a spur. I tie it all together, my belief in God and my resentment for what happened. If I hadn't believed so strongly, I wouldn't have cared enough to resent what had happened, to resent my getting cancer, and cancer getting me. Because I resented it, I needed an answer. The answer didn't come when I wanted it, and it didn't come in the way I wanted it. I'd much preferred God saying to me, "Gargan, it was an organizational slipup. Hold on. We'll straighten it out tonight in your sleep."

Like the story of the lovely nun, Sister Margaret, who, when she died, ended up in the wrong place. She'd been sent to Hell. She promptly telephoned upstairs and got St. Peter on the line. "St. Peter," she said, "this is Sister Margaret. I'm in this *awful* place. There's *such* language. You must come and take me away."

"Strength, Sister Margaret," St. Peter said. "Strength. Just hold on. We won't be long."

But the next day she was still there, so she called again. "This is Sister Margaret," she said. "They're *drinking* now. Please come and get me."

"Courage, Sister," St. Peter said, "just hold on. We'll be picking you up shortly."

The third day she called again. "Hello, Pete? This is Peggy. Forget it."

This is where I am. Forget it.

And anyway, God didn't say that it was a slipup. He had another answer. I was the guy to help other cancer victims. I couldn't do it with a silken voice. I had to have this croak of a voice. All right. So I growl my words, and I resent the way I sound. Which makes me try harder. I speak better today than I did a year ago. I suspect I'll speak better, more clearly, a year from now.

I kept moving about the country. I had other setbacks, but they came from outside. In 1961, Gary Cooper had died, of cancer. The next year, Charles Laughton, of cancer. Fat Charles. I cannot say I enjoyed working with him but, like many actors, he was a far pleasanter human being away from the set than on. So probably was I. Jack Carson died in 1963, of cancer, and so did Richard Barthelmess, and that smiling man, Dick Powell, with whom I'd appeared in the movie, *Broadway Gondolier*, nearly three decades earlier. Worst of all, in 1963, Alec Templeton died of cancer, a blind person with the clearest vision of any man I ever knew.

I kept going, traveling, speaking. People took notice of my work. This pleased me, not because it bloated my ego (I need it not), but because any publicity for me automatically became publicity in the fight against cancer, by the American Cancer Society. In September of 1962, Pope John elevated me to Knight Commander of the Holy Sepulchre, and honored Mary the same way. Later we would be made Knight Commander with Star; finally, Knight of the Grand Cross.

Two months after Pope John had honored us, I received the George W. Buck Memorial Award of the Catholic Actors' Guild, in New York. Merv Griffin and Horace McMahon made the presentation, at the Americana Hotel, with Bert Wheeler, Ed

Begley, and Don Ameche looking on. More important, Ed
and Cooee were there. When Ed had learned of my illness
(so Cooee has since told me), he could not be comforted. "My
brother's work," he said, "his livelihood. What will Bill do?"
Now he saw me speaking again; we spent some time together,
and he heard me pick up the phone and converse. He saw me
not a whit different, except my voice wasn't the same. Meanwhile—and that is the way tragedy is—Ed had become ill. He had
contracted diabetes a few years before; on top of it he now was
suffering from emphysema. None of it, of course, affected his
disposition. He kept right on laughing. He was busy at the bank;
he was busier at home, restoring antique cuckoo clocks, working
on his water colors. So it was a warm and fine visit.

I kept receiving other attentions. The Skeeters honored me as
their man of the year at an annual dinner party at Toots Shor's,
but before they did, they blew me to a marvelous vacation. I
was set up in a fabulous suite at the Plaza for ten days, with no
tab, because of the generosity of Neal Lang, a beautiful fellow,
who managed the hotel. On another occasion the Skeeters took
me out to the Garden State track where the hat was passed, and
the money collected plunked down on a horse. Eddie Arcaro
handicapped the race, and when it was over, I was $1400 richer,
money I later turned over to the ACS. I don't recommend
collecting money for charity and then plunging the kitty on a
nag, but if you insist, you'll do worse than having Eddie Arcaro
handicap the bet.

A whole new life had opened. The curtain had fallen on
thirty-five years of show business, years I had spent entertaining
people. Now it had gone up again, and my role had changed.
Now I was helping people. There is a whale of a difference in
the two roles; before, I'd made my audience laugh. Now I try to
keep them from crying.

The new life filled me with a great love of living. Every minute
was taken up with this new love. To boil it down, I was a happy
man.

23

I Hit the Road

Early in January of 1964, I spoke to an annual crusade kickoff in Salt Lake City, and then returned home to our place on South Elm Drive. Mary and I had become less and less enthralled by life in Beverly Hills. The city of Los Angeles clashes and clatters along, a city on the move, rushing along its burning wheels from one parking lot to another. From afar—say, from a space capsule ten miles above the earth—it must look like a massive colony of ants, hurtling pellmell from one anthill to another, from one tiny hole in the ground to the next. Ants do it more purposefully.

These ants have wheels, and the wheels are powered by gasoline, and a poisonous waste is spewed from the exhaust pipes of these wheeled ant-movers. The waste climbs into the sky, as it does in every city in the world. Except in Los Angeles, the waste usually meets an unmovable object, a thick layer of atmosphere that hangs over the entire city and the entire basin. Instead of climbing toward the stars, the poison hangs overhead and presses down on all the ants. Smog makes the ants cough. It made this ant cough and choke and ache. Mary and I began to talk of moving.

We put aside such talk later that February of 1964. My brother Ed had become quite ill. The diabetes, the emphysema, the years of smoking had all caught up with him.

I flew to New York. I saw Ed at Columbus Hospital. The effort to breathe had begun to strain his heart, and he had an oxygen tank in his room. I spent an hour chatting with him. He looked tired. But he had an unquenchable spirit. He said to me that evening, "I'll get out in a few days."

I nodded. "You bet you will. I'll check in again tomorrow." And I left.

Ed received Communion every morning at the hospital. But this next morning, when a Sister went out to light a candle and bring it back to his room, it was too late.

Cooee called. "We've lost our Ed," she said.

Cooee Gargan is a great woman. She and Ed had been married some twenty-six years. They'd had no children, which is tragedy enough. But Cooee is a practical person, and a woman who refuses to permit grief to undo her good sense. "How silly a funeral is," she said to me. She went to a 14th Street mortuary and she said to the undertaker, "I've got a thousand dollars to spend, and not a penny more. I want a nice funeral, but not a gaudy one." She picked out a casket for $250, and we had two cars, and Cooee got some change back, which is as it should be. We buried Ed next to Mother, in Holy Cross Cemetery. Which also is as it should be. I was my father's son. Ed was my mother's. He had her vivacity, her love of life, her smile, her easy good nature. It wasn't terribly important to Mother that she had her diamond ring back out of hock when Dad was gambling; she could get along just as well without it. It wasn't important to Ed that he wasn't a big Hollywood star, but rather an accomplished character actor. He wasn't a big man, perhaps, in Hollywood terms, but he was big in the ways that counted—big of heart, big of soul.

Like Cooee, I could not let grief undo me. With the help of my desert friends, I'd begun work on Palm Springs' first charity ball for the ACS, to be held April 6, 1964, at the Thunderbird Country Club. Actually, the idea for a ball was Jinx Ray's, and the theme for the ball came from Ruth Valeur, granddaughter of Nellie Coffman, whose legendary Desert Inn was the real beginning of Palm Springs as a world-famous resort and spa. Ruth Valeur, a tall, slender attractive redhead, knows the desert and its people as well as anybody in the area. Ruth suggested a ball with a Spanish theme. "Since it's a fund-raising event, we could call it a Golden Ball, or whatever the Spanish translation would be. *Baile de Oro*. Yes."

And if the idea for a ball was Jinx's, and the theme was Ruth's, the gal who brought the two women together was Mary Gargan, the three of them ironing out details over coffee at a Woolworth's counter.

It took more than that one conference at the 5 & 10. Dan Thornton, former Governor of Colorado who makes his winter home at Palm Springs, agreed to chair the ball. A trio of beautiful women served as vice-chairmen, and the gals—Florence Swanson, Nancy Chaffee Kiner, and Alice Faye Harris—threw a preliminary and private party, for men only, where the men permitted themselves to be tapped for a neat $20,000. Every club in the desert was involved. Volunteer Ball workers sounded like a Who's Who of the desert: Evelyn and Ralph Smith, Marcia and George Barrett, Verle and Ellsworth Vines—he the great tennis champion and then fine golfer, Bill and Mousie Powell, Virginia and Charlie Farrell, Jimmie and Milt Hicks, the Jack Kenastons and on and on; the names I leave out must outnumber by five-to-one the names I have listed. May they forgive me for not mentioning them. I love them all.

We—they—filled the ballroom with the red and gold of the American Cancer Society. Hundreds of red and gold balloons hung from the ceiling, to descend on the 480 guests—a total sellout; we had room for not another soul—seated at tables with gold floral centerpieces, flanked by golden candelabra. Lee Christopher called it "the best damned party you ever saw" on the society page of the Palm Springs *Desert Sun*. I think she was right.

We entertained our guests. Phil Harris, Alice Faye, Allan Jones, Jack Jones, Bob Hope, Desi Arnaz, Buddy Rogers, Harry Von Zell, Fred Waring, Ray Bolger (still the world's most graceful man) doing his soft shoe.

And when the entertainment ended, chairman Dan Thornton

got up and said, "You will be happy to know that the proceeds of tonight's party will exceed $45,000," and I said, "Thank you. For all cancer victims, thank you for saving our lives."

That was all planned. Unplanned, so far as I was concerned, was the handsome golden plaque from the ACS, to me. The plaque read: "To a Gallant Knight in the Cancer Crusade." And even more overwhelming was the presentation by William Clay Ford—Bill Clay is a member of Thunderbird Country Club—of a brand new Ford sedan.

I gulped air, involuntarily, but for a few seconds, nothing came up. Then I said, "For the second time in my life, I've lost my voice."

The music was furnished by Bernie Richards' band—and Bernie gave me a break on his price; it was that kind of night. Mary and I danced. We were show-business people again putting on an act—a series of acts: Buddy Rogers playing the trumpet, the drums, the sax, the piano; Alice Faye and Ray Bolger soft-shoeing together; Bob Hope fracturing 480 people—all make-believe people, doing something totally real. Saving lives. Jinx Ray thanked me for what I'd been doing, in the rehabilitation of cancer victims, and I had to gainsay her. "I'm the one who must be thankful. An actor without an audience is lost. You have given me my greatest audience."

The first annual ball was just that: the first. We've had others, the Red, White, and Blue Gala of 1965; the 1966 party, with Bob Hope the guest of honor, when an inadvertent ticket oversell threatened to push the whole affair out onto the streets of Palm Springs, but which also netted $67,000 for the ACS; the 1967 affair, when Magnavox gave every guest an AM-FM radio, and Ben Heck of Korbel Wineries drowned everyone in champagne, and Ray Bolger danced "Once in Love With Amy," with Alice Faye Harris to a crowd that wouldn't break up at three in the morning; the Ruby Gala of '68 that coincided with Mary's and my fortieth wedding anniversary. God willing, they'll keep coming along, the annual Palm Springs balls, for from them comes money, and from money comes research, and from research, a life is saved.

When I wasn't working on that first ball (and with the help we had, who needed me?), I flew off to other towns, and other crusade kickoffs, other ACS work. In Memphis, on March 30, 1964, I spoke at the Chickasaw Country Club. The day before a Memphis minister asked me to visit a Memphis police officer, J. W. Sumners, at Baptist Hospital, where he lay recovering from a laryngectomy. Officer Sumners received speech help from the Memphis Speech and Hearing Clinic, and when I visited him a second time, I was delighted to hear him speaking, and speaking quite well.

After my Memphis trip, and after the great glorious Baile de Oro was finally desert history, I went off to St. Louis, and then four days later I spoke at another crusade kickoff at the Bancroft Hotel, in Saginaw, Michigan. The cities slipped by in a blur, the days and nights passed, in strange towns, strange hotels, speaking to strange people. But always, the note of urgency remained, and the words had to be comforting. I told them how I had been comforted. "When you're stricken with cancer," I said—in some town, to some strangers who were truly closer to me than many friends—"one of two things happens. If God wants you, He puts His arms around you and takes you. If you live, the nicest things begin to happen to you. The nicest things—the nicest people—have happened to me since I met cancer. And the nicest group of people of good will has been the American Cancer Society."

Sometimes the note of urgency became more intense. As I spoke in Saginaw, or in St. Louis, or as I danced in Palm Springs, someplace outside, and probably very close, a man or a woman lay dying of cancer. So the cities became a blur, but individual people took on sharp edges.

Early in my convalescence I received an artificial amplifier. The instrument helps amplify your speech; it makes a whisperer more easily heard. But the amplifier doesn't make the whisperer speak any louder. It just sounds that way. No artificial instrument is going to do that. You do that yourself, though it helps to have a Mary Gargan along. I never used the amplifier. One day in

1964, on my travels, I ran into a friend of mine, Ed Voynow, who also was a laryngectomee. Ed was using an amplifier.

"You can talk like me," I said. "Try."

He agreed he'd try and we shook hands. I saw him again at the Racquet Club in Palm Springs.

"Hello, Bill," he said loudly. "How are you?" He was still using his amplifier.

I said, "You don't need that thing." I reached to grab it away from him. But I could see by his face—suddenly paralyzed by fear—it wouldn't work. He had to have his crutch. A few months later, I read poor Ed had died of a heart attack. He knew it had been a crutch, and it ate him up, his failure, but he wouldn't try hard enough to succeed.

There are others. Abigail Van Buren—Dear Abby—asked me to see an industrialist who lived in Sutton Place, in New York. He also used a mechanical amplifier.

"Mr. K.," I said, "how do you ever expect to talk if you hang on to that thing?"

But he was too depressed to give it up. He said he felt like jumping out of the window. That was all he wanted to talk about, his depression. And he talked only with his amplifier.

I tried to arrange for him to take private speech lessons.

"I don't have time," he said. "My business won't allow me the time."

So there he was, eaten up by depression, yet driven to make money. Perhaps he had to have this drive. The other drive—to live—was leaving him.

I am no speech therapist. I am not qualified to teach another man how to speak. You need special skills, special education to become a therapist. All I do is try to give a man a boost, try to show him how my own speech therapy, how Dr. Harrington, helped me. I am a sort of cheerleader.

Sometimes this one-to-one cheerleading method works. I was put in touch with a Japanese-American businessman in San Francisco, who'd had part of his tongue cut out when he had his laryngectomy performed. His cancer had gone unnoticed a hair too long, and it had spread. His condition was far worse than mine had ever been. He'd taken speech lessons, but he had no one to speak with. His wife did not speak English. But he had tremendous determination. He made me ashamed of my earlier self-pity. This man knew none at all.

I spent an hour with him. We burped together, and arched our tongues—mine, and what was left of his—and I made all the sounds, slowly, explaining to him what I was doing, as Dr. Harrington had explained it to me.

"One-one," I said.

He grunted and breathed air. He heaved and panted and tried, but no sound came out. Sweat ran down his face and neck.

"One-one," I said. "Come on. One-one."

"Ah ah," he said, gasping, heaving, sweating.

"One-one," I said. "You can do it."

He struggled. His face twisted. I told him to relax. Again he began to work his mutilated tongue around a fleeting passage of air.

"One-one," I exhorted

"Ah-'un," he said, finally.

"Great!" I said. "Again. One-one."

And he said it. "One-one." He said it over and over. One-one. One-one. One-one.

We did two-two. We did the long vowels. I never saw such effort. This is courage. Today, he can be understood, easily.

I got a call from the wife of a man in Red Bluff, California. Her husband had gone to a hospital in Palo Alto, preparatory to his third operation for throat cancer.

"He wants to end it all," she said. "He feels he's such a burden. Would you talk to him?"

I talked to him, over the phone. I spoke, for ten minutes, into this phone, dead except for the sound of his breathing. I said what I had to say, yes, it was awful, and only God knew how many times he'd have to go through the ghastly ordeal, but how could he quit, now? How could he quit on his wife? On his doctors? On himself? He'd gone so far; maybe just a little more would be all he'd have to go. I begged him not to give up. He didn't say a word. Just laid down the phone, finally.

I wrote him a letter. Put it all to him again.

The past two years I've received Christmas cards from him. He's doing fine. He's speaking.

When I was in Chicago, to deliver the speech for the Crippled Children Society, I met two men, one indomitable, one on the verge of suicide. My speech took place at the Palmer House; on the same platform was Roy Campanella, the former Dodger catcher who had been quick as a cat behind the plate but whose career had ended, and nearly his life, when he snapped his neck in an automobile accident. Now he sat in a wheelchair, a man with a smile the size of home plate, a totally self-rehabilitated man.

But in Chicago, I was asked to go to a local hospital, to see and perhaps cheer a business executive who had just been operated on for cancer of the larynx. Now he felt he had nothing to live for. He was, they told me, contemplating suicide. I went. His wife sat by his bed. You could see by his expression he had given up. You get to sense these things. It doesn't take much genius. His eyes were lifeless, his face unsmiling, unmoving. I understood how he felt, because I remembered my own moments when I cried my mute anguish to God. But though I understood, I did not approve, neither his nor mine. Pity gets you nowhere. Self-pity destroys you.

I walked across the hospital room. "You want to give up?" I said. "You want to jump?" I opened the window. "Go ahead."

A gesture. Melodramatic. But it worked. His attention had been caught. A flicker of something—fear, hope, anger?—crossed his face.

I began to speak my piece. Go ahead and jump, if he had to, if he absolutely refused to try to live. It was the easy way out, the coward's. But if he decided to give life a chance, he had wonders ahead of him, a whole life, a new life. I told him of blind people learning to read, legless people learning to walk. Theirs was a worse predicament to begin with. His wasn't so awful. He hadn't really lost his voice. Just misplaced it. It would return, if he worked at it.

"Get well," I said. "We'll arrange speech lessons. You'll speak.

Not beautifully. But you'll speak. Like me. Isn't that better than jumping out of the window?"

His face had changed. Gone was the helpless, hopeless look. A touch of color, a faint sparkle showed. And over his whole body, a look of calm. It works, because these people don't want to cry, don't want to die; they want, desperately, to live, and all they're asking is for someone to come along and tell them there's hope. That's my job. I carry a bag of hope on my back. It's fun. Why *not* me?

A few weeks later, on my way to New York, I dropped by to see him. (Let me blow my horn briefly. I had a flight from Los Angeles to New York, non stop. I thought of the man in Chicago. I changed my schedule to a stopover at Chicago. Why not? I get pleasure out of this. For me, it's fun.) So I saw him. His expression had totally changed. You didn't have to search for a faint sparkle that may or may not have been in his eyes. It was there, all right. He smiled; he had relaxed. He tried to make noises. They weren't good noises, except they were beautiful noises because he was making them. And what a good sign! Just to be trying!

"See you next trip," I said.

ACS arranged speech lessons. Next time through, I called his office. His secretary said, "I'll let you talk to him." He got on. "Where are you?" he asked. Good and clear.

I was at the Admiral Club of American Airlines, between planes.

"I'll be there in five minutes," he said.

In all my years in show business, I never got a bigger kick than from this guy jabbering away at the airport. We both got plastered. It was a beautiful celebration.

But it, too, is a teeter-totter. It has its ups and downs. In 1965, I learned I'd won the Criss Award, Mutual of Omaha's award for individual contribution to health and safety. B. J. Skutt, head of Mutual, gave me the use of his Lear Jet, and I decided to fly on up to Traverse City, in northern Michigan, to see Walter Hagen. Steve Barrie, head of special events for national ACS, was along on the flight, as were a couple of *Life* magazine people, writer Marge Byers, and a photographer.

Walter Hagen had been a hero of mine, one of the all-time great golfers, a man who twice won the U. S. Open, and who won the British Open four times in eight years. Hagen always had a great heart, great courage. It never mattered where he lay, in the rough, deep in a bunker, behind a tree—he always went straight for the hole. He never babied the ball.

Hagen had recently undergone a total laryngectomy, for cancer. I made no appointment with him. I didn't even know where the guy lived, in Traverse City. I checked in to a motel early in the morning, and I asked the motel manager where I might find Hagen. He suggested they might know at a small night club ten or twelve blocks down the street. I rented a car and drove to the club. I ordered a beer. At ten in the morning, even I find it difficult to drink a scotch. (Though not impossible.) A man at the bar said, "I know who you are. You're Bill Gargan. What are you doing here?"

"Looking for Walter Hagen."

"How come?"

"I want to tell him he can speak like me."

The bartender said, "I'll get in touch with him." He came back a few minutes later, and he said, "Haig will be at your motel at 12:30."

I went back. Even in his palmiest days on the golf course, Walter Hagen was not famous for arriving on time.

But he showed up this time, exactly at 12:30. We had a beer together, and we talked. I talked. He had a slate with him. When he didn't use the slate, he whispered.

"Stop using that," I told him. "And stop whispering." I told him I'd arrange for him to have speech lessons.

He was very pleasant, a charming man. He manufactured golf clubs, and he'd brought along a gold putter for me. He said he'd try, but he knew more about himself than I did. Pretty soon he had his second throat operation, and then his third. Cancer, that ravening monster, was still working him over.

It is a teeter-totter. You don't win them all, but you don't lose them all either. Early in 1966, I visited a nine-year-old girl in Montgomery, Alabama. She'd had her larynx removed, which meant if she ever talked again, it would have to be esophageal speech. Except her cancer had gone mad and cut a downward swath into her esophagus. Part of the esophagus had been cut out as well.

I saw the child and told her what I knew. That the surgeons would now build her a new partial esophagus. It would permit her to speak. It would take weeks, and maybe months, before she could make proper sounds, but she had to try. Would she promise to try?

She nodded.

Though God gave her a hand, mainly, she did it herself. She meant that nod. She would try. She did try. Her progress was slow; need I say "painfully" slow? But it was progress. Now she enunciates quite well. She'll make it, that kitten.

24

Through Sleet and Snow and Phlebitis

In November of 1965, I officially joined the ranks of cured cancer victims. Five years had gone by since Dr. Alden Miller had stabbed beneath my epiglottis and come up with a small walnut of carcinoma. His skill with that scalpel had given me the finest five years of my life. Since then, we've added to the five.

We held no celebration of my cure. We'd had celebration enough. I'd just received the Criss Award, which has to be one of the greatest thrills of my recent life, and to my way of thinking the greatest blunder in the history of insurance. The Criss Award, named after Mutual of Omaha's founder, Dr. C. C. Criss, has always gone to people you and I think of as great. Just to give you an idea of who wins the Criss Award, Dr. Jonas Salk got it one year. Dr. Tom Dooley got it another year. The surgeons who developed cortisone, Drs. Kendall and Hench—they got it. And the year before my award, it went to somebody named J. Edgar Hoover.

I'll never forget how I first heard I was to receive the Criss Award. Evidently everybody knew I was to get it before I did. Certainly Bob Hope and Bing Crosby knew, but they were sworn to secrecy. In any event, I was in New York in August of 1965 when a friend, Bill Worthing, conned me into visiting Dr. Charles Mayo, one of the world's greatest and most respected doctors, at his suite in the Waldorf-Astoria.

As we shook hands, Dr. Mayo said: "I guess you're wondering why you're here."

Always fast with the repartee, I replied: "Nice to see you, but the last thing I need *now* is a doctor."

His rejoinder ended my feeble attempt at humor.

"We're going to give you ten thousand dollars, tax free, a medal, and some other things we'll tell you about later."

I stared at him incredulously as he then informed me that a distinguished Board of Judges had selected me as the recipient of the Award.

And that was how I learned I was to receive the great honor.

At first I was so busy on ACS work that I didn't realize the significance of the announcement. Between it and the actual award dinner, I had gone down to Rocky Mount, North Carolina, to help kick off a crusade at an annual dinner meeting of the Rocky Mount-Nash County unit of the ACS. I was so occupied with this chore that it was not until I came back home to Beverly Hills that what was about to take place really hit me. I, William Gargan, ex-actor, current pitchman, was to receive one of the most distinguished awards his country offered. I was overwhelmed.

The dinner was held on October 26, at the Beverly Hills Hotel. The award takes the form of a gold medal and a $10,000 tax-free stipend. Lieutenant General (Retired) James H. Doolittle, the hero of the raids on Tokyo early in World War II, presented me with the gold medal and the check. Over six hundred people crowded into the hotel ballroom, among them such friends as Pat O'Brien, Ray Bolger, Art Linkletter, Bob Hope, Dennis Day, Ralph Edwards, Gregory Peck, George Gobel, and Jack Haley. Hope cracked, "I never thought I'd see the day when an actor could survive Hollywood without being able to talk about himself."

But I could and did talk about myself. I looked along the dais and I acknowledged the VIPs, which was practically a speech in itself—"Right Reverend Monsignor Sullivan, the Reverend Father Reinert, Mrs. Criss, Mr. Skutt, Dr. Mayo, Distinguished judges, Bob Considine, Jimmy Doolittle, volunteers of the American Cancer Society, sweet friends, and Irishmen everywhere—" and I took a couple of breaths. I looked over the huge crowd below the dais, the medal and the $10,000 check in my hand. "I think the only other crowd that ever assembled in my behalf any larger than this one is that group standing right outside the door of the Beverly Hilton now. They heard about the ten thousand dollars. They're my creditors." I thanked Mutual, I thanked Dr. Alden Miller, who brought me through surgery; I thanked Dr. Robert Harrington, who taught me esophageal speech; I thanked Jinx Ray, without whom there might never have been a speech for me to make. I'd survived, through these people, and now I was talking about myself.

After the dinner I tried to give the money to ACS. But as Bob Considine says, cooler heads prevailed. Fortunately. I can wisecrack about it now, but that night I was overwhelmed. I will never forget it.

Five years had gone by since my operation, and I was honored for rehabilitating others. The fact is, I'd truly rehabilitated myself. I am a gregarious man, a fun-lover, a crowd-seeker. Cancer had temporarily cut out the fun, cut me off from the crowds. Now I was back in the swim. It is the ham in me, the actor; you can knock the boy out of show biz, but you can't knock show biz out of the boy. I cannot deny it. I love the attention, the spot on the dais, the warm words people say and write about me. Most of the words are pretty thick, a total exaggeration of the work I do. But I love 'em. In the one-to-one method I find most satisfying, the one person I have treated most carefully, the one person I've rehabilitated, is me.

In 1966, Mary and I moved from Los Angeles. We had sold the Beverly Hills house, finally: also the one at Bermuda Dunes. We found a spot at the La Costa Spa and Country Club, ninety miles down the coast and a few miles inland from the ocean at Carlsbad. Here the hills of the coastal range are soft and lovely. The sea drifts in silently to a cove nearby. The smog does not reach us. The air is clean, cool, and touched with the fragrance of chaparral that clings to the surrounding hills. It is close to the desert communities and close enough to Los Angeles, if we need it; and just thirty miles north of San Diego and its airport. Near us is one of the great medical clinics in the West, Scripps of La Jolla, where I go for my periodic checkups.

At La Costa, we have a racquet club, with four fine courts; a saddle club, with twenty miles of bridle paths that wind through the 3000-acre valley. The Spa features swirl baths, sauna units, herbal wraps, and the whole exotic pampering galaxy of baths, exercises, and physiotherapy. You can be rubbed down Finnish style, Swedish style, with alcohol or with cream. There is a Roman pool, sun slabs, gymnasia, and siesta rooms. Ah, those siesta rooms! The dining room sets aside a section where you can eat a low-calorie diet which, naturally, I avoid like the plague. And from the dining room, you can look out at the 7200-yard golf course where I still slice every other drive, but where I am determined to break ninety again.

Golf has done a great job in helping fight the war on cancer. In 1964, a Bermuda Dunes neighbor, Morty Cohn, introduced the first Bill Gargan "Fight Cancer" Golf Tournament.

"This is the heart of golf country," Morty Cohn said to me one day. "We're going to have a golf tournament to raise money to help lick cancer."

"How about expenses?" I asked.

"There won't be any," Mort replied.

There weren't. Three months later, when that first Gargan Shotgun Tourney concluded with an end-of-the-day cocktail bash at the Bermuda Dunes clubhouse, Morty handed a $5000 check to me. "This represents both the gross and the net take, to help fight cancer."

Through the efforts of Morty, and of Ed Vines and Allan Dauch, everything from prizes to food to liquor to cart and green fees had been donated without cost to the ACS. Including the 5'6" William Gargan Trophy (donated by Ray Ryan), now the perpetual award to the winner of each annual "Fight Cancer" tourney. All I could say was Thank You, and all I could do was buy a purple orchid tree that now stands at the edge of the stone steps leading into the Bermuda Dunes clubhouse.

Another tournament close to my heart was dreamed up by my old friend Angelo (Buzzy) Buzzalino over an after dinner drink at his Rose Restaurant in New York. The first one, at the North Hills Country Club in Manhasset, Long Island, drew about 50 people. It grew each year and now draws the biggest names in show business and the sports world. So far Buzzy's golf tournaments have contributed over $75,000 to the William Gargan Cancer Fund of the ACS.

Since then, we've held tournaments at Indian Wells and at La Costa, and the success of these fund-raisers has bred other similar tournaments in other states. In 1967, the same format was adopted by Mutual of Omaha in Medford, Oregon, which now sponsors an annual "Tournament of Fun" for Oregon's ACS.

But my main activity is on the road. It's become so the ACS prints my itinerary weeks in advance, so Mary and I both know where I have to be and when. Here's the way, for instance, I began the year 1967. On Friday, January 6, I was in Palm Springs for meetings on the fourth annual cancer ball, to be held March 2. I spent the weekend at home, in La Costa, with Mary, and then I flew to New York, for three days of meetings with the American Cancer Society people. On Thursday and Friday of that same week, I attended a meeting in Chicago, and worked on plans for that city's annual crusade. I flew back home to continue work on the Palm Springs ball, and to slip in an evening with Mary, to celebrate our wedding anniversary, at the La Costa Country Club. Monday and Tuesday of the following week, more meetings in Palm Springs; Wednesday and Thursday, a statewide crusade orientation workshop and dinner meeting in Minneapolis; a weekend back home, and then plans for a golf tournament in Carlsbad, beginning eight days hence. On Saturday, February 4, I was in Arcadia, California, to speak at a workshop for nurses at the Methodist Hospital of Southern California. Five days later, the Carlsbad tournament began, with American Airlines picking up the tab. After the tourney, a concentrated series of meetings on the annual Palm Springs ball; then a flight to Lowell, Massachusetts for a weekend at the Parker Lectures; the next day a meeting in Salem, Massachusetts (where I said, "I keep remembering the words of the great poet of this region, Robert Frost, who wrote—'For we have promises to keep and miles to go before we sleep,'—and I told them of my promise to fight that disease, no matter how many miles lay ahead). The next day, a meeting in New York, to remind volunteers of the yearly crusade coming up, and to pep up those who most naturally tend to become discouraged and who might say, "What, another fund-raising campaign?" To them, I say, "This is not *another* campaign. It is the same campaign. The same fight. The endless fight. We are fighting death. We are looking for a cure so we can all put the ACS out of business."

Three days later, the Palm Springs ball filled the Indian Wells Country Club.

Less than eight weeks. Seventeen thousand miles. (I usually do double that, but this was the Palm Springs ball period, so I remained close to home much of the time.) Nine cities. Five states. These are the miles before we sleep. But I love every minute of it and gladly fill my days and weeks and months on a crusade to which I have dedicated myself.

I've been to Hawaii a couple of times for ACS, and I renewed friendships first formed thirty years earlier when Paramount shot that terrible film, *Four Frightened People* on the Islands.

On one trip, I was whisked to the island of Hawaii, where we had a wonderful crusade meeting at Hilo, and then we flew across to Kona, where I spoke at the city's new outdoor recreation center, a beautiful open arena that seats 1500 people. This time, however, it seated just two people. The wrong date had been printed on the invitations and on the placards posted about town. My schedule prevented my making a second date, so I delivered my speech to two crusade volunteers.

More often, however, it's my own fault when there's a foulup.

In February of 1966, I attended the annual Baseball Writers
Meeting in New York, and when the meeting let out, a bunch
of us headed for Toots Shor's, Frank Coniff, Bob Considine,
Toots, and myself. But before I left the Baseball Writers meeting,
I wanted to say hello to a few friends, so Frank, Toots, and
Bob all went ahead. A few minutes later, by myself, I began
to walk up 52nd Street toward Sixth Avenue, a blowy Sunday
night, the sidewalk a thin slick of ice. I had walked past the
new J. C. Penney building when a gust of wind suddenly struck,
and my feet went out and up, and I went down. I threw out
an arm to help break the fall. It broke the fall all right, and
my clavicle as well. Because of the shock of the fall and the
slippery ice, I was unable to get up. I lay there a full five
minutes, and you know what? Nobody came by. Not a soul.
This was New York, this was Sixth Avenue, this was Sunday
night and the lights were bright. It could have been a golf
course I lay on, at midnight. So I got up, finally, and I crossed
Sixth Avenue and went into Shor's, hunched over because of
my broken collarbone. Bob Considine came over. "What's wrong?"
he asked, and I told him, and Bob commandeered one of Toots'
patrons' limousines, and he and Frank Coniff drove me to Roosevelt Hospital. I spent the night at the hospital, and the next
morning, as hospitals will, a woman rolled in a weighing machine at seven o'clock.

"Get up," she said. "I want to weigh you."

Naturally I blew my stack. You weigh newborn babies. You
weigh fat women on diets. I had a broken clavicle. I called
Steve Barrie, at national ACS office, and I said, "Come on
over, and get me out of here," and Steve rushed right over.
Meanwhile, the head nurse got into the act, and a doctor, and
the doctor finally said, "You'll do as well home as in here,"
which really meant he was glad to get that raving Irishman out
of the hospital and out of his hair.

Actually, I had to get out because I had a date that day.
A flu bug can shoot me down, put me to bed, shivering and
feverish and obviously in no condition to get up and speak for

health. A broken wing like this may shelve a bird, but I am no bird. I walk, not fly, and the night before I'd made the doctor on emergency duty tape it, not put it in a cast. Steve Barrie drove me to Queens, for a meeting before eight hundred nurses at Antun's restaurant, a meeting I wouldn't have wanted to miss even if the borough president of Queens had not proclaimed it Bill Gargan Day. So I made the meeting, my right arm in a sling, which made it a cinch to wring sympathy from my audience. I have since considered slipping on a sling in a tough town where my speech seems to be laying an egg.

Some time ago, I was loading my station wagon with supplies left over from the Palm Springs ball, and in the process I felt something snap in my leg. It says in all the pamphlets, a laryngectomee cannot lift loads as he had in the past, because he cannot lock in his breath prior to lifting, the way you can. Well, you learn to lock in your breath fairly well, though admittedly not as well as before, and I hate to have flunkies do my lifting and toting. (Besides, Mary wasn't around.) So I popped something in my leg and a clot formed—phlebitis— and I went to bed with blood de-coagulants for a couple of weeks, throwing my schedule completely out of kilter.

Not quite. I had promised the people of Lawton, Oklahoma, I'd be down there the end of March for a crusade kickoff dinner, and though I knew I couldn't get out of bed, I was still determined to be "present" at that meeting. I'd never spoken at Lawton; the local ACS unit had asked me a couple of times, and I didn't want to turn them down.

So I said to the local chairman of the dinner, over the phone, "How about my doing it the way you and I are talking?"

"How's that?"

"Over the phone. You people attach your public address system to your end, and I'll speak right here from bed. I think it will work."

We did it. I lay in bed at our condominium in La Costa, and while Mary and some of her friends kibbitzed in the background,

I spoke over the phone. It was a kick. I had two audiences, one right in the room, where I could see facial expressions, and the other over a thousand miles away, 290 people at a dinner meeting where I had to listen to laughter and the quality of silence to know how I was doing. I'd learned from the chairman—a very efficient fellow named Maddox—the names of all the people on the dais. Maddox called me at 8:25 P.M., Lawton time—6:25 La Costa time—and told me I'd go on in five minutes. We kept the phone open, and then Maddox said, "Mr. Gargan, I'm about to introduce you. When I say, 'Mr. William Gargan,' you come in."

He launched a brief introduction, spoke my name, and I started talking into the phone.

I sat propped in bed, shuffling through index cards, with excerpts of other speeches Jinx Ray and I had worked over, plus my collection of jokes, stories, and quotations. I breezed. I began by telling them I had promised to speak to the good people of Lawton, and I quoted two lines by Robert Service: "A promise made is a debt unpaid/And the trail has its own stern code." Well, I told them, I had been on that trail now for years, battling the pot roast and gravy at luncheons, fried chicken and gravy at dinner, in towns both big and small. "Recently I was in a town so small they put on the late late *late* show at six o'clock. The only excitement was on Saturday night when people sat on their porches and watched the sewer back up."

In this case, I told them, I'd have to give up the pot roast— or was it fried chicken?—but I could afford to give it up; I was blooming. "A friend told me I'd been putting on weight, and gave me a diet; it's very simple. He said, 'Eat everything you want. Only don't swallow.'"

Which got me serious. I spoke about swallowing and pain, and laryngeal cancer. I talked in general about cancer, and how you had to watch for the seven danger signals. You had to take cancer seriously. Which got me into another joke, naturally. I told about the guy who meets his doctor on the street, and he says, "Doc, I got this pain in my back," and the doctor says, "Come to the office." The man says, "Can't you just give me a pill?" and the doctor shrugs and he says, "Okay, take off your pants."

"Here?" the guy wants to know. "In the street?"

"Why not?" the doctor says. "You asked me to treat you in the street."

So I made the point. See your doctor. See him in his office. See him seriously and at length, and see him regularly.

And I thanked the volunteers. "People like you saved my life," I said. "You have made it possible for me, and for hundreds and thousands of people like me, to live, to work, to lead normal lives. I thank you."

That was my speech, by phone. It took twenty minutes, and I enjoyed myself immoderately. Why not? I called New York the next day and spoke to ACS national headquarters. "You fellows can book me for speeches like that any time."

Later, my phlebitis jumped to the other leg, and I had to have the knees tapped, a much overrated procedure that doesn't particularly hurt and does enable you to lie down and see your toes again. The doctors prescribed exercise this time, rather than rest, so I can't use fat legs as an excuse for sitting in bed and making speeches.

Not that I want to. I like it better the other way. Not only do I see those groups—the kickoff groups, the service clubs—face to face (Omaha on the thirteenth, New York on the fourteenth, Detroit the seventeenth, Seattle the next day, then Fairbanks, Anchorage, Kodiak, Juneau, and back to sunny California, for a golf tournament), but there is always the chance of the bartender or the cab driver or the bellhop saying, "There's this guy in the hospital . . . or at home . . . or at the edge of a cliff. Could you see him?"

Or her. I saw little Becky Dufford one year, on one trip; Becky Dufford was the 1962 ACS Poster Girl, and we chatted together, she and I, she with her beautiful trill of a voice, and I with my croak, about which I made some comment. Since then we have taken to exchanging Christmas cards. Last Christmas, in response to the card Mary and I sent Becky, we got this one back:

Dear Mr. Gargan,

I should very much like to return the heartfelt thanks you sent to me in your Christmas Greeting, as the thrill of meeting you is something I will treasure all of my life. I should also like to say that your voice isn't funny, it is beautiful, because it brings cheer, hope, encouragement and education to millions. Please do not stop crusading now, Mr. Gargan, because without people like you, people like me might not be alive. So thank you again.

Becky E. Dufford.

That's really why I do it. Why I don't stop crusading. Just as long as there are Becky Duffords around, how can I stop?

And, of course, I do it because I haven't changed very much. I'm still the guy who chases and finds fun, chases and nails down laughs. I'm still the guy who enjoys attention; I guess I'll always be an actor.

In 1967 several events took place that must rank high on the list of things that have happened to me. First was the Creighton University Award, that fine Jesuit school's Distinguished Citizen Citation, presented—so the award read—"to William Gargan for outstanding achievement in drama and for courageous efforts to overcome a disability to help others by his example."

Another award that thrilled me—and perhaps thrilled me more was a unique one. I went to prison for it, the Huntsville, Texas, prison, where 1600 inmates had formed a foundation in honor of a reporter named Harry McCormick; McCormick had exposed prison conditions in Texas, had fought to have them improved, and then he'd died of cancer. So the inmates collected $1200 in 1967, and I went down there to speak to these odd and wonderful cancer fighters. Wonderful? You bet. The $1200 they collected represented 75¢ per capita, which made these inmates the most generous single community in America, in the war on cancer. The state of Nevada had previously led, with an outlay of 18¢ per Nevadan; California was close behind, with 17¢

per capita. Now these men in prison had gone far beyond those figures, and I complimented them. Yes, a wonderful gesture. And odd. The man who introduced me was a lifer, a three-time loser who had been released from jail not too many months before, determined to go straight, but when he got outside, he found he was lonesome in a world now strange to him. So he committed a minor crime, phoned the police, and let himself be picked up. He was happy, in for life. But more wonderful than odd. The men gave me a plaque. A prisoner made this plaque, out of a plain piece of pine, a likeness of me copied from a newspaper photograph, and inscribed with the words: "Thank you for your courage."

Becky Dufford is why I do it and that is why I do it.

But on November 12, 1967, the most thrilling moment of my life took place. You must remember that with all my work I am and always have been an actor. It's a different league from those I played in when I was Martin Kane on television or Red Regan in *The Animal Kingdom* on the stage or in the hundreds of roles I'd played in the movies. But I'm still an actor at heart.

Knowing this you can understand my feelings when the Screen Actors' Guild selected me Man of the Year for 1967. This is an honor I especially cherish because it came from my peers—actors and actresses who knew what made me tick since they were spurred on by the same drive that made me go. These were my people and they were honoring me!

At the Hollywood Palladium, I thanked Guild president Charlton Heston; I thanked Gregory Peck, Dennis Day, Bob Hope, Bob Carson, and countless others whose names I am not including here, but they must know I love and honor them all. I thanked them all for the award. "At times like this it matters very little that I have lost my *voice*," I said. "For what could I do with a voice if I don't have any *words?*"

I linked my current work to my past work, acting. "I'm not acting any more, but that's because my agent upstairs wrote 'Finis' to my acting career before the public could do it . . . more cruelly. I lost my voice—but I still have my feet. And if sometimes I find myself running pretty hard for the cancer crusade, at least that's the *only* thing I'm *running* for."

The work, I said, wasn't much different from acting. "One good thing came out of my experience with cancer: For years my bride sat up nights worrying that I'd get my throat cut in the acting business. Well"—Jack Benny pause; nervous laughter starts; I go through and over—"we don't worry about *that* any more."

And I got serious. "Today, when I travel back and forth across the country, people ask me what I'm doing in the cancer fight. I guess the only answer I can give is that I've seen the face of the enemy—and because I won my battle, I think I was spared to help other people fight. Besides, who ever heard of an Irish Dove?"

And I got truly serious. I harkened back to my days at Warner Brothers. "In the days long before we had catchy names for a celebrity's particular friends—I refer to names like the 'Rat Pack' and 'Arnie's Army'—I had a bunch of good pals who took some pleasure in calling me the 'Big G.' And human nature being what it is, I recall being privately pleased to be called the Big G. It took a major calamity in my life to prove what I should have known all along—that there is a Bigger G."

That's what I said to 1900 actors and actresses when they gave me their annual award "for outstanding achievement in fostering the finest ideals of the acting profession," and when they gave me their plaque, with the bronze masks of tragedy and comedy.

I don't know now how I was able to talk because I was all choked up. But then as Mary had said so many months before "He's talking very well tonight, don't you think?" Talk I did but as Mary and I went home that night I knew words could never express my feelings. Only my heart could. And it was filled to overflowing.

Epilogue: Why Not Me?

Cancer.

The ancient Greeks thought the spreading cancerous growths moved like the claws of a crab. They called it the crablike disease, *karkinos*. From which we get the word carcinoma. Cancer. Except sometimes it moves not at all slowly like a crab, but rushes about furiously, like a rabid dog.

It is an old disease. It is as old as life, as old as death. Older, in fact, than man. The runaway cell preceded man's existence. It is found in the bones of animals that roamed the earth millions of years ago; it is found in every kind of living thing, plant, animal, man.

Man does not understand the dynamics of cancer, as yet. How does the cancer cell break the usual rules of growth? What makes it grow out of control, when normal cells proceed so orderly? Why should the cell multiplication rate change so crazily—one cell become three or four or fifty? Why are the cells so weirdly shaped, so wrongly sized—some pygmies, some giants? Why do these cells form useless tissue, while normal cells form useful tissue? And why do they not stop multiplying? Mostly, the last. Why does cancer spread so unmercifully?

We will know, someday. That is what it is all about. A quest for knowledge. Knowledge costs money. Ask the college of your choice. And so I go out into the towns of America, with my hand outstretched. On my federal income tax form one recent year, where it asks "Occupation," I wrote: "Pickpocket." That is what I do. I go around picking pockets, for money. It has to be done this way, privately, with private people asking other private people to help. The Department of Health, Education, and Welfare gets six billion dollars a year, under the federal budget, but of this, just a trickle is for health, and of that trickle, just a drop goes into cancer research. More money is spent on researching and fighting hoof-and-mouth disease, and frankly, not enough money is spent even on that. In man's odd hierarchy of values, learning to kill by bullet or bomb, or to avoid being killed by bullet or bomb, is far more important than learning to cure.

So we beg and borrow and take what we can, to fight this disease. The American Cancer Society collects fifty million dollars a year to fight cancer. Fifty million. This is the equivalent of a mere 2¢ a month from every American.

Every sixth death in the United States is caused by cancer. Cancer strikes one person in every four, two families in every three. Sometimes I say in a speech: "Medical statistics are human beings with the tears wiped off." The statistics are you, your loved ones, your neighbors. Look about you. Are there four in your family? One of you will get cancer. Look to each side of you. A family to your right, another family to the left. And your own. Of these three families, only one will escape a brush with cancer.

Fifty million Americans now living will one day have cancer.

In all the wars in our history, we have not lost one-twenty-fifth as many men, killed and wounded, combined.

So I beg. I pick pockets.

But the begging is not just for money. One simple plea is for speed. Please hurry up. That lump under your armpit, or on your breast; that thread of blood in your stool; that chronic soreness in your throat—take it to your doctor. That oddly colored discharge; that sore which will not heal; that darkening or enlarging mole or wart. Please. Go. Your life may be at stake.

Of course much of the worry is needless. Lumps are puddles

of fat that melt away; the streak of blood comes from a crack in dry skin; the wart is a wart is a wart. Huck Finn could cure it as well as your doctor.

But why not find out you've been a worry wart? Let the sore throat be laryngitis. Find out, and breathe easy.

But find out. I beg.

Of every six people who get cancer, only two survive. Yet if all six went to their doctors early enough, instead of two surviving, three would survive. Instead of a third surviving, half would survive. Catch the cancer early, and tear it out in its entirety, and your chances are bright indeed. But let those multiplying demons spread through the lymph channels and bloodstream to other parts of the body, and your chances are dim. Why gamble? I beg.

I beg for more.

I beg for education. Lately, I have become a mite tired of one part of my job. Fund-raising. Yes, it is vital, and it must be done, and I will keep doing it. But sometimes I am frustrated by it. We collect money, in part, to treat cancer *victims*, to buy laryngectomees magic slates and pay for their speech lessons.

More and more, I want to catch that laryngectomee before he ever has to learn what the word means. The cures of cancer are two in number, and two only. Each is gross. You cure it by radiation, or by surgery, or by both. Either you shoot X-ray or cobalt into the diseased area and gun it down, then and there, or you carve it out with a bloodied knife. Yes, I am a cancer cure, but I have no larynx. Yes, that woman across the street is a cancer cure, but she has no breast. He has no leg; she has no uterus; he has one lung; she has no tongue. Cures?

The walking wounded.

So more and more, I want to get out on the street and meet the cancer cure before he has to be cured.

Not all cancer can be spotted easily, in advance, by someone walking down the street.

But some I will spot. You carry it in your pocket, or your hand, or between your lips. Cigarettes.

In Anchorage, Alaska, I spoke to a group of teenagers.

That so many people smoke is to me incredible. That so many children smoke is sickening. By the twelfth grade, fully half of our children smoke. Yet it ought not surprise us. We older people like to think we just didn't know what we were doing when we began to smoke in our youth. Today, we have the Surgeon General's report; we have a dozen other reports that tell us, Yes, there is a definite link between smoking cigarettes and spitting up a cancer-rotted lung, a link between cigarettes and throat cancer, a link between cigarettes and heart diseases, between cigarettes and a dozen other ailments, any of which might kill someday. When we were young—we keep saying— we didn't have all these facts.

Yet we called cigarettes coffin nails.

We knew.

We laughed and curled a smoke ring into the sky.

I brought the evidence with me to Anchorage. I had smoked two to three packs of coffin nails a day, for thirty-five years. I squirmed with guilt, before these teenagers, so beautiful and straight and sturdy, God's images, all of them.

"My father and mother smoke," one child says. "Why can't I?"

"I'm sorry about your mother and father," I say. "But I'm not worried about them. If they don't have the brains or the determination to stop, I feel sorry for them. But I can't help them. It's you I'm worried about. If you haven't started smoking, I beg of you. Don't. If you have started, I beg of you. Stop."

"But why?" they ask. "It's 'in' to smoke. Everyone does it. We don't want to look like fools, like oddballs."

I produce the evidence.

"Would you rather look like me?" I ask gently. "And sound like me?"

. . . So that's how it goes, on the cancer circuit, these days and these years. I raise what money I can, and I educate what little I can. Meanwhile, I continue to rehabilitate myself. It remains a selfish act, catering to the person I know best. I told you how I've always wanted to sing? Well, I sang.

At the first Palm Springs ball, we arranged a little songfest, after all the other business had been attended to. Fred Waring was around, and nobody whips up a glee club any better. So Fred whipped, and Desi Arnaz, Bob Hope, Buddy Rogers, Allan Jones, Dan Thornton, Ray Bolger, and I—William Gargan, *basso profundo*—harmonized.

Rather, they harmonized. When they reached the last note, I was permitted to come in, all by myself, solo.

I sang my one note.

Everybody got up and left.

I like to think it was because the ball was over, but in the succeeding Palm Springs balls, nobody has asked me to sing again.

I don't care. Inside, I'm singing.